The Blue Sky Boys

American Made
Music Series

DICK SPOTTSWOOD

UNIVERSITY PRESS OF MISSISSIPPI • JACKSON

www.upress.state.ms.us

The University Press of Mississippi is a member of the
Association of American University Presses.

Manufactured in the United States of America

First printing 2018
∞

Library of Congress Cataloging-in-Publication Data

Names: Spottswood, Richard K. (Richard Keith) author.
Title: The Blue Sky Boys / Dick Spottswood.
Description: Jackson: University Press of Mississippi, 2018. | Series:
American made music series | Includes bibliographical references and
index. |
Identifiers: LCCN 2017036812 (print) | LCCN 2017037466 (ebook) | ISBN
9781496816429 (epub single) | ISBN 9781496816436 (epub institutional) |
ISBN 9781496816443 (pdf single) | ISBN 9781496816450 (pdf institutional)
| ISBN 9781496816405 (cloth: alk. paper) | ISBN 9781496816412 (pbk.:
alk. paper)
Subjects: LCSH: Blue Sky Boys. | Country musicians—United States—Biography.
Classification: LCC ML421.B673 (ebook) | LCC ML421.B673 S66 2018 (print) |
DDC 782.421642092/2 [B]—dc23
LC record available at https://lccn.loc.gov/2017036812

British Library Cataloging-in-Publication Data available

Dedicated to the memory of Barbara and Perry Westland, who loved the Blue Sky Boys.

Praise for the Blue Sky Boys

I grew up just outside Atlanta, Georgia, and I could . . . and did listen to the Blue Sky Boys virtually every afternoon on WGST Radio. There was something about their impeccable harmonies, plaintive songs, and straightforward musicianship that spoke to me from an early age. Listening to their recordings today, I can easily conjure up those old memories and warm feelings.

They might not have been the biggest, brightest stars on the horizon, but their music and their contributions definitely mattered.

They did then and they always will.

—BILL ANDERSON
GRAND OLE OPRY
COUNTRY MUSIC HALL OF FAME

I was a big fan, though never fortunate enough to meet them—came close several times when our family was doing radio work over the country in the 1940s. Seems like our paths never crossed. The Blue Sky Boys were two of the unsung heroes of country music. To my knowledge, they were the very first to sing their type harmony, switching the lead and harmony back and forth with each other. Certain songs they would do this harmony more than others, but always tastefully. And most importantly the highest compliment I could pay them is, "They were original."

—THE LATE SONNY JAMES
COUNTRY MUSIC HALL OF FAME

Bill and Earl Bolick of Hickory, North Carolina, were only eighteen and sixteen respectively when they recorded "There'll Come a Time," but their musical integrity always displayed a maturity beyond their years.

Rock-ribbed devotees of genuine old-time country music, they recorded several of the finest versions of British broadside ballads ever preserved. They are among the finest, if not the finest, examples of the sincerity and dignity of mountain music.

—RANGER DOUG, RIDERS IN THE SKY

When I first had a radio at home, the first duets and trios I heard were by the Blue Sky Boys. I always go by the Starday people and say I've got to have one of the Blue Sky Boys' latest albums. I take it home and play it over and over and over.

—JIMMY MARTIN, 1964

Their sunny name notwithstanding, the Blue Sky Boys gravitated to the dark side. Their unerring sibling harmony was almost dreamlike and made them perhaps the all-time finest brother duet. Along the way, they saved many ancient songs from extinction.

—COLIN ESCOTT

Those of us who grew up in, or listened outside of, the listening range of radio stations in the Carolinas, southern Virginia, or east Tennessee had to rely on local disc jockeys or a record shop to gain exposure to the Blue Sky Boys. In my case, it was the RCA Victor shop in Baltimore that agreed to allow me to listen to a Blue Sky Boys 78 rpm in one of their listening booths—and I was literally blown away with their gentle and extremely smooth harmonies, incorporating a third part by way of Bill Bolick's mandolin. Bill and his wife Doris were kind enough to allow me to visit them in their North Carolina home in the early 1970s, where I asked Bill how he was able to add a third-part harmony to his and Earl's duets: "Did it just come naturally?" "Well no, I really had to work on that," was Bill's quick and honest response.

Meeting them and getting to see them in a live performance only began several years later, when I was able to see them perform live at a festival in Virginia. Despite long periods of separation they came very close to perfection in both their choice of material and their brotherly harmonies.

But perhaps the most overlooked aspect of the Bolicks' contribution to American mountain music is the wealth of good material they produced over a fairly short span of years. Personally, I believe that Bill Bolick collected, and generously passed along to others, more good songs than any other artist outside of A. P. Carter of the original Carter Family.

The book you hold in your hands is long overdue and it will finally provide real insight into one of this country's finest pioneering music teams.

—BILL CLIFTON

DANIELS, WEST VIRGINIA

Sincere thanks to a great writer and my good friend Dick Spottswood for sharing his wonderful story about the life and times of the Blue Sky Boys. I never had the pleasure of meeting Bill and Earl Bolick. However, I've been an avid fan since their first recordings. One that really stands out is "I'm S-A-V-E-D."

I've had the pleasure of reading this wonderful story about Bill and Earl and heartily suggest everyone should read it.

—MAC WISEMAN

Contents

Preface

William was never at a loss for words. I think William took that from Daddy; I think that came from Daddy's side. If you asked him for his opinion, I think he would tell you. Earl was more of the quiet type and not that outgoing.

RUTH BOLICK SIGMON, HICKORY, NC, SEPTEMBER 20, 2010

BILL AND EARL BOLICK WERE ONLY TEENAGERS WHEN THEY FIRST performed publicly in 1935 as brother duets were becoming increasingly popular on radio and records. As the Blue Sky Boys, their gentle harmonies, wistful hymns, and sentimental songs explored themes of longing, alienation, and regret that had flourished in Victorian parlors and music halls decades before they were born. They called attention to their songs more than themselves, and their closely blended voices and accompaniments were spare and unobtrusive. As Bill Anderson says, they were never headliners, but they'll never be forgotten either.

When country music became an identifiable genre in the 1920s, performing family groups were an important source of talent, and organized themselves for recording, broadcasting, and local stage opportunities. A few, like the Carters, Stonemans, and Pickards, had regular media access and acquired local and regional prominence, but child-rearing and domestic requirements limited other family women's ability to be away from home. Nevertheless, country music and family values have remained closely entwined, and many families are active today, particularly in the gospel music sphere.

Families were supplemented by brother acts in the 1930s, usually self-accompanied duets who could travel and perform by themselves or with others, and who didn't require large salaries until they either acquired a measure of fame or began to have families of their own. The Allen

Brothers from Chattanooga were the first country brother duo to enjoy a measure of success, although they were a quirky, non-harmonizing novelty act who recorded blues-flavored originals from 1927 until their appeal faded during the Depression.

The Delmore Brothers from northern Alabama wrote more bluesy songs and broadened their appeal with comic and sentimental tunes, and close harmony singing. An initial disc made for Columbia in 1931 sold poorly, but they reappeared in 1933 to record "Brown's Ferry Blues," coupled with a reissue of the Allens' "A New Salty Dog" for RCA's low-priced Bluebird label. "Brown's Ferry" took the Delmores to the Grand Ole Opry and sparked a career that lasted until Rabon's death in 1952. Homer and Walter Callahan from western North Carolina had a comparable hit with "She's My Curly Headed Baby" in 1934, and were in and out of music for most of their lives. When Bill and Earl Bolick became the Blue Sky Boys and made their first records in 1936, they joined the Delmores and the influential Carlisle Brothers, Dixon Brothers, and Monroe Brothers, all on RCA Bluebird. The brothers Wade and J. E. Mainer were Bluebird regulars, too, though they never sang duets.

All had significant radio careers that boosted record sales and live show attendance, producing income streams that provided modest livelihoods. The Bluebird brothers' influence persisted in the later music of the Louvin, Bailes, Armstrong, McReynolds, Wilburn, Osborne, and Stanley Brothers into bluegrass and other popular formats after World War II.

Other 1930s sibling duets were from the Midwest and southwest, including the Shelton Brothers from East Texas and De Zurik Sisters from Minnesota. The Overstake Sisters (a.k.a. Three Little Maids) and Girls of the Golden West were from Illinois, and starred on the WLS *National Barn Dance* at various times from 1933 into the 1940s, and all featured mid-western and western-style vocal harmonies.

I was in my early teens, living in Bethesda, Maryland, near Washington, DC, when I discovered the Blue Sky Boys. My adolescence began just as the duo was retiring from music in 1951, but I actively sought old copies of their records and was always happy to hear one on local country music shows. Though their influence occasionally lingered in bluegrass and country styles, their compelling, heartfelt singing and understated instrumental accompaniments were unlike any other music I knew. In 2010 I learned from Gary Reid that the Bolick family wanted to have a book written about the Blue Sky Boys. I volunteered, thinking the project would be a conventional third-person narrative, piecing together as much who, what, where, and when as I could gather. But I soon learned that over the years Bill Bolick provided numerous spoken interviews and written accounts of his music, life, and career, and he was unsparing in his appraisals of all aspects of the Blue Sky Boys story and the country music world of the 1930s and 40s. I learned to appreciate his eloquence and passion, his memory of details, and how well he placed them within the perspective of the times. To make maximum use of them, I have woven parts of Bill's multiple narratives into a single account that presents much of the Blue Sky Boys story in his voice. I have edited to eliminate repetition and so-called "crutch" words and phrases, adjust pronouns, correct obvious misspeaking, and to add or subtract small words to enhance the flow. Bill's extended quotes are italicized and unattributed when their context is clear; those from others are credited as appropriate.

Special thanks are due to family members Steven Bolick, Larry Settlemyre, the late Doris Bolick, the late Ruth Bolick Sigmon, and to Linda and Alan Justice for help, patience, hospitality, and encouragement. Gary Reid of Copper Creek Records introduced me to Alan and provided stimulus and inspiration for this entire project. Lorrie Westland has created an online video that celebrates the Blue Sky Boys with images and music. Mary-Jo Cooney, Bill Malone, Fred Bartenstein, and an anonymous reader have reviewed this work in draft form and made solid observations, suggestions, and corrections.

Mary Katherine Aldin, Rob Bamberger, Julay Brooks, John Broven, Jay Bruder, Bob Carlin, Bill Clifton, Stuart Colman, Wayne Daniel, Paolo Dettwiler, Tom Diamant, David Diehl, John Dodds, the late Ernest Ferguson, Kevin Scott Fleming, Ranger Doug Green, Lorrie Westland, Kitsy and the late Pete Kuykendall, the late Eric LeBlanc, Kip Lornell, Greil Marcus, the late Ben Niblock, Kevin Owens, Ina and the late Ray Patterson, Linda Penniman, Kinney Rorrer, John Rumble, Walt Saunders, Bob Shea, Mark Slobin, Richard D. Smith, Aaron N. Smithers, Jeremy Stephens, Chris Strachwitz, Eddie Stubbs, Charles Travis, Stephen Wade, Leslie Weidenhammer, Steven Weiss, Richard Weize, Mac Wiseman, and Marshall Wyatt have helped out in many ways, and each has contributed vital links to the chain.

Introduction

DURING THE 1940S, COUNTRY MUSIC WAS RAPIDLY EVOLVING FROM traditional songs and string band styles to honky-tonk, western swing, and bluegrass, via radio, records, and film. The Blue Sky Boys resisted the trend, preferring to continue performing folk and parlor songs, southern hymns, and selected new compositions that enhanced their trademark intimacy and warmth. Their instantly recognizable style was fully formed in 1936, when their first records captured their youthful harmonies and spare guitar and mandolin accompaniments. Other successful 1930s brother duets inspired imitators, but none could duplicate the Bolick brothers' emotional appeal and distinctive Catawba County (NC) accents. Even their last records in the 1970s retained their magic sound, decades after other brother duets had become history.

As their story unfolds, we'll learn that the Bolicks were far from being rural throwbacks or idealized folk specimens of an isolated society tied to ancient beliefs and customs. They grew up after World War I in a mid-sized, progressive North Carolina mill town whose opportunities afforded their family a comfortable middle-class lifestyle. Bill and Earl chose performing careers while still in their teens, gladly leaving menial hometown jobs behind when they discovered music was something they could do well. It eventually earned them devoted fans throughout the world, whose loyalty has endured from the Blue Sky Boys' professional years into our own time.

Their father Garland was a mail carrier who embraced old hymns and folk songs, and actively encouraged his sons' interest in them. Bill was six and Earl four when Garland brought home a radio in 1924 for his family, who enjoyed *National Barn Dance* broadcasts on Saturday nights from WLS in Chicago. These were supplemented with the hymns and country songs that Garland loved, and Bill inherited his father's passion for traditional music.

Fourteen of Garland's favorite hymns were among the ninety songs Bill and Earl placed on 78 rpm records between 1936 and 1940. In those days they were free to choose the songs they and their audiences liked without interposition from record producers and song publishers, who dominated music in Nashville after 1942. The comic title of a 1938 *Collier's* article, "Thar's Gold in Them Hillbillies," became reality as wartime copyrights, contracts, and publishing rights to new songs were secured and profits accumulated. As we shall see, the country music business eventually worked against the Blue Sky Boys, whose postwar records often featured professionally crafted tunes they did not like and rarely performed.

In those days the Blue Sky Boys were little known outside the southeastern states. Their broadcasts were limited to local stations in Georgia, the Carolinas, and southwest Virginia, and their records were only regionally distributed. Northern folk music and bluegrass aficionados began to discover the Bolicks after they retired from music in 1951 and their out-of-print records became collectible. When they made two reunion LPs in Nashville for the country market in 1963, a few folklorists arranged festival appearances and more records, new and reissued. A 1965 Capitol set, *Presenting the Blue Sky Boys,* contained traditional songs selected by a young folklorist, Ed Kahn. Good as it was, it failed to appeal either to the country music audience or the folk revival. Beyond hard core fans, the record's sales were negligible.

Traditional songs had dominated country music when it was first heard on radio and records in the 1920s. It was still a new genre, and initially marketed in catalogs with descriptors like *Old Familiar Tunes* (OKeh 1925), *Familiar Tunes Old and New* (Columbia 1926), and *Old Familiar Tunes and Novelties* (Victor 1930). In the 1930s "hillbilly" became a default name for the music, even though some (including the Bolicks) viewed it as demeaning. Bluebird and Decca catalogs called it *Hill Billy* or *Hillbilly,* but Columbia Records' Vocalion and OKeh products were called *Country Folk and Sacred Songs* in 1938, and later *Country Dance* [and] *Folk Songs* (1942) and *American Folk Music* (Columbia 1948), as the industry sought to invest the music with more respect. The "country and western" tag was adopted in 1949 and shortened a few years later to "country" when Nashville became its center and western music was perceived as a separate entity.

In the 1920s and '30s, Vernon Dalhart, the Carter Family, Ernest Stoneman, Bradley Kincaid, and other prolific record makers reclaimed old songs from sheet music, hymnals, broadsides, and songbooks. They could often be recorded without royalty costs after copyrights expired, or when attribution could be evaded by reshaping songs or altering titles. Resourceful musicians routinely recycled old music when radio and records demanded a constant supply of fresh material at low or no cost.

Nineteenth-century composers like Gussie L. Davis (1863–1899), Will S. Hays (1837–1907), and Henry Clay Work (1832–1884) were no longer household names in the 1920s, but their successful songs lingered in memory. Quite a few were reborn as country classics, including "Maple on the Hill" and "In the Baggage Coach Ahead" (Davis), "We Parted by the Riverside" and "Jimmie Brown, the Newsboy" (Hays), and "Grandfather's Clock" (Work). Work's "The Ship That Never Returned" (1865) supplied the melody for "Wreck of the Old 97," which commemorates a train accident that occurred nearly forty years later.

Pioneer country artists often relied on memory or improvisation to provide melodies for their texts, and many tunes lost their distinctive Victorian era contours when they were reborn as country songs. Wade Mainer kept most of the words to "Maple on the Hill" (1880) but replaced Gussie Davis's melody with a simpler one when he recorded it in 1935. It displaced the original and is still sung today.

Even professional folklorists provided occasional grist for the mill. Ernest Stoneman learned and recorded "The Wreck on the C and O" from John Harrington Cox's *Folk-Songs of the South* (1925), and the Texas cowboy singer Carl T. Sprague carried a copy of John Lomax's *Cowboy Songs* (1910) in his guitar case. Bradley Kincaid, Bascom Lamar Lunsford, and Buell Kazee learned folk songs from printed collections and professional songsmiths revisited, revised, and copyrighted old ballads like "Naomi Wise," "Frankie and Johnny," and "The Strawberry Roan."

Carson J. Robison (1890–1957), from Oswego, Kansas, and a blind Methodist preacher from Atlanta, Rev. Andrew Jenkins (1885–1957), were prominent among country music's 1920s songsmiths, creating quantities of material for expanding record catalogs. Both excelled at novelties and topical songs inspired by train wrecks, celebrity deaths, criminal trials, and other sensational events. A Texas-born New Yorker, Vernon Dalhart (born Marion Try Slaughter, 1883–1948), was a professional tenor who put many of their songs on records. His previous résumé included everything from Tin Pan Alley to operatic roles in Puccini and Gilbert and Sullivan productions. He embraced country music in 1924 when his "Prisoner's Song" became a novelty hit and his voice training ensured that he could be easily understood in areas of the country where record buyers might otherwise have had trouble understanding southern regional dialects.

Dalhart dominated country record-making between 1925 and 1927, appearing in one New York studio after another, often in company with Carson Robison, performing multiple versions of songs for competing labels, with professional musicians doing their labored best to sound down home. Dalhart's records sold throughout the English-speaking world but his singing lost some of its appeal after he separated from Robison in 1928. By then, record makers were routinely traveling to Atlanta, Charlotte, and other southern locales to capture the region's music closer to home. Resourceful producers like Frank Walker at Columbia and Ralph Peer at OKeh and Victor discovered new stars like the Carter Family, Stoneman Family, Gid Tanner's Skillet Lickers, and Jimmie Rodgers for record companies that had paid little attention to regional music in any form before the 1920s. These pioneers were the first to have a lasting influence on country music, reflecting the tastes and feelings of people who preferred to hear music they knew from performers they understood. Peer had a particularly good ear for promising talent and songs, and he led frequent recording trips to southern and southwestern locations between 1923 and 1932, when he left the record business to build a major music publishing house. By then, country music was an essential component of the radio and record industry.

The Blue Sky Boys

Origins, Family, and Childhood

THE BLUE SKY BOYS COULD TRACE THEIR ROOTS BACK TO EIGHTEENTH-century German immigrants who settled in Pennsylvania and elsewhere, establishing farms and related industries. Their family name was spelled Böhlich in the Old World; in America the variants include Balch, Balich, Boalich, Bohlich, Bohlig, Boleck, Boley, Bolich, Bolick, Boliek, Bolig, Boligh, Bolih, Bolish, Bollich, Bollick, Bollig, Bolligh, Bolock, Bolsch, Boulch, and Bowlick. A website traces the family tree back to Johan Adam Bolch, a shoemaker who sailed from Rotterdam to Philadelphia with his wife Anna Christina and two children in 1753, along with his brother Andreas Balch. In 1754 a half-brother, Johan Georg Bolch, made the same voyage.

Even before the Revolutionary War, restless settlers began to move on to western North Carolina, where the German presence remains a component of the southern Piedmont region to this day. Johan Adam Bolch's family took up farming before 1770 and his son Jacob later simplified the name to Bolick. Catawba County development was expedited after 1865, when the South sought to rebuild industries and revive an economy shattered by the Civil War. New textile mills throughout the region prompted the growth of cotton farming and railroads, and the town of Hickory developed a furniture industry that still thrives.

By the twentieth century, Hickory supported a comfortable middle class and Lenoir-Rhyne College, a prominent Lutheran institution that would one day include Bill Bolick among its students. West Hickory was an industrial suburb where the Blue Sky Boys' parents, Garland Bolick and Annie Hallman, met as children when both worked at Ivey Weavers, a cotton mill located between the railroad tracks and First Avenue SW. It was one of several locations where the photographer and social activist Lewis Wickes Hine took disturbing photographs that documented juvenile working conditions as part of a campaign to reform child labor

Young workers at the Ivey Weavers cotton mill, Hickory, NC, 1908. Photograph by Lewis Wickes Hine. Courtesy of Library of Congress, Prints and Photographs Division, Washington, DC.

laws in 1908. A few years later, Garland briefly worked in Ivey's Southern Desk Company, building school and church furniture.

The Blue Sky Boys' father Garland Henry Bolick (1890–1977) was the sixth child of Abel Bolch/Bolick (1837–1908) and his second wife, Elenora Euphemia Dellinger Bolick (1851–1927), who farmed in rural Catawba County before moving to West Hickory in 1901. On February 13, 1910, Garland married Annie Elizabeth Hallman (1892–1988), daughter of David Plonk Hallman (1855–1926) and Nancy Missouri Froneberger Hallman (1861–1935). Bill and Earl's siblings were James (1911–2003), Myrtle (1913–1998), Carl (1916–1992), and Ruth (b. 1926). Myrtle married Russell Settlemyre and Ruth married Glenn Sigmon.

William Anderson Bolick (October 29, 1917–March 13, 2008) and Earl Alfred Bolick (November 16, 1919–April 19, 1998) were the fourth and fifth of Annie and Garland's six children. Bill was born at home and thought Earl was, too. The brothers were exposed to music from church, friends, and neighbors, supplemented by mid-1920s Saturday night radio barn dance shows.

Radio brought stimulating new sounds to remote areas, influencing the Bolick boys and other North Carolina musical children, including Thelonious Monk, Max Roach, John Coltrane, Nina Simone, and Billy

Bolick children, 1925. Left to right: Carl, James, Earl (age 5), Myrtle, and Bill (age 7). Courtesy of Larry Settlemyre.

Taylor, all major jazz figures after World War II, and contemporaries of the Blue Sky Boys. Starting in the 1920s, professional dance bands led by Kay Kyser, Les Brown, Tal Henry, and Hal Kemp entertained in the Triangle region (Chapel Hill, Raleigh, Durham) and elsewhere. Bill and Earl could hear these and other competing popular music styles but, with their father Garland's encouragement, they preferred to learn the old music that had flourished where they lived before they were born.

The Bolick family lived in a West Hickory area called Mill Hill, where small homes were built for Ivey mill workers. Bill remembered that before he was old enough to go to school his grandmother Elenora Bolick cared for the children while Garland and Annie worked at the mill. Garland took a correspondence course and studied with a tutor to broaden his education and earn a better living. He became a substitute mail carrier after passing a US Post Office exam in 1918. When he was hired full-time around 1923, the family moved from Mill Hill to 24th Street SW, "three or four houses down the street from the church," as Bill recalled. Garland's increased income allowed Annie to leave the mill, and he delivered mail until he retired on May 9, 1955. Eventually Carl Bolick, Glenn Sigmon (Ruth's husband), and Bill had Post Office careers, too.

Bolick family house, Hickory, NC, completed in 1929. Photograph by Leslie Weidenhammer, 2010.

In June 1929 the family moved to a spacious new two-story brick home on a seven-acre parcel of land on Old Shelby Road, now 33rd Street SW in Hickory, where they remained until the end of their long lives. As Bill recalled,

We moved out in the country about four or five miles from town. We had a small farm, seven acres, I think. We raised our own vegetables and had a cow and things like that. I did quite a bit of farm work when I was growing up, because my uncle next to us had a pretty good-sized farm, and I helped him quite a bit. We traded work because we didn't have a horse or a mule to do the plowing. So usually they did our plowing for us, and we helped in the fields to make up for it.

In 1975 Bill and Doris Bolick built a new home on a lot next door to his parents. The next one over had been occupied by Bill's sister Ruth and Glenn Sigmon since the late 1950s. His older sister Myrtle and Russell Settlemyre lived in a fourth house at the end of the row.

Annie and Garland had been raised as Methodists. Garland attended the First Church of God (of Anderson, Indiana)* when its building in

---

* "First Church of God" is a name adopted by unconnected congregations and denominations in southern and midwestern areas.

Bill (left) and Earl at the new house, 1929. Courtesy of Larry Settlemyre.

Hickory was completed in 1908; Annie attended with him following their marriage in 1910. A wall plaque there today cites them as charter members as of January 22, 1912.

Music was part of the church's attraction. Garland looked forward to the annual singing conventions where he learned hymns that the Blue Sky Boys performed later on. Bill remembered:

Our parents were religious almost to the extreme, so about half the songs we do are hymns. They didn't believe in tongues or anything like that, but they were very strict. They didn't believe in wearing jewelry, no going to the movies or any kind of slang words. No drinking and no smoking—that was just out of the question, although all of my mother's people used tobacco in some form or another. My father didn't believe in sports too much, although he did buy us a set of boxing gloves when we were just kids because we were picked on quite a bit. The kids had a habit of calling us "old saints" and it was a little bit tough at times.

Earl recalled, *"On Sunday mornings we'd wake up hearing* [Garland] *singing hymns,"* and Ruth remembers that *"They were always singing till the boys left home."* Bill:

Left to right: Ruth, Bill, Carl, Annie, Earl, James, Garland, and Myrtle, late 1930s. Courtesy of Larry Settlemyre.

Family reunion, 1965 (L to R): Ruth Bolick Sigmon, Earl Bolick, Bill Bolick, Carl Bolick, Myrtle Bolick Settlemyre, James Bolick, Annie Bolick, and Garland Bolick.

My father knew quite a number of old time hymns. He attended singing schools and learned—I don't know whether it was round or shaped notes (this do, re, mi, fa, so, la, ti, do stuff), or both. He had old-time hymn books and by using this method he could get the tune to practically any song we wanted to know. Our father was instrumental in teaching us a lot of old-time hymns but he didn't play any type of musical instrument.

We never celebrated Christmas like it is today. We always had a Christmas tree; the decorations were homemade. I knew there was no Santa Claus ever since I can remember. We always had a church service on Christmas Eve and a church play that we attended. Then after church we would go home and they would give us presents, which usually was one present [each]. *I remember them buying me a little toy airplane that I could wind up and it would go around the floor in circles. I thought that was great—I couldn't have been over seven or eight years old.*

They always gave what they called a treat, which was a bagful of fruit—grapes and a little candy to [everyone in attendance]. *I kind of looked forward to that because I didn't get anything like that otherwise.* [At home] *we would have an apple or an orange and my mother always made a fruitcake, fudge, and several different kinds of candies. I remember her making a coconut candy that I liked very much. It never quite hardened and when you ate it your fingers would get sticky—but it was very good!*

My mother could play the piano by ear and the old-time organ. She also said that when she was a girl she could play the autoharp but, as we never owned one, I never heard her play anything on it. In later years, for my older sister Myrtle, we bought a piano and my mother could play a few numbers by ear on it. I think she knew more old time songs than she sang. I recall my mother singing a few numbers like "Bonnie Blue Eyes," "Cripple Creek," and possibly "Get Along Home, Cindy," but usually it was only a few verses that she knew.

The Church of God held less appeal for the Bolick children as they grew older. James joined the United Methodist Church when he moved to Kannapolis, North Carolina, as an adult, and Myrtle and Ruth joined different denominations after their marriages. Bill and Earl dropped away when they left Hickory, though they remembered the church and drew on its music. Half of their pre-1960s discography is devoted to gospel songs, and two or three hymns were essential to their daily fifteen-minute radio shows. Several came from *Reformation Glory* (1923), the Church of God hymnal when Bill and Earl were children.

Bolick family hymnal, 1923. H. A. Sherwood, A. L. Byers, and Barney Elliott Warren, *Reformation Glory: A New and Inspiring Collection of Gospel Hymns for Evangelistic Services, Shape Note Edition.* Anderson, IN: Gospel Trumpet Company, 1923.

I learned the tunes of a few songs from my maternal grandmother Hallman. When she would visit, I continually aggravated her to sing me some of the old songs she knew, even after she was in her seventies. She knew a lot of old songs, but she could maybe only remember a verse or a chorus of them. But I learned the tunes to a lot of songs and picked up the words later on. Two I think I learned from her were "Bonnie Blue Eyes" and "Two Little Frogs."

Grandmother Nancy Hallman lived a few miles outside of Hickory. When she came to visit, Bill would get his guitar and sit with her to learn words and tunes to old songs they both loved. Taking note, Garland ordered a book of folk songs for Bill from the magazine *Literary Digest.* When Garland bought a radio in 1924, the family could receive broadcasts from WJZ (New York), WLW (Cincinnati), WSB (Atlanta), and KWKH (Shreveport). Bill especially enjoyed the Saturday night *National Barn Dance* from WLS in Chicago that debuted April 19, 1924, one week after the station first went on the air.

We never had a phonograph. My father got one later on, but that was after we left home [in 1935] *and started entertaining. We did have one of the very first radios in West Hickory, a set which, as I remember, took two dry-cell and one wet-cell batteries. It was in a cabinet and you had to set three dials in order to tune in a station. The superintendent of the church had a radio, and I think he talked my father into buying one.*

There weren't too many stations in operation back then and, contrary to what most people think, there was very little country music on the air. We used to listen to the WLS Barn Dance *in Chicago before the* Opry *came on WSM. I thought the* Opry *was pretty poor when it started. It had a lot of fiddling and didn't have much singing. WLS was the station* [we preferred] *on Saturday nights. It was only a 5,000-watt station but you could pick it up on the old battery set we had. My parents would let us sit up until they signed off the air.*

There was a fellow, Chubby Parker, who used to play on the WLS Barn Dance. *He picked the five-string banjo and sang with it. I have heard some of his old recordings, and now I don't think so much of them. But at that time I really thought he was something. He sang mostly comedy songs. After Bradley* [Kincaid] *started singing over WLS, I never heard Chubby Parker again.*

Frederick R. "Chubby" Parker (1876–1940) and Kincaid (1895–1989) were part of a varied *National Barn Dance* menu that included pipe organ solos, regional comedy, pop crooners who specialized in nostalgic favorites, and quaint novelties that appealed to midwestern tastes. The entertainment was relatively upscale in comparison with Nashville's *WSM Barn Dance* that hired emcee George D. Hay (1895–1968) away from WLS in 1925. In 1927 he renamed it the *Grand Ole Opry,* dubbed himself "The Solemn Old Judge," and embraced the vigorous southern string-band

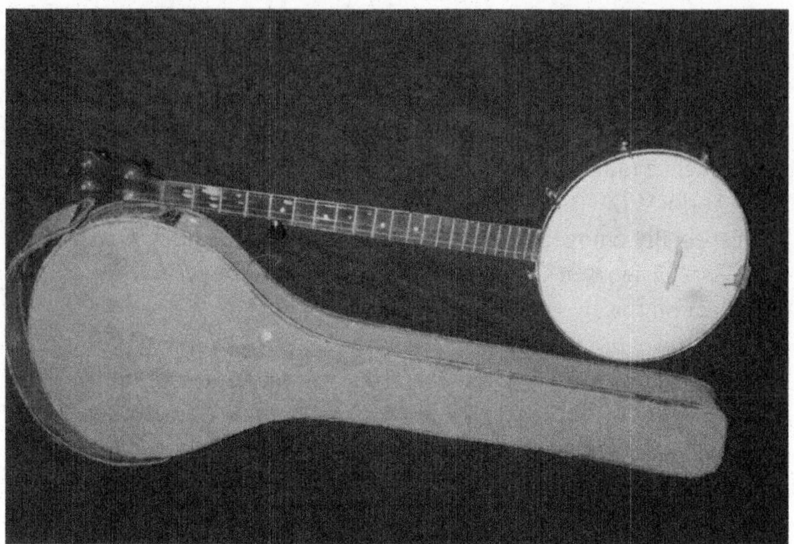

Bill's first banjo. Photograph by Charles Travis.

music that was more to his liking. Chubby Parker's banjo-picking *Opry* counterpart was the consummate showman Uncle Dave Macon, whose raucous, no-holds-barred performances left the sedate Parker in the dust. Nevertheless, it was Chubby who inspired Bill to take up music.

I decided I would like to learn to play the banjo, so I aggravated my father to buy me a five-string banjo when I was nine or ten years old. He ordered me one from Sears Roebuck as a Christmas gift. It cost four dollars and maybe ninety-five [cents], *including a canvas case—I still have it.*

I didn't learn anything about the banjo for three or four years. There was a fellow named Hugh Reinhardt who worked at the Southern Desk Company, a factory that made school furniture, and attended the Church of God we went to in West Hickory. He was a pretty capable musician. He could play piano pretty well, and the cornet. His main instrument was the fiddle, although he could play practically anything with strings on it. He came from back over there in the south mountains somewhere and he was self-taught, but he could read notes and play just about anything. When I was twelve, my dad got him to teach me a few chords on the banjo and how to tune it with a low bass, the fourth string [tuned down to C].

I liked to sing very much. I would hear songs on the radio, write them down, and remember the tunes. I seen the banjo wasn't what I wanted and so I talked [my daddy] *into buying me a six-dollar guitar. It was an orange-colored thing and the neck was sprung, but it was so pretty* [that it] *was the one I wanted. I remember where I bought it, over here in Long View at a furniture place. I took a few lessons from Hugh on it. Hugh picked with a thumb and three fingers on "New Casey Jones" and "Spanish Fandango," and that's the way I play the guitar. He had a brother named Luther that was supposed to be very good on the guitar, but he had a reputation of boozing a little and my father wouldn't let me get close to him.*

After three or four lessons, I learned about all Hugh could teach me. I bought a chord book and learned myself and taught Earl to play guitar. He plays altogether a different style than I do, because I play with three fingers and the thumb and he just uses the thumb pick. Earl was going to play the mandolin and my dad bought him a little cheap one, but he would never fool with it, so I started trying to learn it. All I knew was that it was tuned like a fiddle. I didn't fool with it much because I played the guitar most of the time.

More Early Inspirations

AS A CHILD, BILL REMAINED LOYAL TO WLS, LEARNING MUSIC STYLES he would later adapt and improve on. Lacking a family phonograph, pioneer record stars weren't part of his early music education, though he became familiar with them later on.

I liked a lot of old timers—Riley Puckett, Bradley Kincaid, Mac and Bob, Karl and Harty, Doc Hopkins, Charlie Poole. I liked Cliff Carlisle, possibly even more than I did Jimmie Rodgers. I particularly liked the Carter Family, although I didn't hear much of them until the late 1930s, when we tuned them in from XERA in Del Rio, Texas. I especially liked the Delmore Brothers and old Fiddlin' Arthur Smith—he was unique. A lot of old timers had their own style; they could sing the same songs and yet not sound like the person that they learned them from.

There are ones that never did any recordings and were only heard over the air. I recall speaking to Doc Hopkins when we were out in California [in 1965], *about a fellow named Roy Faulkner,** *a singing cowboy who used to play over KTHS in Hot Springs, Arkansas, for Dr. Brinkley, this pseudo-doctor that ran this clinic out there and later opened up these stations in Mexico.*

I don't think there was any Jimmie Rodgers or Carter Family influence on our style, although we did some Carter Family songs. I could have been influenced by two blind singers who used to be on WLS, Lester McFarland and Bob Gardner. These two blind musicians didn't sound much like country singers, but they sang very pretty songs and Mac played some of

* Faulkner (The Lonesome Cowboy, 1911–1981) sang on behalf of the infamous goat gland "doctor" John Brinkley at KTHS. They moved on to southwestern "border blaster" stations, which Brinkley owned from 1928 through the 1930s, that beamed powerful signals from over the Mexican border at twice the power permitted in the United States.

the prettiest back-up mandolin that I have ever heard. They gave me an idea of developing second harmony on mandolin to the tenor I'm singing with Earl.

In 1931 the *National Barn Dance* welcomed two influential brother-style duets who played their own mandolin and guitar accompaniment. Lester McFarland and Robert A. Gardner (aka Mac and Bob) lived in an era when Riley Puckett, Rev. Andrew (Blind Andy) Jenkins, Blind Lemon Jefferson, Blind Blake, Blind Alfred Reed, Blind Willie Johnson, and others promoted visual handicaps as part of their public image. Mac (1902–1984) was born in Gray, in southeastern Kentucky. Bob (1897–1978) came from Oliver Springs, near Oak Ridge, Tennessee. They met in 1915 at the Kentucky School for the Blind in Louisville. According to their songbook, by 1921 they "united their forces into a harmony duo, and began singing together in public appearances."

By the time they came to WLS, Mac and Bob had been successful for several years. They were smooth performers whose simple, direct style helped their Brunswick and Vocalion records and songbooks sell in enviable quantities. Their first coupling, "There's No Disappointment in Heaven" and "When the Roses Bloom Again" (1926), was a double-sided hit that became one of the best-selling country records of the decade, and both titles later became fixtures in the Blue Sky Boys' repertoire. Mac and Bob were no less accomplished in radio, performing at WNOX (Knoxville) from 1925 to 1931 and intermittently on WLS until they retired in 1950. *Mac's and Bob's WLS Book of Songs (Old & New)* was published when they joined the station in 1931 and appeared regularly in new editions thereafter. No fewer than seventeen songs in the Blue Sky Boys discography can be traced to Mac and Bob songbooks and records.

The Bolick family's radio in Hickory probably couldn't pick up Mac and Bob's 1920s Knoxville broadcasts, but Bill heard them often after they joined WLS. Their bland, over-articulated singing lacked regional appeal and tended to fall back on standard barbershop harmonies. Still, as Bill observed, clear diction and many good songs enhanced their appeal, and their influence on the Blue Sky Boys and other brother-style duets in the 1930s was considerable.

Mac and Bob had followed the earlier lead of an unlikely pair of Chicago building contractors, Perry Kim and Einar Nyland. They weren't country stylists, but they made half a dozen influential gospel discs with mandolin and guitar accompaniment between 1920 and 1923 for the

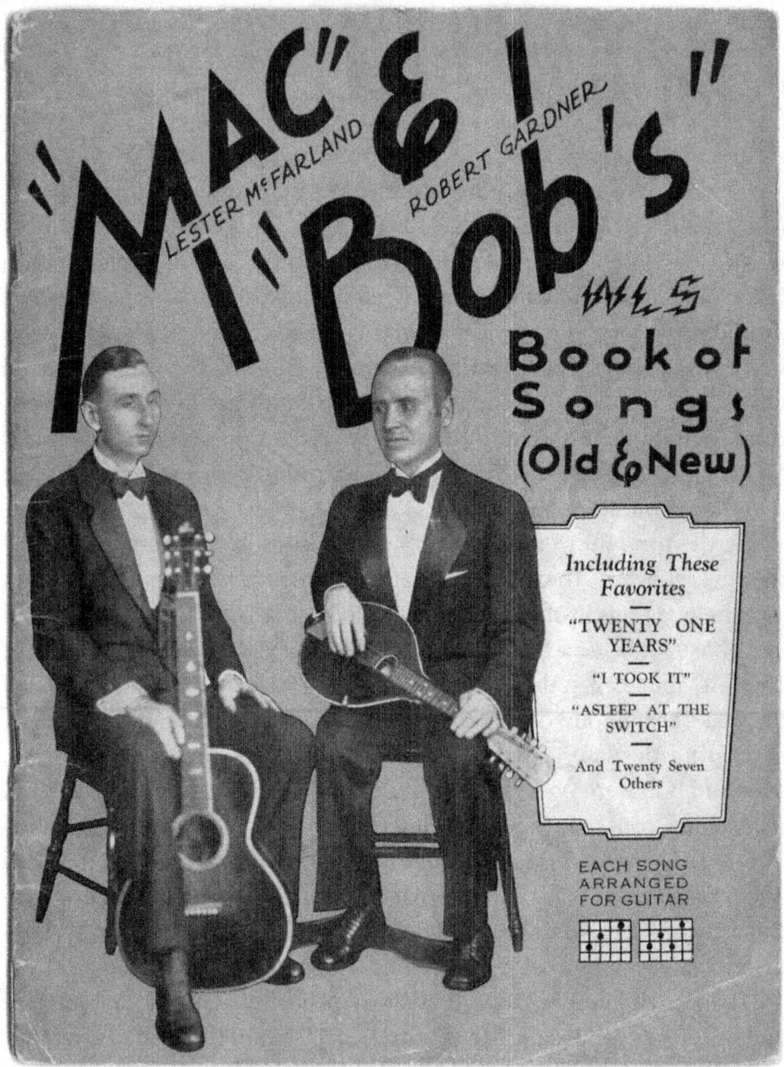

Mac & Bob's WLS songbook, 1931. Courtesy of Alan Justice and Marshall Wyatt.

Rainbow record company in Winona Lake, Indiana, owned and operated by the prominent singing evangelist, composer, and music publisher Homer Rodeheaver (1880–1955). Joseph Scott has written online that "a licensed minister and house contractor named Perry Kim lived on 111th Place in Chicago, and a house carpenter named Einar Nyland lived nearby on 111th Street. Kim was born in Holland on Dec. 2, 1876, per his draft card, and moved to the U.S. in 1899. Nyland was born in Norway about 1889 and moved to the U.S. in 1901." Kim and Nyland sang in a dated declamatory style favored by the first recorded singers in the 1890s. Nevertheless, their version of "There's No Disappointment in Heaven" (1922) undoubtedly inspired Mac and Bob's first record in 1926, and both Bob Wills and the Blue Sky Boys recorded it again in the 1930s.

Another influential duet, Karl and Harty, preceded Mac and Bob on WLS by a few months. Karl Victor Davis (1905–1979) and his partner, Hartford Connecticut Taylor (1905–1963), were both born in Mount Vernon, Kentucky, and teamed with Doc Hopkins as the Krazy Kats on WHAS (Louisville) in 1929. The trio became part of the Cumberland Ridge Runners at WLS in 1930 and recorded as the Renfro Valley Boys for the Paramount and Broadway labels in 1931. Davis was a talented songwriter whose "I'm Just Here to Get My Baby Out of Jail" (1934) and "Kentucky" (1941) were hits for Karl and Harty before becoming signature songs for the Blue Sky Boys.

Though more country than Mac and Bob, Karl and Harty were also plain vanilla singers who lacked energy and imagination in their vocal arrangements and instrumental backups. Even so, Bill Bolick heard the potential in their songs, and the Blue Sky Boys learned them from radio and promotional sheet music from publisher M. M. Cole in Chicago. Bill's record collection held only three prewar Karl and Harty discs and he rarely mentioned them to interviewers, but nineteen of their songs were covered on Blue Sky Boys records. Charlie and Bill Monroe also appeared on the *National Barn Dance* stage during the Depression years, but only as square dancers. Current tastes have consigned Mac and Bob and Karl and Harty to footnote status in country music histories, and we can only imagine the impact the Monroe Brothers might have made if their fiery music from the mid-30s had been aired on WLS a few years earlier.

The 1930s and the Call of Music

BILL BOLICK WAS FIVE WHEN HE ENTERED FIRST GRADE, AND TEN OR eleven when he was promoted from sixth to eighth grade. When he graduated from Hickory High School on May 4, 1933, he received a Gibson Kalamazoo guitar and gave his old guitar to Earl. Bill was just fifteen and employment prospects were few, so he worked as a stockroom clerk in F. W. Woolworth's basement in downtown Hickory, earning $3.50 for a sixty-hour week.

Bill pursued his extracurricular music education with Richard (Red) Hicks (1918–1987), who lived nearby in Long View. Hicks knew Earl from school and liked to stop by and pick with Bill, who called him both Richard and Red. Their collaboration would have unforeseen consequences for each.

We lived on the outskirts of Long View, right next to Hickory. You might even call it a suburb of Hickory. Red carried the newspaper by here and played the banjo. I thought he was great because I had never heard anyone play a banjo. He would stop by after he delivered his route and we started playing a little bit together. Richard never did sing any at that time. I would go over to Richard's some nights.

He took me over to Lute Isenhour [1913–1968] *who lived close to him. Lute was living with his mother-in-law and he played the five-string banjo. Lute was originally from around Taylorsville and married a girl in Long View. He was really wonderful to me. He played with a thumb and two fingers. He played a lot like Earl Scruggs and chorded some like Charlie Poole, putting in those runs on his bass strings—back then a banjo seldom took the lead in a band. He could play just about anything he wanted and he was one of the best banjo players that I have ever run across. He and Snuffy Jenkins reminded me a lot of each other.*

Bill and Lute Isenhour (with banjo), 1935. Courtesy of Alan Justice.

We kind of took to each other. Lute was almost five years older than me, and he liked the way I picked the guitar. Lute knew more songs than anyone I'd ever heard over the radio. Where he learned them I do not know. I didn't think to ask him because at that time I was only fifteen or sixteen years old. He knew them from the raunchy to the sacred—he knew more raunchy songs than anybody I ever heard!

He and I and Richard played and started singing some songs together. At first he sang tenor, and I sang lead and played the guitar (at this time I don't even think I owned a mandolin). I learned "Little Bessie" and, I believe, "Short Life of Trouble" from him, although I don't think that Earl and I sing the same version that Lute and I sang. He was the first I ever heard sing "A Wild and Reckless Hobo" and several old-time numbers like that. We changed our versions of various songs. If we heard another version or worked out an arrangement we liked better than the way we originally done it, we changed it.

Back: Ollen Benfield, Homer Sherrill. Front: Lute Isenhour, Arthur Sherrill. WBT, Charlotte, NC, 1934-35. Courtesy of Alan Justice and Marshall Wyatt.

Occasionally we would switch and [Lute] *would sing the lead and I would sing the harmony. People seemed to feel our singing was better when I sang harmony, so I started singing harmony with Lute all the time. In '34 and the early part of '35 we got to playing around the neighborhood and singing together. Once in a while we picked up extra money playing for square dances; Lute and I and the Hicks boy usually played together on those.*

In 1935 Lute was playing Saturday nights over WBT on the Crazy Water Crystals Barn Dance *in Charlotte with Homer Sherrill and the East Hickory String Band. The band* [included] *Ollen Benfield, a good guitar player for chording. Arthur Sherrill, Homer's brother, played the mandolin*

Flatiron Building, Asheville, NC, 1920s. Courtesy of Jay Bruder.

and strictly chorded with the band. Homer was a real good breakdown fiddler and Lute played the five-string banjo. They really had a good old-time band.

Early in '35, Old Man Fincher, J. W. Fincher, who headed the Crazy Water Crystals Company out of the two Carolinas and Georgia, elected to sponsor them on the Crazy Water Crystals program in Asheville over WWNC. This was the only station in the city at the time and was a 1,000-watt station, but it had quite a bit of coverage. There weren't too many radio stations then and even a small station covered quite a bit of territory. There was no one in the outfit that could sing, with the exception of Lute, and Fincher informed Homer that he would have to get someone that could. As Lute and I had done quite a bit of singing together, Lute suggested that they get me.

They let the Benfield fellow go and I started with the Crazy Hickory Nuts (the Crazy, of course, coming from the Crazy Water Crystals). I may have played with them one time on the Crazy Water Barn Dance, *but I think I actually started when we moved to WWNC, on top of* [Asheville's] *Flatiron Building. The station only had one triangular studio. I was picking the guitar at that time and I sang "Barbara Allen," "After the Ball," and a lot of old train songs. I stuck more or less to ballads; Lute and I sang duets even though our voices didn't harmonize well. I don't remember the exact time we were on the air, but it was around mid-afternoon.*

I was just seventeen and I had never worked at many jobs except around the farm. When they offered me ten dollars a week, I jumped at it because I was working for an auto body shop and making four and a half dollars a week. When we first started, I had no thought of making my living that way. Because I really was so young and everything, I don't think I realized the potential that we had. It was a day-to-day thing, just a living that we were doing.

Crazy Water, Odysseys with Homer

BILL'S RECRUITMENT COINCIDED WITH THE HICKORY NUTS' TRANSItion from Saturday night appearances on WBT's *Crazy Barn Dance* in Charlotte to a daily sponsored live noontime show on WWNC. It's not clear when one engagement ended and the other began, and they may have overlapped. The band was led by Homer Lee Sherrill (1915–2001), from Sherrills Ford, southeast of Hickory, where he learned the fiddle as a child. As he recalled, "I used to fiddle for my daddy to help him sell watermelons. By noon all ours would be sold and we'd leave the other farmers standing out in the hot sun."* After the family moved to Hickory, Homer's father worked in a furniture factory.

In August 1933 James Wesley Fincher arrived in Charlotte as the regional agent for Crazy Water Crystals, an aggressively marketed laxative from Mineral Wells, fifty miles east of Fort Worth, Texas. WBT's 50,000-watt signal allowed Fincher's daily fifteen-minute broadcasts to be heard across the region.

Fincher sponsored J.E. Mainer's Crazy Mountaineers weekdays at noon on WWNC and on WBT's *Crazy Barn Dance* Saturday nights from March 17, 1934, through November 9, 1935. At various times the *Barn Dance* cast also included the (Crazy) Tobacco Tags, the Dixon Brothers, Dick Hartman's Tennessee Ramblers, (Snuffy) Jenkins' String Band, the Monroe Brothers, Homer Sherrill's East Hickory String Band (later the Crazy Hickory Nuts), and other regional talent. The show moved to WPTF in Raleigh from February 29, 1936, through January 16, 1937, when it left the air for good.

In Georgia and the Carolinas, Fincher placed local talent on many small stations. Bill Bolick, who was never fond of him, nevertheless

---

* Pat J. Ahrens, *A History of the Musical Careers of Dewitt "Snuffy" Jenkins, Banjoist and Homer "Pappy" Sherrill, Fiddler* (Privately published, 1970).

Crazy Water Crystals container. Courtesy of Marshall Wyatt.

conceded that Fincher "really put country music across on the early radio shows throughout North Carolina and the South." Elsewhere, Crazy Water Crystals sponsored Bob Wills and his Texas Playboys over KVOO in Tulsa, Roy Acuff's Crazy Tennesseans on WROL in Knoxville, Doc Hopkins on WLS and WBBD in Chicago, and even a young Hank Snow over CHNS in Halifax, Nova Scotia.

When Bill joined the East Hickory Nuts, he still owned the amateur-grade Gibson Kalamazoo guitar he'd received two years earlier at his high school graduation. When musicians at WBT called it a Gibson reject, Garland came to Bill's aid and found him a 1928 Martin 028 guitar (serial number 36548) for seventy-five dollars. Comparing the Hickory Nuts with other acts on the *Crazy Barn Dance,* Bill concluded that his own outfit was less than outstanding:

The band really wasn't very popular or very good, and wasn't run with any business sense because we were all kids. I was just seventeen and Homer was nineteen. After you were on the air a certain length of time, [Fincher] *expected you to make personal appearances and make as much as he was paying you. When you did that, he would cut out your salary and no longer pay you. I always referred to him as the "Old Man." I imagine he was in his sixties. He was a nice looking fellow for his age and he was a very sharp dresser.*

Bill's new Martin, 1935. Courtesy of Larry Settlemyre.

Homer and I had a little difficulty about the way I played the guitar. Lute liked it [but] *Homer didn't. The old man got on Homer about why we weren't doing good up there. We really weren't—we couldn't get bookings, we weren't drawing a lot of fan mail, and he was very disappointed in us. When he came for a rhododendron festival in June* [1935], *Homer said, "Well, the whole thing is Bill's guitar playing. Bill picks the guitar with a funny style. He uses three fingers and his thumb, and his style isn't adaptable to our way of playing, so Bill is the one that's causing us not to be a hit."*

So the old man called me on the carpet and said, "Bill, you're going to have to change your style of playing the guitar. Homer says it's causing the group not to go over." I told him, "Mr. Fincher, it's like this: I'm not going to change my style of guitar playing. I've been highly complimented by Fisher Hendley, who runs your barn dance on Saturday night, about the way I pick the guitar. But," I said, "Since you feel so strongly about it, I'll just quit."

Lute and I quit in late June or July 1935 and Fincher took the show off the station [WWNC]. *Arthur Sherrill had left some time earlier, as he didn't like being separated from his family. I don't know how long we were*

Bill's Martin today. Photograph by Charles Travis.

up there—three, four, five months, possibly. When I quit, Lute quit, so that kind of broke up the whole outfit. Although we hadn't been particularly popular, the station was impressed by the way we behaved, even though we drew only fourteen, fifteen, sixteen pieces of fan mail a day, maybe not that much. They asked if we'd be interested in coming back to the station if they could get something worth our while—in other words, a sponsor. We told them that possibly we would.

When they quit, Lute suggested that Bill "whip Homer's ass." Instead, they both returned to Hickory where Lute took a job with Hickory Overalls and Bill took a hitchhiking trip through Virginia and Maryland for several weeks. Returning home, he reconnected with Earl, who had left school and run away while Bill was in Asheville, taking Bill's old Kalamazoo guitar with him when he hopped a freight train and headed west. Their sister Ruth remembers, *"We didn't know where Earl was. He didn't finish high school and he just took off with an older fellow from the west. They caught the trains and hoboed. William had gone off with somebody to make music. William said, 'I'll never go off anymore without Earl' and he was true to his word."**

Earl was just fifteen but the hobo experience had matured him. Observing that Bill had earned money from playing music, Earl resolved to

* Ruth Bolick Sigmon, Hickory, NC, September 20, 2010.

follow his example. After Bill showed him some basic techniques, Earl took to the guitar and made progress with it. The brothers became serious about developing music together and their parents encouraged them, in part to keep Earl from leaving home again.

Earl and I sang a few songs together, mostly with two guitars. People thought we were pretty good and had a different style of harmony, which encouraged us a little. I taught him chords but he developed his own style. Earl was very good at keeping time. He didn't make many bass runs—every once in a while he might give an up stroke. He was the only one I ever played with and, after I got used to it, I liked it. He said what I was doing with finger picks was too hard—he didn't like to exert himself. Up until World War II, either Red Hicks or I tuned his guitar for him.

They soon built a repertory, starting with their father's hymns and adding old songs Bill had learned from Lute Isenhour. They practiced so rigorously that their mother Annie recalled in 1974, "I liked it, but there was so much of it when they first started to learn. I never did say anything to them but sometimes I'd get so tired of it I just wanted to stop up my ears!"

Earl and I chose songs to suit our personal taste. Both of us realized that, in order to produce good, clear harmony, we had to sing at a moderate pace to be understood—and softly, if our voices were to blend. We strove to keep the harmony and lead separate. We tried to keep our natural God-given voices and didn't try to see how high or how loud we could sing. I learned to reach high notes without increasing the volume of my voice. On radio stations we worked, control men would tell us we were easier to ride gain with than anyone they had ever worked with. They seldom had to touch the controls to bring us up or down.

The Monroe Brothers came to WBT in Charlotte in the summer of 1935, just Charlie and Bill and Byron Parker, who did the announcing. I don't know that I heard the Monroe Brothers at that time, because we were on WWNC in Asheville around noon, at about the same time the Monroes were on WBT. But, as a result of the Monroe Brothers making the mandolin popular, people would write in and say play the mandolin more.

Byron Parker (1911–1948) had met the Monroes at WAAW in Omaha, Nebraska, in 1934, where he hosted their radio appearances for Texas Crystals, a mineral laxative product that unsuccessfully challenged Crazy

Water Crystals for market share. They moved on to WIS in Columbia, South Carolina, and WBT in Charlotte, where they left Texas Crystals for Crazy Water Crystals, and briefly joined WBT's *Crazy Barn Dance* cast before moving to WFBC in Greenville, South Carolina, for most of 1936. They were at WPTF in Raleigh, North Carolina, from February 1937 through June 1938, when they broke up the act. They even worked for a week at WGST in Atlanta in February-March 1936 before being replaced by the Blue Sky Boys.

Meanwhile, Lute and Bill were back in Hickory while Homer hung on at WWNC through the summer of 1935 with banjo player Mack Crowe, but they weren't a success. Then Homer heard from JFG Coffee, who had previously sponsored the Callahan Brothers at WWNC from 1934 through early 1935, when they moved to WHAS in Louisville, Kentucky. JFG agreed to back a new show at WWNC that October.

[A station representative] a*sked Homer if we would be interested in* [another] *program over WWNC, sponsored by the JFG Coffee Company of Knoxville, who would pay us ten dollars a week each. Anything we made on personal appearances would be our own. Homer heard that Earl and I sang together. I asked him if he had seen Lute and he said he had, but I found out later that he hadn't. He and Lute didn't get along. Lute wasn't interested because we hadn't done too well before, so Earl and I went up there with Homer. Earl knew C, D, and G chords on the guitar. We had never sat down to practice and I doubt if we knew half a dozen songs that we could sing together.*

We were trying to get along on ten dollars a week. That seems very little but at that time ten dollars was pretty good. You take the average textile worker around here, if they worked forty hours a week, they only made twelve dollars. And you could hire just about anyone for any kind of work for a dollar a day. So ten dollars really sounded okay—did to me! I was working at that time in an auto building place for $4.50 a week. All I had to do at WWNC was play fifteen minutes a day. We could get room and board for five dollars a week. You could get your laundry done for fifty cents; we didn't have many clothes. So that left you about $4.50 a week and that was a fortune to me. We were known as the Good Coffee Boys, John, Frank, and George. I don't know which I was, Frank or George, but I think Homer was John.

This outfit consisted of Earl, myself, and Homer. We weren't there long before we became very popular, drawing from forty to a hundred letters or more a day. WWNC had never seen anything like it. No group there had come close to drawing that much fan mail. It was a surprise to me because I didn't think we were that good. We turned to radio in the first place when we couldn't get other jobs that paid as much as the ten dollars a week we were getting.

At that time we didn't have an automobile, so Homer bought a '29 Whippet. It was a good looking car, but my daddy had owned a four-cylinder Whippet and that thing gave trouble all the time. [After Homer bought one] *we were afraid to make personal appearances because we were afraid we'd break down on the road.*

Finally, when its radiator froze and burst on a cold day, the Whippet became history. The Good Coffee Boys remained without transportation for the rest of their stay at WWNC, but their daily broadcasts allowed them to develop the music they would soon perform as the Blue Sky Boys.

We sang with the mandolin and guitar, or two guitars. Our style was so different from the Crazy Hickory Nuts that I don't believe many listeners realized that two of us [Bill and Homer] *were former members of that group. We sang religious songs and songs that told stories, like "The Knoxville Girl." We didn't sing too many western or frivolous songs. We were the first group that was popular with religious songs. We found they were so popular with our radio audience that we kept singing them through the years.*

We started getting requests for songs using the mandolin because the Monroe Brothers had made the public conscious of the instrument. I don't think I knew over three or four songs on the mandolin but, in a short time, I discarded the guitar and started playing the little cheap mandolin my dad had bought for Earl. It had cost less than ten dollars. I didn't know anything about it; I was just trying to teach myself. From the very first I never simply chorded while we sang. I worked to develop a sound that would be similar to a third voice while I was singing harmony with Earl. We always felt the singing was more important than the instrumentals, and we tried to develop a style of playing that would enhance our voices.

Bill Bolick drew on his earlier inspiration, Lester McFarland, in adding a harmony part on his mandolin. It was a straightforward, elegant style that inspired other young players like Ernest Ferguson (1918–2014), Jethro Burns (1920–1989), Paul Buskirk (1923–2002), Ira Louvin (1924–1965),

Ray Patterson (1926–2012), and Red Rector (1929–1990), who preferred Bill Bolick's melodic and harmonic approach to Bill Monroe's warp-speed virtuosity.

Ernest Ferguson was initially attracted to the Monroe sound in the mid-1930s, and tried to emulate it until he joined Johnnie and Jack in 1940, when Johnnie Wright encouraged him to develop his own style. Citing Bill Bolick's solos and harmonies and Paul Buskirk's phrasing as his models, Ferguson's 1945–47 records with the Bailes Brothers show how well he'd absorbed both styles.

WWNC, WGST, 1935–36

WE [THE GOOD COFFEE BOYS] *DIDN'T STAY AT ASHEVILLE BUT ABOUT six months. When Old Man Fincher found out we were doing so well, he asked us to go to Atlanta and play over WGST. It was owned by the state—GST stood for the Georgia School of Technology. The only thing he knew about us was that we were very popular. I don't think he realized until we got there that we had worked for him previously. WWNC had been so nice to us that we hesitated, but Homer, Earl and I left Asheville in March 1936 and went to Atlanta. We were guaranteed twenty dollars* [per week] *each, but we made much more than that.*

A Mrs. Hingle was there; the movie star Pat Hingle was her son. She ran the office for Crazy Water Crystals in the Arcade Building on Whitehall Street. We didn't know that Fincher was going with Mrs. Hingle and that they were planning to get married. She wanted to name us the Blue Ridge Hill Billies—Homer, Bill, and Earl. She was a nice lady and I liked her.

Her office had a water fountain doctored with Crazy Water Crystals, and Fincher and Mrs. Hingle both drank from it. She became the Hill Billies' agent, accompanying them to schoolhouse shows, placing poems and her picture in a songbook that Fincher subsidized, *Songs and Poems by the Blue Ridge Hill Billies,* and taking a quarter of their income off the top.

The Monroe Brothers had been [at WGST] *but they didn't stay long; I think we took the same spot they had. I don't think they ever worked for Crazy Water Crystals after that time. I would never say we were as popular as the Monroe Brothers, but I believe we were closer to the people. WGST was a 1,000-watt station when we first went there; it was a 5,000-watt station in 1938. We were bucking* (i.e. competing with) *WSB, a 50,000-watt station. Not a lot of people listened to WGST like they did to WSB. To get listeners*

Earl, Homer Sherrill, and Bill were the Good Coffee Boys in 1935–36 and the Blue Ridge Hill Billies in the spring of 1936. Courtesy of Alan Justice and Marshall Wyatt.

you had to pick them up by hand and mouth, so to speak, and I know we were the only act that was ever really successful on WGST.

We had a tremendous reception down in Georgia—yes, we did! We were on the top floor of the Ansley Hotel and we had so many people up there to see us broadcast that you had to get a pass [to get in].

The Monroe Brothers were only at WGST for a week and played their final show at 12:15 P.M. on Tuesday, March 3, 1936. Bill, Earl, and Homer, formerly the Good Coffee Boys and now the Blue Ridge Hill Billies, succeeded the Monroes at 7 A.M. the next morning, and remained for the

Postcard of the Hotel Ansley, Atlanta, GA, home of WGST studios, 1930s.

next two and a half months. On the air, Fincher described them as backwoods mountaineers, even though their theme was the 1925 Hawaiian pop song "Drifting and Dreaming." The Bolicks didn't much care for the stereotyping, but at Fincher's insistence they dressed in overalls and straw hats for publicity photos, personal appearances, and even broadcasts.

We would go to the Crazy Water Crystals office and change into overalls and stuff. And then we would walk four or five blocks to WGST, carrying our instruments with everybody staring at us. This lasted for about a week—they knew we didn't like it.

Bill's Hembree mandolin. Photograph by Charles Travis.

It was a nice station, head and shoulders above WWNC. In a short time, we were drawing a tremendous amount of mail. We started getting requests right off—I think it surprised Old Man Fincher. We were having large crowds at what few public appearances we made. We had schoolhouses running over. The Blue Ridge Hill Billies—they were something!

I purchased the first mandolin I recorded with at an Atlanta pawn shop. It sounded so much better than the one I had been playing, a production-line job that could have been equaled anywhere for six to ten dollars. I understand it was made by a fellow named E.M. Hembree and I think I paid eighteen dollars for it. I thought the tone was beautiful and I used it on our first two recording sessions.

When we first went [to Atlanta], *Fincher offered to sell us a car on time without making a down payment. He had two cars in good shape and he said, "I'll sell them to you for four hundred dollars. Take either one—one's a Ford and the other's a Nash." He said he'd take five dollars a week as payment, so we jumped on it because it gave us a chance to start making personal appearances. We took the Ford because it was sportier looking. It was a black two-door with red wheels, I believe, silver rims. Oh, it was top of the line!*

Most show dates we played were east and north of Atlanta. I remember playing five or six places in Tennessee and about the same in North Carolina. We played south and east of Atlanta to a range of forty or fifty miles, as far east as Augusta, and occasionally in South Georgia, but most people in these areas didn't know there was another station in Atlanta besides WSB. We played quite a number of dates in eastern and northern Alabama.

When J. W. Fincher learned that Victor and Bluebird producer Eli Oberstein was planning a visit to Charlotte to make records in June 1936, he arranged an audition for the trio, just as differences between him, Homer, and the Bolicks were coming to a head. Bill and Earl approached Fincher about excluding Homer from their duet records, but he refused to go along.

Old Man Fincher asked if we would like to make records. "Of course we would," I thought. So he said, "I know a talent scout at Victor in Charlotte. I'll tell him about the mail you're drawing and have him tune in to your program. I think he could pick up WGST and if he likes you he'll get in touch with you." So he saw the scout and the scout wrote us. We picked out a few numbers for Homer to fiddle; the rest of the songs Earl and I sang, and they were the ones we got requests for. Homer seldom got requests for fiddle tunes.

Fincher's talent scout was Van H. Sills, manager of RCA distributor Southern Radio Corporation's record department, who vetted and scheduled performers in advance of Oberstein's visits.

Earl and I didn't think we should give Homer an equal split on the recording contract because on our radio shows Homer had just been playing breakdowns and things like that. He couldn't play backup fiddle and when Earl and I sang he got us off our harmony, so we thought it best not to let him play while we sang. We talked the situation over and he said, "That'll be all right. I'll play a couple of fiddle tunes and we'll do like we've been doing on the radio shows." Everything seemed okay.

Then he went to Mr. Fincher and told him Earl and I were trying to keep him from making phonograph records. At the time we were living with Mrs. Hingle and [Fincher] *was down there for a weekend. We were all sitting at the table and he jumped all over Earl and I. He said we were getting too big for our britches, that we thought we were a lot better than what we were. He didn't give us a chance to defend ourselves; he really poured it on right there at the table in front of Mrs. Hingle and her kids. He said that from now on Homer would be the boss of our outfit.*

Eli Oberstein. Courtesy of David Diehl.

Earl and I didn't say anything. After it was all over, we were upstairs in our room and Homer said, "Well, I didn't know he was gonna do like that [or] *I wouldn't have said anything about it." And I said, "Well, Homer, you did."*

We stayed a couple of more days but things weren't right, so Earl and I moved to a rooming house. We went on like that for a week. That didn't work out, so Earl and I came on back home. We were making very good money and it was difficult to make this decision. We were, perhaps, a little too proud for our own good, but never during our entire career did we continue working for anyone we didn't feel was treating us fairly. While Mr. Fincher may have possessed some admirable qualities, he was a very vindictive person.

Fincher promised to get replacements, two fellows who went by the names Shorty and Mack. On his arrival back in Charlotte from Atlanta, he got in touch with Van Sills and told him that Earl and I were no longer working together, that Homer, Shorty and Mack would fill our recording engagement. He told Van quite a number of things, said we copied the Monroe boys and we weren't too distinctive in our styling.

When the group broke up, Earl and Bill left WGST and went home to Hickory to prepare for recording, unaware that Fincher had cancelled their audition. On Tuesday, June 16, 1936, Garland took the day off from work and brought Annie along to visit her sister in Charlotte while their boys were making records. It was the day they met Eli Oberstein and a day that would change the direction of their lives and assure their place in history.

The old Victor Talking Machine Company was producing country and "race" records only on an irregular basis before 1926, when Ralph Peer agreed to work there for a dollar a year while securing copyright control and publishing rights to music he produced. Those songs became the foundation for his profitable companies, Southern Music (ASCAP) and (after 1939) Peer International (BMI). His celebrated first recordings of the Carter Family and Jimmie Rodgers in 1927 were moneymakers that stimulated profitable new markets for Victor and others in the South and Southwest.*

Peer copyrighted every song that wasn't already nailed down and, by intent or error, poached a few that were. In the 1930s, new country songs were increasingly written by performers themselves—notably Alton Delmore, Cliff Carlisle, Karl Davis (of Karl and Harty), Dorsey Dixon, John Lair, Bob Nolan, and, in Canada, Wilf Carter and Hank Snow. By 1940 Floyd Tillman, Cindy Walker, Mel Foree, and others were becoming even more skilled at the craft, and at learning business and professional practices of the broader popular music industry.

As Peer's publishing empire expanded, it didn't take his bosses at Victor long to recognize that they were giving away the store. Even though he made Victor the strongest country label of the late 1920s, he was eclipsed in 1930–31 by his assistant Eli Oberstein, who achieved a power base at RCA by cutting corners and elbowing Peer aside. Oberstein's new game plan included evading copyright royalty payments whenever possible, often by retitling popular songs on records for country audiences, and hoping no one would notice.

---

* *Ralph Peer and the Making of Popular Roots Music* by Barry Mazor (Chicago Review Press, 2015) summarizes Peer's life and career.

By cutting production costs, Oberstein created stable and sustainable bottom lines in the early 1930s, when the Depression forced other record operations into mergers or finished them off entirely. Though budget labels flourished in the 1920s, price cutting then was anathema to Victor, who retailed its discs at seventy-five cents until 1931–32, when competitive price cuts became essential to survival, even for the industry's flagship label.

At some point, Victor began to press independently produced Crown discs that retailed for twenty-five cents. Near the end of 1931, the company started to keep written records for each Crown release in its files. Elektradisk and Bluebird lines followed Crown in 1932; none of the three were publicized as Victor products. Elektradisk received limited distribution and the label quietly expired early in 1934.

A new Bluebird series was launched in April 1933 as a Victor byproduct, retailing at thirty-five cents and serving briefly as a house label for Woolworth stores. Under Oberstein's direction, Bluebird went into general distribution as Crown quietly disappeared by summer's end. After January 1934 new RCA country, blues, and Tex-Mex releases appeared exclusively on Bluebird, sharing catalog space with second-tier pop singers and dance bands. The label soon became a competitive player, especially when the Montgomery Ward chain re-pressed Bluebird and occasional Victor masters for retail and catalog sales on its own label, discounting them to as little as twenty-one cents each when purchased in quantity.

Ralph Peer captured country music and blues closer to home when he took portable recording equipment to Atlanta, Savannah, Memphis, and New Orleans in February and March 1927, inaugurating an ongoing series of southern recording expeditions that lasted until February 1932, when negligible Depression record sales no longer justified the effort. Oberstein resumed the practice in 1934 on Bluebird's behalf, traveling to San Antonio in March and Atlanta in August. He returned to both cities in 1935 and added New Orleans to the schedule. He first visited Charlotte in February 1936 to record the cream of southeastern country talent, including Mainer's Mountaineers, the Carlisle Brothers, the Monroe Brothers, the Dixon Brothers, the Delmore Brothers, Riley Puckett, and Fiddlin' Arthur Smith. Sales of their records prompted a return in June, when Eli added the Blue Sky Boys to the roster. Bluebird scheduled regular releases of their records for the next five years and re-pressed all but a handful on the Montgomery Ward label until 1941, when the mail order and department store retail chain left the record business.

Southern Radio Corporation, Charlotte, NC, 1930s. Courtesy of Andy Merck, Bear Family Records.

Record making in the 1930s produced a large body of classic performances in multiple genres and regional styles. Eli Oberstein supervised thousands of blues, country, gospel, Acadian French, and Tex-Mex records through 1938, setting up portable disc mastering equipment to capture local talent in hotels, warehouses, and other commercial spaces in southern cities. Bluebird remained marginally active through the war until 1946, when its artists were either dropped or placed on the company's full-priced RCA Victor label and Bluebird became inactive.

In 1936 RCA's temporary studio was on the second floor of the Southern Radio Corporation building at 208 South Tryon Street in Charlotte.

The Blue Sky Boys arrived at their appointed time on June 16, expecting to perform songs they'd prepared. But, because of J. W. Fincher's mischief, Oberstein tried to show them the door.

*Eli Oberstein wasn't expecting us when we arrived at the recording studio. The place was kind of a dump. You should have seen it—it was a kind of auditorium with a little stage. There was a place draped off where the engineer worked while we recorded. When we walked in they were recording the Dixon Brothers.**

We sat down and were listening, and Earl picked up something to read. After we had been there a while, Eli Oberstein, the A&R man for Victor, came back and said, "What in the hell do you think this is, a reading room?" He was pretty rough about it. Earl was pretty high tempered and he told Eli he didn't give a damn what it was. We told him we were supposed to record and Eli said, "You're the Bolick boys?" I told him that we were, so he said, "You are not supposed to record—we were informed that you cancelled your recording date." We told him we hadn't been notified about it and he said, "Well, your date's been cancelled. I had notification that you all had broken up and wouldn't be recording."

By that time I was getting pretty well disgusted with the whole situation. Eli wasn't too congenial and he said, "You're the boys who copy the Monroe Brothers, aren't you?" I told him, "No sir, we do not copy the Monroes. I haven't ever heard the Monroe boys," and I'm not sure that I had, because it was less than a year after they hit this part of the country. He said, "Well, just stick around a little while. Being as you're here, we may as well give you an audition." I said, "Well, if you want us to," but we were just about out of the mood of making records.

Earl and I went up on that little old stage they had. You should've seen the primitive recording stuff they used. They had something like a music stand with a red light on it. They had an RCA ribbon mike. The records were made on twelve-inch wax discs. As you sang through the microphone, the disc went around and [a stylus] *cut a groove in that wax.*

He said, "When this red light goes on, you start singing. When it goes off, you be sure to stop. We would like for the songs to run about two and a half minutes to three minutes and twenty seconds." He had a little curtained

* Bill's memory is contradicted by the day's recording logs, which show the Brown Brothers duet recording six tracks on the morning of June 16. The Blue Sky Boys followed from 1 to 3 pm, and Cliff and Bill Carlisle from 3 to 6:15. The Dixon Brothers session took place a week later on June 23.

off place in the corner. He went back in there and we played "Sunny Side of Life" for him. We had sung one verse and we were just singing the chorus when he came out from his little booth. I said to myself, "That's it, I'll just put 'em back in the case." But he said, "Oh, that's great, you boys really got something different. Whoever said you sounded like the Monroes sure didn't know what they were talking about. I think we can sell a lot of records."

Oberstein's surprise was understandable. The Monroes and Bolicks were both brother duets whose specialty was harmony singing with guitar and mandolin, but the resemblance ended there. As we've noted, the Monroes emphasized high-speed dexterity, tuning their instruments above standard pitch and singing near the top of their ranges. The Blue Sky Boys were just as intense, but they focused their exceptional voices and harmonies on slower, thoughtful songs that they performed in comfortable keys.

Oberstein had the Bolicks record ten tracks in two hours, using Bill's new Hembree mandolin while Earl played Bill's Martin 028 guitar. "Sunny Side of Life" came from the 1923 Church of God hymnal *Reformation Glory* and, coupled with one of Garland Bolick's favorites, "Where the Soul Never Dies," was the first Blue Sky Boys record. Both sides were hits. When "I'm Just Here to Get My Baby Out of Jail," "Midnight On the Stormy Sea," and "Down on the Banks of the Ohio" were released a few weeks later, they too more than held their own.

The first record we put out undoubtedly sold pretty well because Victor put out a flyer that called us "The New Hillbilly Kings," and it said that in the amount of time this record had been out it had sold more than any other group.

When we started to record, Eli told us, he said, "Were I you boys, I don't think I would use the Bolick Brothers. We have so many brother acts recording now: the Dixon Brothers, Monroe Brothers, Callahan Brothers, Delmore Brothers. If you can think of something else I would use another name." He and I sat there and discussed it. We got the blue from the Blue Ridge Mountains and the sky because that country is known as the Land of the Blue Sky. So that's how we came up with the name Blue Sky Boys. He told us that beneath "The Blue Sky Boys" he would print "Bill and Earl Bolick" in parentheses.

After that Eli always treated us pretty nice, I thought, maybe a little nicer than most of the groups that would come in there. He never spoke one harsh word to us, I guarantee you that! He knew times were rough [so] *he came to me and said, "If you need any money, Bill, to carry you over wherever you are, just write me and let me know, and I'll send you some." It would have been an advance on royalties. I said, "I might want more money than I'll sell records," and he said, "You just let me worry about that!" I never did call on him, but there were several times I thought about it.*

Homer Sherrill's reconstituted Blue Ridge Hill Billies, with Everett "Shorty" Watkins (mandolin) and Kinman "Mac" McMillar (guitar), recorded ten titles for Bluebird six days later on June 22. Homer returned to WWNC for the summer before teaming briefly with Wade Mainer and Zeke Morris. He recorded with them on October 12 when Oberstein returned to Charlotte, and even sang bass harmony on five titles. Like the Bolicks, Wade and Zeke had severed relations with J. W. Fincher and moved on after parting amicably with Wade's brother, J. E. Mainer, who chose to keep working for Fincher. Bill and Earl replaced Wade and Zeke with J. E. that summer, after Bill took time out for surgery to cure a blocked nasal passage and tonsillitis.

Immediately after we finished our first recording session, June 16, 1936, I went to an ear, eye, nose, and throat clinic in Charlotte. For the past few months I'd had difficulty breathing through my nose and my throat had been giving me a lot of trouble. In fact, the morning we left Hickory for our session, I couldn't breathe enough through either nostril. With constant use of an inhaler, I managed to open both passages just a little. After an examination, I was informed I needed cartilage removed from my nostrils and my tonsils removed. I remained in the hospital for three or four days. I was told not to sing any at all for six to eight weeks, and then start back gradually.

In late August or early September 1936, J. E. Mainer came to Hickory to see if we would go to work with him. Earl and I were over on our brother's farm, cutting wood and selling it for four dollars a cord. I'd seen a car coming at a distance and it looked like J. E. Mainer's, a '34 Ford with yellow wheels and a trunk on the back. He was working for Crazy Water Crystals on a small station in Charlotte, WSOC. We told him we weren't interested in working for J. W. Fincher again, but he insisted that we would actually be working for him and not Mr. Fincher.

J. E. had a group at that time but evidently they weren't doing well. We really needed the work as my operations were quite expensive. We hadn't worked anywhere in about three months and agreed to work with him. All monies were to be divided equally. Another thing upon which we agreed was that we would be known as The Blue Sky Boys. At this time we had two or three records on the market and felt if ever we were to get anywhere, we couldn't afford to be changing our name. He could refer to the entire group as J. E. Mainer's Mountaineers, but whenever we sang a song we were to be introduced as The Blue Sky Boys, Bill and Earl Bolick.

I also said, "You are going to have to tune down your fiddle, J. E., because we can't sing as high as you tune." Earl and I tuned our instruments to about standard key. When J. E. tuned to G, he was actually in A, too high for the way we sang. We finally agreed that Earl and I would tune in standard and J. E., his guitar and banjo players would keep their instruments at a higher pitch.

It's not clear how the Mountaineers sounded with instruments tuned at competing pitches, but it was a factor in terminating their brief stay with J. E.

It is possible that we were with him a month, but I think it was three weeks at most. First, although J. E. asserted that J. W. Fincher had nothing to do with his hiring us, on our arrival in Charlotte he insisted that we go to the Crazy Water Crystals office and talk with Mr. Fincher. The meeting was civil, although we quickly realized that Mr. Fincher was the one who had sent J. E. to hire us. He wanted us to understand that J. E. would be our boss, a fact we already understood. We realized we had made a mistake but we decided to make a go of it.

A WSOC announcer emceed all the programs, including the commercials, artists, and songs. We were never introduced as the Blue Sky Boys but as Bill and Earl. We mentioned this to J. E. but he insisted he had told the announcer to introduce us as the Blue Sky Boys and would talk to him again. But during our entire stay with J. E. we were never introduced as the Blue Sky Boys on radio or personal appearances. We were never allowed to look at the fan mail. J. E. picked it up and always took it home with him.

We could see that things could never work out and told J. E. we thought it best to leave. We were making enough money to get by but we didn't hesitate to quit working for anyone when we felt we weren't being treated fairly. I think J. E. was relieved when we quit but I learned later that

Mr. J. W. Fincher was outraged and vowed he would never give us another chance to work for him. I have held no ill feelings toward J. E., but it disturbed me that he hadn't dealt fairly with us in describing the circumstances under which we would be working with him. I still believe the only reason he hired us was at the insistence of Mr. J. W. Fincher, and he wanted no part of anyone that didn't want to be called J. E. Mainer's Mountaineers.

Mainers and Bolicks aside, Fincher had other, more pressing problems. The *Crazy Barn Dance* moved from WBT to WPTF in Raleigh, where it lasted from February 1936 until January 1937. By then the product was coming under scrutiny of the Food and Drug Administration and President Roosevelt's Undersecretary of Agriculture Rexford G. Tugwell, who singled out Crazy Water Crystals for special scrutiny in a campaign to stamp out medical advertising quackery. Fincher ended his sponsorship of radio programming in 1936 and the product was history by 1940.

We left [J. E. Mainer] *in the late summer or early fall of 1936. Not long after we returned to Hickory we received a letter from Eli Oberstein, wanting us to record again in October. We were surprised, as we didn't expect to be recording again so soon. We had no idea how our recordings were selling, as we weren't due to be paid royalties until November. We had little time to prepare for the session, as we hadn't been singing too much due to the circumstances I have described. We mainly chose songs with which we were familiar and hadn't been recorded by other artists.*

The Bolicks' second session took place only four months after their first, and it was Eli's third visit to Charlotte that year. He was there on six occasions between February 1936 and January 1938 and recorded the Blue Sky Boys on four of them. Three two- to three-hour sessions would be scheduled on a typical day and, like other groups, the Bolicks were expected to produce ten or twelve titles per session. Bill wasn't happy about the casual way their records were made. He felt that neither Eli nor Earl was fastidious about details, and he was frustrated by them both.

Earl was not one to practice too much. He didn't worry about me having to harmonize with him or about my playing the mandolin. He didn't worry at all, didn't bother Earl a bit, so we didn't do too much rehearsing. I notice a lot of little bobbles and stuff when I listen to the records. I could have done better if Eli had let us do them over. He'd say, "Let's just go through this."

I thought it was to get a level and he'd say, "That's good." I'd say, "Did you record that?" and he'd say, "That's all right; that's the way hillbilly music is supposed to sound." What can you say to a man like that? After the war the union took more part in the recording [when sessions were more strictly controlled and] *they would only allow you so many hours. It was nice to make records, but you made little money off them. You only drew one penny royalty on a record and the company took a certain amount for breakage out of that.*

After our second recording session in Charlotte on October 13, 1936, Earl and I made no effort to get back on radio. We borrowed our father's car and made a trip to Knoxville to see if the JFG Coffee Company would be interested in having us again. We had learned from the JFG salesman in Asheville area that the company's sales had increased greatly while we were working for them over WWNC in Asheville and thought they might like to have us again. We went to the plant and talked with Mr. Goodson, owner and manager of the company. He was very nice to us and recalled our having worked for them in Asheville. He called his son into the office and both listened while we sang several songs for them.

They seemed very impressed and Mr. Goodson asked if we would do their radio program over WNOX that day. After presenting the program we went back to the plant. I felt that, because of our youthful appearance, Mr. Goodson hesitated to hire us. He wanted us to remain in Knoxville for several weeks and play his program. He told us he would pay our expenses while we were there. We would gladly have done this, but we had to get our father's car back. Too, I think we were too proud to admit that we didn't have enough money with us to pay for even one night's lodging. We returned to Hickory and never followed up this opportunity. Had we done as Mr. Goodson suggested, I'm sure he would have hired us to present his programs over WNOX. At this time I'm pretty certain there were no other live country acts on the station and we would have been successful. I still recall Mr. Goodson being nice to us and I never forget anyone who treated us in that manner.

Homer Redux

SOMETIME IN JANUARY OR EARLY FEBRUARY OF 1937, HOMER SHERRILL came to see us. Crazy Water Crystals had taken all their programs off the air, and he was unemployed. He had been working with Wade Mainer and Zeke Morris, and with Fincher's son Tom, [announcer] *for the Crazy Water Crystal Company over various stations since we had separated in early June of 1936. They were broadcasting from WPTF in Raleigh.*

Homer wanted us to return with him to WGST in Atlanta. He said WGST had told him they would give us sustaining time [i.e., without commercial sponsorship], *as no other group on the station had seemed as popular as us. We were hesitant about working with Homer again. He had been the cause of my confrontation with Mr. J. W. Fincher when I was working with the Crazy Hickory Nuts over WWNC in Asheville that had caused me to quit the group. Also, he had directly been the reason for our disagreement with Mr. Fincher in the spring of 1936.*

Homer apologized profusely for the way things had turned out in Atlanta and promised that nothing like that would ever happen again. He said he had a 1932 Model B Ford coupe that was completely paid for and all he asked of Earl and me was to pay our part of expenses to keep it in running order. As soon as we started making personal appearances, he would trade it in on a more comfortable car. The coupe had only one seat and riding conditions weren't too pleasant for three people. We could pay our part of the equity he had invested in the coupe and we would all be equal owners of the new car. Before agreeing to work with him again we made a strict pact: from this time on it would be one for all and all for one. Under these conditions we went back to work with Homer over WGST.

It was hard to get going good over WGST as we were working on a sustaining basis and personal appearances were hard to get until you built up an audience. We were paid only when we had a sponsor and this was usually ten dollars weekly per person. At least half of the time, we played

(L to R) Earl, Homer Sherrill, and Bill, sponsored on WGST by an Atlanta auto tire retailer, 1937. Courtesy of Alan Justice and Marshall Wyatt.

free of charge in return for the privilege of announcing where we would appear in person.

We were bucking the powerful 50,000-watt WSB, which had a regular country music program, the Cross Roads Follies. *It had five to ten times more coverage than WGST, four to six groups of country music entertainers, and a booking agency. We usually attained listeners by people telling other people about our programs. I recall many listeners telling me that they had never tuned in WGST until we came there.*

After we had two or three records on the market, publishing companies began to send us sheet music and songbooks. If I felt any of the material was suitable for our style of singing, I usually held on to it. We received all kinds of music including jazz, orchestra, and classical.

I decided I would try to learn to read music. I felt it a shame that we were receiving so much material and were unable to put any of it to use. I started taking lessons from Ernest Hodges, who taught violin and banjo. He now taught music and made violins. He knew more fiddle tunes than anyone I had ever known. He knew many jigs, reels, polkas, and hornpipes,

1937. Courtesy of Ben Niblock.

and he was the best five-string banjo player I had ever seen or heard. His banjo playing ranged from "Coal Creek March" to the classics. I used the mandolin as my instrument for learning. Ernie was an excellent teacher and in a very short time I was able to read simple music in most major keys. If we received a song I thought would be good for us, if I had any trouble with it, I would take it over to Ernie. He would play it over several times for me and help me with the rough spots. I would usually learn new songs and teach them to Earl.

After we had been at WGST several months, Byron Parker, the Old Hired Hand, came to see if Earl and I would go to work with him. He had been Charlie and Bill Monroe's announcer and manager since they first came to the Carolinas. I never had the opportunity to listen to their programs very much but I do remember that he would say in this old folksy voice: "Yes sir, folks, you're listening to the boys that can't be beat and can't be tied, Charlie and Bill Monroe." [When] *they would go out he would say, "Oh, we had to have the house stretcher last night—we really stacked them in there."*

He told me he was splitting with Charlie and Bill, or already had. He said Charlie's wife was going to take care of the business and Charlie and

WGST banner with Bill's Martin 0028 guitar and Hembree mandolin. Photograph by Charles Travis.

Bill felt they didn't need him any longer. He offered us a weekly salary plus a percentage of personal appearance receipts. The salary alone was more than we were making at that time. Too, we knew we would be booked almost solid on appearances. I'm sure we would have worked out a good deal with him, for I really feel he wanted us to work with him.

I told him we were interested, but Homer Sherrill was working with us at that time and we had agreed to stick together. I will quote almost verbatim the words he spoke, "You don't need anyone else. If you will come with me, I'll make you famous just like I did with the Monroe Brothers." When I told him I didn't think we could go without Homer, he said, "If that's the only way you'll come with me, I'll take Homer. However, I don't think we can work him on a percentage basis." Earl and I decided we couldn't accept his offer because of the conditions under which he would hire Homer. No one that has ever worked with Earl and I can truthfully say that we ever went back on our word or wrongfully treated them in any way.

Parker parted company with the Monroes in the spring of 1937 and became a staff announcer at WIS in Columbia, South Carolina, where he remained until his untimely death at 37 in 1948.

Bill's 1937 Martin mandolin. Photograph by Charles Travis.

Things went pretty well for us on WGST after we got started good. Although show dates weren't plentiful we had fairly good crowds at most of them. WGST got us a sponsor that paid us the weekly sum of ten dollars each.

I managed to pay off my hospital bills from the previous year. I also purchased a Martin mandolin. On our first and second recording sessions I had used [the Hembree] *homemade mandolin I had purchased at a pawn shop in Atlanta. I always thought it had a beautiful tone but it was very thinly carved. The arched top was almost paper-thin and gradually it kept sinking in. I had it repaired several times but I knew I would have to get another mandolin. The* [1929] *Martin I purchased was a Model 20. I have always liked its mellow tone and I still have it in my possession. I understand that less than three hundred of this model were produced. Mine is one of the few with an ebony pick guard. It has curly maple sides, a curly maple curved back, and a spruce arched top with a genuine ebony fingerboard and bridge.*

I kept the Hembree mandolin and around 1990 a fellow came by who told me he thought he could repair it. He never succeeded in restoring it the way it was originally built, but he put an adjustable bridge on it and a pick guard. It still sounds good, but not quite with the original quality.

Bill's Martin Model 20 mandolin (serial number 14322) is the one seen in Blue Sky Boys photos from 1937 onward. When he first spotted it at the Cable Piano Company showroom in Atlanta, it was offered for

1937 poster. Courtesy of Alan Justice and Marshall Wyatt.

seventy-five dollars, or ninety with a case. It was more than he could afford and he decided to wait awhile. He and Homer saw it again after a showroom fire reduced the price to sixty dollars, including the case. Homer loaned Bill the money and they walked out with the Martin. Bill featured it on the Blue Sky Boys session in August 1937 and it remained his instrument of choice for the rest of his life.

In May of 1937 we received a royalty check from RCA that allowed us to make a substantial down payment on a big Oldsmobile. It wasn't new but it was in good condition and roomier and more comfortable than any car we had owned previously. Homer didn't quite live up to his promises regarding the use of his auto and had purchased a larger and roomier car, but not under the partnership basis. We agreed to drive our car 2,000 miles and Homer would drive his car 1,000 miles. Each would pay his own car expenses.

Homer married an Atlanta girl and told us he would like several days' vacation to take his bride to Hickory to meet his parents, relatives, and friends. He was to return in three or four days. When this time had passed, plus two or three more days, we got in touch with Homer's wife's people, who informed us that Homer was working with the Morris Brothers over WPTF in Raleigh. They seemed shocked that we knew nothing about this. We could hardly believe that Homer would do a thing like that. To the best of my knowledge we had had no disagreements of any consequence and things seemed to be going very well. I suppose Homer's added responsibility of marriage was partially the cause. I feel he thought he could make more money by going with the Morris Brothers to WPTF. He often told Earl and I what large crowds they had and how easy it was to book appearances when he had worked there with Wade and Zeke in 1936. After the pact we had made I don't think he had the nerve to face us. We never again worked with anyone on a partnership basis.

Homer married Doris Lyle on June 27, 1937, and recorded with the Morris Brothers as Wiley, Zeke and Homer in 1938. In 1939 he replaced fiddler Verl Jenkins (1901–1969, Snuffy's older brother), who had earlier replaced J. E. Mainer in his own band at WIS in Columbia, South Carolina, after members became impatient with J. E.'s drinking. When Homer joined, they renamed themselves the WIS Hillbillies and appeared on Bluebird records in 1940 as Byron Parker and his Mountaineers, confirming the announcer's managerial leadership. Parker himself wasn't a musician and, after his untimely death in 1948, the band became the Hired Hands, adopting Parker's radio moniker in his memory. Homer Sherrill remained with them for the rest of his career.

Homer did cause us to lose our sponsor at WGST [when] *they tuned in and found that only Earl and I were there. They wanted to know why Homer had left. We couldn't give them a good answer because we really didn't know. This put us working again on a sustaining basis. We didn't immediately try to get someone to replace Homer. An old-time fiddler, Charlie Bowman, was living in Atlanta at that time and we hired him to help us with our personal appearances. Charlie was a good showman but we didn't feel his type of fiddling suited our music too well, and he didn't work on the radio programs.*

Charlie Bowman (1889–1962) was an accomplished contest fiddler with broadcasting and vaudeville experience, who made influential records in the 1920s with his brothers and Al Hopkins' Buckle Busters.* As with Homer and J. E. Mainer, Bowman's old-time fiddling was more suited for hoedowns and dance tunes than the harmony backup style Bill preferred for Blue Sky Boys songs.

---

* *Fiddlin' Charlie Bowman* by Bob L. Cox (University of Tennessee Press, 2007) is an illustrated biography by a family member.

The Blue Sky Boys Almost Retire

THINGS WERE PRETTY HECTIC FOR US AT THIS TIME. A WGST STAFF announcer had always handled our radio shows and Homer emceed our personal appearances. He was approximately two and a half years older than me and we usually let him take care of the business of the group. Amid all this confusion, RCA wanted us to record again on August 2, 1937. I was afraid we might run into Homer while we were in Charlotte. Earl had told me he was going to confront Homer about the way he had treated us if he saw him. I think he would have gone much farther than that. Earl was usually a quiet, easy-going person, but since the time he had run away from home on an extended hobo trip at the age of fifteen, he didn't allow people to push him around. I knew if we ran into Homer there would definitely be trouble. As usual, it was up to me as to what songs we would record. Again, we simply chose songs we were familiar with and songs we felt hadn't previously been recorded, especially as duets.

A short time after our recording session, we wrecked our car on the way to a personal appearance. Fortunately no one was seriously injured, but the car was badly damaged [and needed] *a month or longer to be repaired. We were working on a sustaining basis over WGST and this placed us in a difficult situation. We did get friends to take us on several show dates, but the future seemed bleak. Although we were drawing more fan mail than all of the other fan mail WGST received, they wouldn't* [pay] *us until we were able to make personal appearances again. This is no reflection on WGST. Very few radio stations at this time would give you across-the-board time on the air.*

We thought it best to quit radio and go back home to Hickory until our car was repaired. Many radio stations, especially in the South, were opposed to our type of music and felt it was strictly beneath their dignity. It was popular with their listeners but they frowned upon it and tried to hold country musicians down. [We were appearing] *in country schools or in small towns I considered wide places in the road. A lot of teachers, principals, and higher-ups felt that this music wasn't conducive to a good way of life and they were opposed to it. Our sponsors were religious organizations or outside organizations that got permission to use these schools. Had we dared to approach a college or university about making an appearance, we'd have gotten tossed out on our ear.*

After we returned [to Hickory], *I decided I would give up entertaining. Although I have always enjoyed bringing people happiness, I felt this type of life wasn't meant for us. I returned to Atlanta to get our car and we sold it several months later as we didn't have money to keep up the payments. Earl and I worked at various odd jobs but nothing steady.*

We didn't start back into radio until the following year. In December 1937, a fellow from a prominent family nearby, Carroll Hollar, stopped to visit. He asked why Earl and I had quit radio as he understood we were doing well. I told him WGST had told us we could have a sustaining spot on the station anytime we wanted to return. He told me he had a new car and would like to go back to Atlanta with us as our booking agent. We could use his car on personal appearances for a reasonable mileage fee. He felt by keeping us booked five to six nights weekly, he could do well financially. In addition he hoped to clear some money on the car mileage. It appeared to be a good opportunity to get back in the entertainment business but, as I stated before, I really wasn't interested in doing that.

Several days later my father came to me, telling me he had overheard my conversation with Carroll. Earl was considering joining the Navy as we couldn't find regular work. He had gone to the recruiting office in Statesville to see about enlisting. My father said this was worrying my mother. He told me she had worried herself sick when Earl had left on his hobo trip in 1935, when I was with the Crazy Hickory Nuts in Asheville. He didn't want her to go through that again and wanted me to reconsider Carroll's proposition. I told him I didn't feel that Carroll had the experience to obtain bookings for us on a full-time basis and, as soon as the novelty wore off, he would come back to Hickory. We would be left without the means to make personal appearances and we would have to go through the same experiences again.

My father kept pleading with me until I agreed to give it one more try. We talked with Richard "Red" Hicks about going to Atlanta with us. He played almost any musical instrument and I had played with him often in previous years, when he carried the newspaper and would stop by after finishing his route and we would play together. We had played a number

Probably WGST, Atlanta, ca.1938. Courtesy of Alan Justice and Marshall Wyatt.

of square dances together. Richard was glad to get the opportunity and he worked with us for two years and ten months.

About the last of December 1937, Carroll, Richard, Earl, and I left for Atlanta. I hadn't contacted WGST as I was certain they would give us sustaining time on the air. We began our programs around January 1, 1938, and stayed until the last of 1939. As usual, we started receiving a lot of fan mail and it was only a short time until we were playing several personal appearances a week.

This time their stay at WGST would be unencumbered by Homer Sherrill and J. W. Fincher, who were finally out of the Bolicks' lives for good. When they began their new show at WGST, they adopted "Are You from Dixie?" as their theme for the first time.

Publicity photos from the time still show Red, Bill, and Earl in checked shirts, though with neckties instead of overalls and straw hats. Other images from that time to their last performances in the 1970s capture the Blue Sky Boys in conservative business suits, reflecting their professionalism and the respect they sought for their music and themselves.

Red Hicks and Uncle Josh, 1938–40

*WE HAD HARDLY GOTTEN STARTED IN ATLANTA WHEN WE RECEIVED A letter from Eli Oberstein wanting us to record in Charlotte on January 25, 1938. We hadn't given much thought to making recordings and, prior to coming back to WGST, we had done little singing since we had made our last recordings. Again, most of the song selections were left up to me. I picked songs that we liked and were familiar with, and songs we felt hadn't previously been recorded.**

As Bill predicted, the arrangement with Carroll Hollar lasted only a few weeks before he returned to Hickory, taking his car with him. Garland came to the rescue and loaned his boys a 1936 Ford sedan. Richard Hicks stayed with them, working on salary and lending variety to their shows with current popular and cowboy songs. Soon they began to feature vocal trios, something they'd learned to enjoy a few years earlier, singing informally with a neighbor back in Hickory.

We patterned our trios after the way Earl, Lloyd Price, and I sang. Lloyd was the son of a Lutheran minister and had lived approximately half a mile from us. He had a good bass voice and really enjoyed singing. We sang a lot of old hymns together—Earl would sing lead, Lloyd bass, and I would sing tenor. Lloyd taught me the words to "Are You from Dixie."

When Red Hicks joined us in 1938, he would take the lead, Earl would sing bass, and I would sing tenor, and it gave a rather pleasant effect. It

---

* On the following day the *Charlotte News* dispatched Cameron Shipp to report the sessions on the tenth floor of the Hotel Charlotte. His article, "Expert Comes Here To Direct Making Phonograph Records," appeared in the paper's late edition that day (January 26, 1938). Shipp observed a session with Claude Casey's Pine State Playboys and spoke with Oberstein and recording engineers Fred Lynch and Raymond R. Sooy, the latter a Victor employee since 1903 who died later in 1938.

wasn't like a quartet and it wasn't like most trios. We done most of our hymns as trios and we got a heck of a lot of requests. We practically always used a fiddle on our radio programs, with the exception of the time that Red Hicks was with us and he picked the guitar. But Eli didn't want anyone else to record with us and neither did [his successor] *Frank Walker. They didn't want us to use anything except the mandolin and guitar.*

With Red's voice leading, the Blue Sky Boys trio featured many gospel songs, reflecting their background in the Church of God, the tastes of their listeners, and the superior quality of the hymns they chose. By 1938 Bill was a polished, tasteful mandolinist who could play melody, harmony, and lead dance tunes to run out the clock on their broadcasts. He could be self-effacing and proud of his skills at the same time:

I never considered myself a mandolin player. I was never around anyone that played a mandolin and I had to learn on my own. I didn't have the opportunity to listen to anyone enough to copy them. I could play the mandolin pretty good. I could play a lot of hornpipes and stuff like that, but I used to be nervous when we recorded and I really didn't play to my full ability.

Bill had worked out some rudimentary comic routines in 1935 with Lute Isenhour and the Crazy Hickory Nuts. When Red joined the Blue Sky Boys they experimented further, first with him and then with Earl, who created a hilarious alter ego named Uncle Josh that surpassed everyone's expectations. He became an essential feature of the live shows the group regularly hosted.

The comedy role of Uncle Josh developed in the late 1930s. Prior to this, Earl and I played comedy on our personal appearances. We played either blackface or rube. Blackface was very messy and the burnt cork was hard to remove. At that time, blackface comedy was a common thing and no stigma was attached to it. Most acts that worked out of Atlanta either used blackface or rube comedy. Rube comedians used only a limited amount of makeup that wasn't too hard to remove. Red Hicks had no experience on radio or stage, but we hoped that with a little experience he would make a good rube comedian. Red's attempts were disastrous and we realized he was not an answer to our problem. Earl didn't want the responsibility of an emcee, so the lot of comedian fell to him.

Earl was one of the best comedians I have ever seen. He was good at blackface, rube, or anything else he chose to be. The biggest job was getting him to do it. Earl, as Earl, couldn't do a thing on the stage. He was backward about talking and he would never sing a song by himself. But when he was Uncle Josh, Earl was a different person.

Many people in our radio audience thought he really was an old man. On our stage shows, he blacked his front teeth, wore an old crumpled hat, eyeglasses without lenses, and attached gray sideburns and a gray goatee. Our mother had made him a long slit tail coat. He wore large brogan shoes, each on the wrong foot.

While Earl was dressing for his Uncle Josh role, I would usually sing a solo, usually a comic one, tell a joke or two, [or another] *member of the group did his specialty. After the comedy routine we usually played a fast tune and started our closing routine.*

From the very first, [Uncle Josh] *was a hit with our radio audience. A daily chat with him on our programs turned out very successful. I didn't emcee our radio programs until possibly June of 1941. Prior to that, the radio stations had done our announcing. Announcers liked to kid with Uncle Josh and one in Raleigh was always trying to get something on him. Thinking of North Carolina, he said, "I'll bet you don't know where one seventh of all the tobacco in the world is grown," and Uncle Josh said, "In the ground."*

Several people have asked me why we used the name Josh. I never gave much thought to the matter. The name Uncle Josh simply seemed to fit the character. The comedy was spontaneous and none of our radio programs were rehearsed. Our sponsors liked him to say something about their product. When we made up to ten programs in one session, as we did on those [1946–7] *transcriptions, you can imagine how difficult it would be to think of something entertaining to say.*

As for comedy on our stage shows, people expected more than singing and playing, especially in the thirties. Life was tough back then and people wanted to be entertained. Radio performances brought people out to see you, but comedy brought them back when you made a return engagement. I can recall playing the Cobb County Court House in Marietta, Georgia, as many as six times in the same year. Each time we had a full house.

As Uncle Josh, Earl helped the group develop a solid stage show that lasted for seventy to ninety minutes, depending on audience reaction. A program opened with songs for thirty-five to forty minutes, beginning with "Are You from Dixie." Then Earl would get in costume offstage while Bill and Red sang solos or told jokes. When Earl reappeared as Uncle Josh, Bill was his straight man in half-hour skits. When Curly Parker worked with them, he'd play "Pop Goes the Weasel" as a trick fiddle solo. Leslie Keith, the fiddler who appeared with them from 1949 to 1951, added a bullwhip routine and became a comic foil for Uncle Josh.

Earl's inspired caricature was deeply embedded in American folklore, especially in New England, where rube comics with Old Testament names like Si (or Cy), Reuben, Josh, Ephraim, Ebenezer, and Hiram dominated rural nineteenth-century humor. In 1830 the newspaper editor and humorist Seba Smith (1792–1868) created Uncle Josh Downing (of Downingville, Maine) for the *Portland Courier.* Uncle Josh received comic letters in colloquial style from his nephew, Major Jack Downing, in New York and Washington, conveying Jack's views on politics and urban life to relatives back home.

In 1875 character actor Denman Thompson created Joshua Whitcomb in a short sketch about New Hampshire village life. When Joshua reappeared in Thompson's and George W. Ryer's 1886 play *The Old Homestead,* Calvin Edward Stewart (1856–1919) learned the role as Thompson's understudy. When Thompson revived the play on Broadway in 1904, a reviewer described Joshua as "the old farmer who comes to town and balks at nude Venuses, shakes hands with the lackey, and stares at high buildings."*

By then, Cal Stewart had already appropriated the caricature for himself, performing popular monologues in Downing/Whitcomb style as Uncle Josh Weathersby on hundreds of phonograph records from 1897 through the rest of his life. Stewart placed his rural character into unfamiliar situations: at Coney Island or a "Base Ball" game, in a Chinese laundry, department store or museum, at the opera, on streetcars, automobiles, and steamboat excursions, riffing on his supposed naïveté, and letting culture clash inspire the comedy. He was as familiar to 1900s record buyers as Jack Benny was to radio listeners in the 1940s. Earl Bolick may or may not have known about those records but, at any rate, he moved Uncle Josh from Down East to the rural south, where his hayseed comedy acquired a combative tone and became even funnier.

Seba Smith or Cal Stewart would have recognized Earl immediately. His portrayal of a quaint old rustic who told corny jokes, sang comic

* *New York Times,* September 6, 1906, p. 7.

Uncle Josh (Cal Stewart). Courtesy of Archeophone Records.

verses to fiddle tunes, bragged about his women, and thought he knew everything, made him a superior comedian whose character was as voluble as Earl himself was inscrutable. Brief dialogues between Uncle Josh, Bill, and WGST staff announcers survive on 1946–47 radio transcriptions. Earl revived him once more at the Blue Sky Boys' 1964 concert at the University of Illinois, to the great delight of the audience.

Parenthetically we should note that Burkett Howard "Buck" Graves (1928–2006) became another comic Uncle Josh when he worked with Lester Flatt and Earl Scruggs in the 1950s and '60s. He was a good

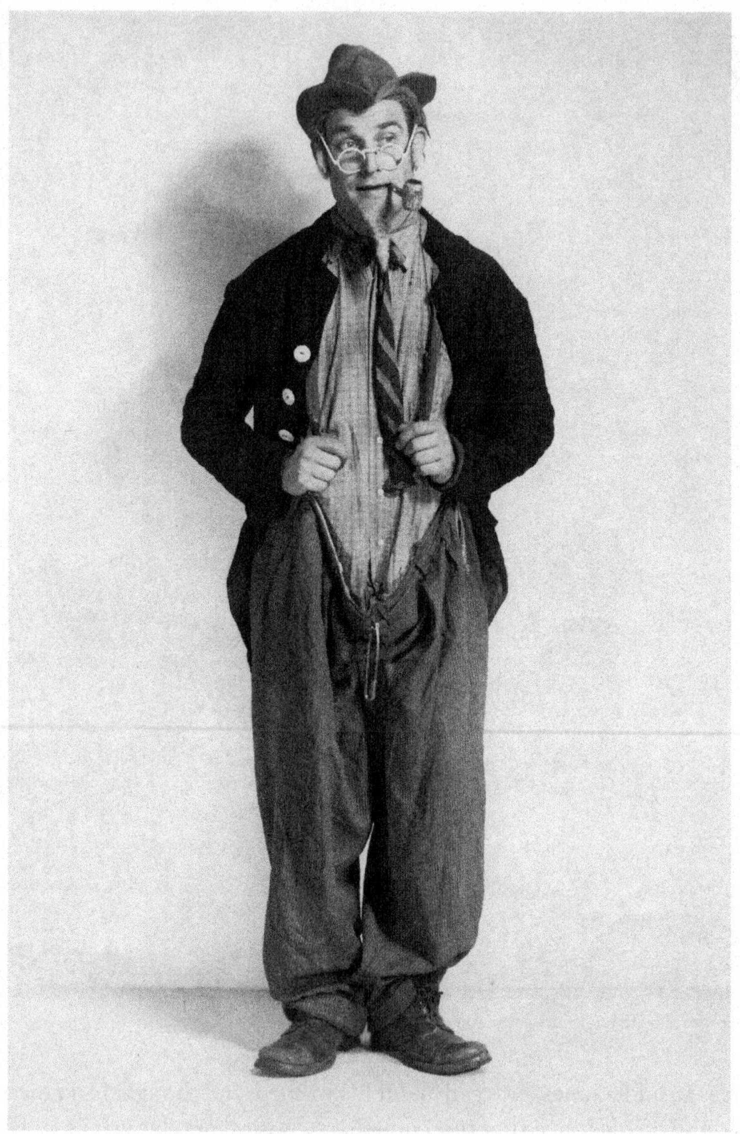

Earl as Uncle Josh, 1938. Courtesy of Alan Justice and Marshall Wyatt.

mandolinist and trend-setting Dobro player, and he teamed with bass player English P. (Jake) Tullock Jr. as Cousin Jake and Uncle Josh, with Jake as the rube comic and Josh in the straight man role. His 2012 autobiography *Bluegrass Bluesman* is credited to Josh Graves, the name he adopted with the Foggy Mountain Boys.

New Records, More Radio, Good Times, 1938–41

RCA'S LAST PREWAR CHARLOTTE RECORDING SESSIONS WERE HELD IN January 1938. Because of a dispute between RCA and Local 342 of the American Federation of Musicians, the Blue Sky Boys and other Bluebird artists next recorded in September in Rock Hill, South Carolina, thirteen miles from Charlotte. Decca Records apparently satisfied union requirements when a team came to Charlotte in June 1938 to make new records by ex-Bluebird artists the Carlisle Brothers and Carter Family. Bill claimed that Decca producer Dave Kapp tried to poach the Blue Sky Boys from RCA as well.

Eli Oberstein's last known meeting with them was at their January 25, 1938, session. He resigned (or was fired) from RCA on February 27, 1939, and started Royale and Varsity (1939–40), Elite (1941), and Hit (1942–45), beginning a series of budget labels that went into and out of eclipse for the rest of his life. He returned to RCA from 1945 until 1948 and died in 1960.

Eli's replacement at RCA in 1938 was veteran Columbia Records producer Frank Walker (1889–1963), who had supervised historic 1920s sessions with Bessie Smith, Blind Willie Johnson, Charlie Poole, and in Atlanta with Blind Willie McTell, Gid Tanner's Skillet Lickers, Barbecue Bob, Riley Puckett, Peg Leg Howell, Clayton McMichen, and other regional stars. Walker hosted RCA's Rock Hill sessions in September 1938 (including the Blue Sky Boys) and then conducted regular Bluebird sessions in Atlanta through October 1941. His co-producer, Dan Hornsby (1900–1951), was an Atlanta radio personality who had speaking roles on Skillet Lickers comedy records in the 1920s, worked at WGST during the Blue Sky Boys' residencies in the 1930s and '40s, and served as a local agent for RCA.

One of Bill and Earl's most loyal WGST fans was Ruth Walker (no relation to Frank), who lived seventy-five miles east of Atlanta in Greensboro, Georgia, where she listened almost every day to their morning shows at 8:30 or 9:30. On May 9, 1939, she began a diary of Blue Sky Boys programs, listing whatever they performed six days a week through May 9, 1940.

She usually identified solo features by Red and Bill, though she did so less often as the year progressed. She noted that Bill had an emergency appendectomy at the end of November that sidelined him for three weeks. In his absence Red Hicks and Earl soldiered on, reinforced by a group called the Hidden Valley Ramblers and a few rare solos from Earl.

At the same time, the Blue Sky Boys were preparing to relocate. In those days country music professionals often moved between cities and radio stations, where they performed until their appeal began to wane. Residencies could last from a few weeks to a few months, or until attendance at live appearances dropped off. The Bolicks' two-and-a-half-year run at WGST had been exceptionally long, but by the close of 1939 it was time for them to move on.

After his recovery, Bill returned for two final shows on December 22 and 23; on December 27 the group debuted on WPTF in Raleigh, a prestigious 5,000-watt CBS affiliate that had hosted the *Crazy Barn Dance* briefly in 1936 and dominated the regional radio market. Its call letters stood for "We Protect the Family," station owner Durham Life Insurance Company's slogan since 1927. The Blue Sky Boys prospered there through May 1941 and enjoyed abundant show dates. Ruth Walker could still hear them in Greensboro, and she faithfully continued to log their songs.

I might mention that we made an audition transcription and sent it to WPTF in Raleigh in order to try to get on there, because we were getting played out around Atlanta. They sent the transcription back without saying a word, so we figured that they weren't interested. Then, while I was still in bed recovering from my operation, Graham Poyner, the program director of WPTF, called me and said if [we could] *be there on the 27th of December, that they had a sponsor for us and would like to have us. Through Homer playing there we knew that was good territory. I told* [Poyner] *that if my doctor said it would be all right that we would come. He told me that if I took care of myself, everything would be all right. As a result, we moved to WPTF approximately December 27, 1939.*

When we went to WPTF we made more money than anyplace else. The station had a good reputation and terrific coverage, as good as any

THE BLUE SKY BOYS
RADIO STATION

Dear Friends:

We have received your request for an appearance, and wish to inform you we are available the date of ______________________.

Our terms are:

We receive sixty-five per cent (65%) of the door receipts. Admission prices are: Adults 25c. Children 12 years and under 15c. Circulars will be printed for you at the cost of ($2.00) two dollars. This is to be paid from the sponsors part of the proceeds, the night of the show. If you prefer, we will pay for the circulars provided we are allowed seventy per cent (70%) of the gross receipts.

We shall regard this letter as a contract, and if the date is satisfactory, please fill out the blank spaces below, along with your signature, and return to us at your earliest convenience. If we do not receive a reply from you in regards to this on, or before ______________________, we will assume you do not wish us to hold the above date open for you any longer.

Thanking you for your kind consideration, and awaiting your early reply, we remain,

Very truly yours,
The Blue Sky Boys.

Town ______________________

Name of building ______________________

Percentage ______________________

Sponsor ______________________

Signature ______________________

"We got so many requests for personal appearances that I had to get a printer to print me out a form."

5,000-watt station at that time, and it was the only station in that part of the country. It reached up into Virginia and clear down to the coast in South Carolina and as far [west] *maybe as Morganton* [North Carolina].

We first worked for a fertilizer company in Goldsboro at 1:15 in the afternoon. When that played out they let us keep our time. We could put on our program and advertise our show dates but they did not pay us. They didn't pay very much anyway. Most stations in the South only paid entertainers

ten dollars a week. A top entertainer got about twenty-five dollars a week. That was considered a very good salary. Most so-called hillbillies (I never liked that name because it threw off a little on the people)—most country musicians were not paid by the station. If they got a sponsor, the sponsor paid so much a week.

After a month and a half, we played six nights a week and within six weeks we were booked for six months solid. We usually played [within] *a radius of three to four hundred miles of the station and traveled back each day* [for live broadcasts]. *Sometimes we traveled two thousand miles a week; other times we could play close to the station. We bought four new cars in one year. We could have been booked up to a year but most sponsors couldn't obtain a building that far in advance. We got so many requests for personal appearances that I had to get a printer to print me out a form.*

We charged fifteen, twenty-five cents and got 65 per cent of the receipts. We charged two dollars for posters we sent out, which came out of the sponsor's proceeds the night of the show. If they wanted us to pay for posters, we received 70 per cent. You'd be surprised at [how many opted for] *70 per cent and had us pay for them. We played mainly schoolhouses. If we'd take in $150 at the gate, it was a fortune. We'd mostly get change—we didn't get many bills.* [A man might] *have four or five kids and I'd think to myself, God, I wish I could let you in free, but I had to make a living too.*

I couldn't handle the mail; it was too much for me. By the time you answered a few letters, put on your radio program, and got ready to go to your personal appearances, you put in a lot of hours. The Delmores, the Monroes, the Mainers, the Morris Brothers—all the big acts had been [at WPTF] *and the program director* [Graham Poyner] *told us we drew more fan mail than any other act that had ever been on that station. When you got fifty to a hundred letters a day, opened them up, read them, paid attention to what they said and the numbers they requested, it took a lot of time. I don't know how we did that. I always handled all the business.*

With their increased income the Blue Sky Boys could afford a couple of professional upgrades. For several years Earl had played Bill's Martin 028 guitar. When he wanted a more substantial instrument, Garland found him a discounted 1940 Martin D28 (serial number 75371) for about $150. Through much of the 1930s the Bolicks worked in country schoolhouses and other venues that still lacked electricity. The Rural Electrification Act of 1936 gradually brought power to remote communities, and Bill and

Earl bought themselves a basic Bogen sound system with a microphone, amplifier, and two speakers to accommodate larger audiences.

Red Hicks left the Blue Sky Boys in October 1940 and retired from professional music. When he met the Country Music Foundation's Douglas B. Green in 1973, Hicks was employed by the Federal Aviation Administration at Nashville's Metro Airport. He brought along the Ruth Walker diary and Green edited it for publication in the *Journal of Country Music.* In 1977 Green became Ranger Doug, celebrated straight man of the comic cowboy team Riders in the Sky.

Off to War, 1940–46

WHEN RED HICKS LEFT THE BLUE SKY BOYS, HE RECOMMENDED SAMuel "Curly" Parker (1919–1986) as his replacement. Parker was working with the Holden Brothers band at WPTF and had become Earl's friend. The Bolicks paid him twenty-five dollars a week. Curly wasn't a hot hoedown fiddler but Bill valued his tasteful backups and harmonies that blended with his mandolin. His straightforward singing allowed the Blue Sky Boys to keep the vocal trio arrangements they'd developed with Red.

When Curly Parker joined us in late 1940, he had done very little singing. With a little encouragement and practice he soon became a good lead singer. I think his voice blended with ours better than anyone else who ever worked with us. We tried to work Curly on our last session previous to going in the service, but Dan [Hornsby], *Frank* [Walker], *and Eli* [Oberstein] *were opposed to anyone else working with us.*

The WPTF engagement lasted until the final week of April 1941, when the Blue Sky Boys left after feuding with Graham Poyner, who resented their prosperity.

I think he thought we were making more money than we actually were. [When we owned] *four new cars within a one-year period, I don't think that set well with him, especially when one of them was a Packard. I had some acts tell me that he didn't believe in someone strapping a guitar around their shoulder and making more money than the manager of the station. I don't know why he didn't like us; we tended to our own business and kept to ourselves.*

Bill's friend Charles Travis adds:

Curly Parker (fiddle) with the Holden Brothers, WPTF, Raleigh, NC, ca. 1940. Courtesy of Marshall Wyatt.

The Blue Sky Boys were performing five nights a week to large audiences and beginning to prosper. They traveled in Lincoln and Ford automobiles and joined the Businessmen's Association at the YMCA so they could have access to the swimming pool, sweatboxes, and masseurs. Earl developed an interest in flying, took lessons and acquired his private pilot license. [Charles Travis email to me, November 19, 2012]

I didn't owe anybody anything and we were sitting on top of the world for a change. We had a little money in the bank, two new cars, and a lot of nice clothes. We always dressed in regular business clothes. We never wore a cowboy hat, western-style hat, riding britches, boots, or anything like that. Once in a while we would wear checkered shirts, but usually we wore white shirts and ties. I was taught to dress as neat as you could when going anywhere. There were times when we didn't have very nice clothes, but we did the best we could. Most of the time we wore suits alike if we could get them, especially Earl and myself.

Mr. Poyner seemed to resent all this and kept bringing other acts on the station and moving us to less enjoyable spots. Noon was the best time to be on [but] *he pushed us onto a six-thirty or six-forty-five spot and gave new groups spots around noonday. They were no extreme competition to us and didn't hurt our crowds or fan mail.*

Mr. Poyner kept shoving us to such bad spots that he eventually drove us out. Before leaving, [we learned that] *Joe Oswald from KWKH in*

Shreveport was interested in us, and [we made] *a transcription to send him. When* [Poyner] *found out that we were planning to leave, he wrote me a letter. Instead of coming and talking to me like a man, I went to our box and found a letter. I opened it. I didn't know who it was from. It wasn't even the station's stationery.*

He said, "This is to inform you that the six-thirty (*or six-forty-five*) *spot will no longer be available after such and such a date." I don't remember just what the exact date was. In other words, he was cutting us off a week or two earlier than we had planned to leave. He went on to say, "I am using this means of informing you with thoughts that you might like to use this letter as a future recommendation. I have found the Blue Sky Boys a sober, industrious group," and a few more words like that.*

Well, when I saw the thing, I was so mad I couldn't see straight. I went into his office and slammed it on his desk. I said, "We don't need a letter like that, so I'm bringing it back to you." He turned real red and said, "Well, if that's the way you feel about it." I said, "That's just the way I feel about it." He hardly spoke to us from then till the time we left. The last day we were at WPTF, he announced our program and didn't mention that it would be our last.

The draft at that time was getting a little close. We thought if we're drafted right away, it's going to be pretty bad for us to go all the way down to Shreveport, so we'll try a station closer by. The Monroes had worked over WFBC in Greenville, South Carolina [in 1935-36]. *They did well there, so I figured maybe that would be a good station for us. I went and talked to Jim Reid, the program director and a heck of a nice guy. He later came to WPTF in Raleigh and became mayor of the city.*

We went to WFBC about the middle of May 1941 and drew fantastic fan mail there. We had thirty minutes [at 6:30] *in the morning and fifteen minutes at noon. We were drawing four to five hundred pieces of fan mail a day and the station said it beat anything they had ever seen. I'm sure we would have been booked solid within another month. I gathered up several days' mail, carried it in to Jim Reid and told him that with a response like that we should have no trouble getting a sponsor. He agreed and said he would get to work on it immediately. He also agreed to allow us to sell pictures, books, or anything along that line on our radio programs.*

Not long after that, Jim called me where I was rooming and asked if I could come to the station and talk with him. When I arrived he told me we would be given a substantial raise beginning next week. Canada Dry was going to sponsor our show and pay us eighty-five dollars a week, by far the largest amount we had ever been paid. I know of no outfit that had been offered that high a salary prior to World War II.

The station was pleased and we were to start the program within the next week or so. About that time, I got my draft notice. When I showed it to Jim he said, "Well, before we go through with this deal with Canada Dry, we'd better hold up and see whether you'll have to go or not." It was only a very short time before I had to go. They gave me very little notice, possibly two or three weeks. We had to sell a Packard and a Ford for practically nothing. When we came out those cars would have cost many times that.

In no more than two weeks we were in the armed forces and didn't return to entertaining for over four and a half years. [When I was drafted,] *Earl joined because it was only supposed to be for a year and we felt it would be better for him to volunteer so we could come out together, but it wound up almost five years we were in the service. I was in the Pacific area about eighteen months. I was in the initial landings on Leyte Island in the Philippines and Okinawa.*

I got out of the Army on Christmas Day of 1945. Earl got out a little earlier, since he had a few more points because of being wounded so many times. He won the Silver Star and the Purple Heart. He was shot with shrapnel and got his legs banged up pretty bad.

The Battle of the Bulge, or Ardennes Offensive, was launched in Belgium by Germany in December 1944. The Allies were taken by surprise and it became the largest battle of the war. German forces were defeated the following month, but only after thousands of Allied casualties and deaths. Earl was an experienced paratrooper by that time but, as his son Steven Bolick relates,

The wind caught him and others, blew them into some rocks, and there were a lot of broken bones. He messed his knees up. Sometimes they didn't know if they were going to make it or not. I remember Dad saying there was a lot of death, but he wouldn't elaborate. [telephone conversation, October 15, 2011]

In the Blue Sky Boys' 1947 songbook *Favorite Hymns and Folk Songs,* Bill briefly summarizes their wartime résumés:

Bill was inducted at Ft. Bragg, North Carolina. He took basic training at Ft. Eustis, Va., and Camp Davis, N.C. He served with the 85th A.A.

Earl in army dress uniform with paratrooper badge, Bill in khaki uniform, 1941–42. Courtesy of Larry Settlemyre.

[Anti-Aircraft] *Regiment in Newport News, Va., and with the 79th A.A. Regt. in Hartford, Connecticut. Serving a year and a half overseas in the Pacific Theatre, he participated in the initial landings on Leyte Islands in the Philippines* [in October 1944] *and Okinawa* [April 1945]. *While overseas he served with the 485th A.A. (A.W.)* [Automatic Weapons] *Battalion. He was discharged from service Christmas Day, December 25, 1945, after serving 4 years, 4 months and 14 days.*

Earl was inducted at Ft. Bragg, N.C. He took basic training at Fort Monmouth, New Jersey, and Ft. Jackson, S.C. with the 8th Signal Company. Volunteering for the Parachute Infantry in August, 1942, he took training in Fort Benning, Ga., and Alliance Air Base, Alliance, Nebraska. He served two years overseas in the European Theatre with the 507th Parachute Infantry Regiment, participating in the initial parachute landings of the invasion of Normandy [June 1944], *and the jump across the Rhine. He also participated in the Battle of the Rhineland and the Battle of the Bulge* [December 1944–January 1945]. *Earl has been cited with numerous medals and decorations, including the Purple Heart with Oak Leaf Clusters, the Silver Star, and Distinguished Unit Badge. He was discharged from service September 22, 1945, serving a total of 4 years, 1 month and 10 days.*

While Bill was fighting in the Pacific he was not forgotten back home, where a friend decided to be a matchmaker. Because of the war, Bill didn't actually meet Doris Eileen Wallace for a few years. She remembers how they were introduced:

I worked in Bellaire [Ohio] *in a beauty shop for a girl, and her brother came home on leave. He told me he had just the boy for me, and I said, "Oh, I bet you do!" He gave me Bill's address, the girls dared me to write to him, and I did. We corresponded all during the war. He was discharged Christmas Day, 1945 and, either in January or February 1946, he came to see me. He rode the Greyhound bus all the way from Hickory to Bellaire. I had never heard of the Blue Sky Boys. Bill sent me the first record they made after the war. I did play it but I don't remember what the song was.* [telephone conversation, September 6, 2010]

Bill was lucky to have a penpal back home in the form of an attractive lady who was sending letters to him in the South Pacific. Events in their lives would further prolong Bill and Doris's courtship until their marriage in 1957.

New Songs, New Rules, 1946–48

INEVITABLY BILL AND EARL RETURNED TO MUSIC WHEN THEY WERE discharged, hoping to reclaim at least part of the loyal following they'd enjoyed before the war. Their singing sounded relatively old-fashioned as country music evolved in the postwar years, but committed fans nonetheless continued to cherish their unique harmonies and spare eloquence that evoked the days before the sounds of honky-tonk took country music from mountains and meadows to urban streets and smoke-filled bars.

When the Bolicks resumed performing in 1946, there were still audiences for Roy Acuff, the Mainers, Molly O'Day, the Bailes Brothers, Bill Monroe, Charlie Monroe, and others whose music predated honky-tonk. The Blue Sky Boys made common cause with them but, unlike the others, they'd fought overseas for a long time and the road back wasn't easy. As Bill ruefully observed,

The war ruined us in more ways than one. It kept us out of the business for five years and we had to start all over. We were separated [from each other] *all that time and things were different when we got out of the Army. We hadn't played and sung in so long, and* [only] *one of our records had been put out during the war. So I guess we were kind of forgotten.*

After we were discharged, we spent approximately three months at home with our parents. We had Curly Parker come up from Georgia to Hickory and rehearse. We practiced our singing and playing every day. Earl and Curly had changed quite a bit and I guess I had, too. We hadn't sung or played our instruments and didn't know if we could still harmonize together. It was as if we had never been in the entertainment industry at all. We started entertaining so early in life that we never learned any other type of work. The only thing we felt we could do was get back into the entertainment business. We didn't really know what else to do.

We gave auditions at radio stations, but several were like the old days—they didn't even want to talk with us. We first went to WBT in Charlotte but you had to belong to the local union and they had their groups already. On our way up to WWVA, we went by WRVA in Richmond and talked to the program director. He told me he couldn't listen to us right then, but he would have the station make an audition transcription. Their budget was at its limit and he couldn't pay us right then. But, if we would agree to play show dates, he would work something out with us later. So we made the transcription and left it for him.

We went to WWVA in Wheeling. Pete Cassell was on the air when we first walked in the studio. I knew Pete quite well; I'd worked several show dates with him in Atlanta. He introduced me to Paul Myers who said, "I'd like to listen to you," so we gave him an audition. He said, "Yeah, I'd like to have you boys, and I'll give you thirty-five dollars a week apiece. The only thing about it," he said, "some of these acts up here got rich during the war." He said some of them wouldn't make half of their programs in the morning. They would claim it was because they had been out and hadn't had any sleep, so the station decided the best thing to do was to cut everybody down to three personal appearances a week. I didn't like that much, so I said, "Well, I'll study it over." Pete was there and said, "If he wants you, you can get fifty." I talked to Myers and I said, "Being as you've cut down on personal appearances, I don't believe I can come for thirty-five dollars a week." I said I thought fifty dollars apiece would be good and he said, "Well, we can work that out," so I had the job if we wanted it. I wished a thousand times we'd taken it.

Another audition at WVOK in Birmingham resulted only in an offer for free broadcast time, so Bill and Earl set out again for Wheeling, stopping in Atlanta to revisit WGST. An old friend, John Fulton, had been promoted from program director to station manager. He welcomed them enthusiastically and persuaded him and Earl to pick up where they'd left off in 1939.

Things seemed as they did prior to World War II. They seemed delighted to see us and offered us a weekly salary of fifty dollars apiece. That almost knocked me down, a small station like that offering as much as they had at Wheeling. After taking all offers into consideration we decided to start back at WGST.

With Curly Parker, after 1945. Courtesy of Alan Justice and Marshall Wyatt.

Earl, Bill, and Curly Parker returned to Atlanta for a fourth and final stay at WGST from March 25, 1946, through February 1948. Earl's ties to Atlanta became permanent after he met Elizabeth Geraldine (Gerry) Bennett of Tucker, Georgia, at a performance, and they were married on October 12, 1946.

The Blue Sky Boys were fortunate that their broadcasts were still popular, because they had to contend with new protocols in the world of record making that limited their choice of songs. The 1942 formation of the Acuff-Rose song publishing house in Nashville demonstrated the financial value of copyrights and contracts, and country music rapidly began to earn money from them. The operation was underwritten by *Grand Ole Opry* star Roy Acuff, supporting the vision of the veteran pop song writer Fred Rose (1898–1954), who understood country music and invested it with commercial savvy. His own songs helped Acuff-Rose expand and he actively pursued new material from promising young writers. With $25,000 from Roy and Mildred Acuff, a formal partnership was created on October 30, 1942, with Mildred (1914–1981) the active participant and Acuff partner of record.

Acuff-Rose was formed in the wake of a ten-month licensing rate dispute between broadcasters and the performance rights organization ASCAP (American Society of Composers, Authors and Publishers) that licensed compositions for radio, film, and other modes of public performance. John Rumble, senior historian at the Country Music Hall of Fame, explains, "The broadcasters and ASCAP had failed to come to terms over ASCAP's proposed licensing rate hike of 50 percent over the existing rate. So, at midnight on Dec. 31, 1940, the contract expired. Without a new contract in place, radio could not legally broadcast any song licensed through ASCAP" (email to me, October 19, 2015).

Through most of 1941, the action prevented major network broadcasts of music licensed by ASCAP. Radio interests had taken preemptive action in 1939 by forming Broadcast Music, Incorporated (BMI), a competing organization that assembled a catalog of its own. ASCAP's membership included few country songwriters, but BMI actively welcomed them. It was an ideal opportunity to monetize country music and Acuff-Rose was well placed to take advantage of it. After its doors opened in 1942, commodified music became as vital to Nashville as it was in New York.

Fred Rose was a versatile and prolific composer who avoided attaching questionable claims to old songs, as Ralph Peer had done in the 1920s. Instead, Acuff-Rose embraced honky-tonk songs and win-the-war anthems that generated revenue from airplay and record sales. Pre-BMI songwriters like Alton Delmore (who lauded Rose in his unfinished autobiography *Truth Is Stranger Than Publicity*), Cliff Carlisle, and Dorsey Dixon came largely from the performing ranks and their songs were rarely copyrighted in the 1930s. Rose mentored Delmore when both worked at WSM in Nashville and further nurtured beginning professional writers like Jim Anglin, Mel Foree, and Jenny Lou Carson (Lucille Overstake) in the 1940s. Others, like Walter Bailes, Marty Robbins, and Hank Williams, could write as well as they performed. All placed original songs with Acuff-Rose and its growing roster of Nashville competitors.

John Rumble praises Rose for providing "a publishing home for other important singer-songwriters, including Ira Louvin of the Louvin Brothers. He nurtured the early solo career of Martha Carson as well. The most famous early songwriters associated with Acuff-Rose were Boudleaux and Felice Bryant" (email to me, March 24, 2013).

Fred Rose is best remembered for his collaborations with Hank Williams, touching up his songs and contributing a few of his own to Hank's repertory. With his son Wesley, Fred successfully pitched several of

Hank's hits to Columbia Records producer Mitch Miller, who turned them into successful pop productions for Tony Bennett ("Cold, Cold Heart"), Jo Stafford ("Jambalaya"), Rosemary Clooney ("Half As Much"), and Frankie Laine ("Hey, Good Lookin'"). Rose's own pop hits began in 1920 with "Sweet Mama (Papa's Getting Mad)," recorded by Duke Ellington's orchestra and the Original Dixieland Jazz Band. Later hits included "Red Hot Mama" and "Honest and Truly" (both 1924), "Flamin' Mamie" (1925) and "'Deed I Do" (1926). Several of his exceptional jazz compositions were recorded by 1920s celebrities: "Deep Henderson" (King Oliver), "El Rado Scuffle" and "Deep Trouble" (Jimmie Noone), "Mobile Blues" (Muggsy Spanier with the Bucktown Five), "Black Maria" (Carroll Dickerson, Fletcher Henderson), and "Here Comes the Hot Tamale Man" (Freddie Keppard with Doc Cook).

Rose suffered from alcoholism in the 1930s and turned to Christian Science when he was in recovery, moving between Nashville, Chicago, and New York. His first country songs were composed in Hollywood after 1938 for Gene Autry and included "Be Honest with Me," "I'll Be True While You're Gone," "Tweedle-O-Twill," and "Ages and Ages Ago." Following the establishment of Acuff-Rose, he composed:

We Live in Two Different Worlds
Texarkana Baby
Roly Poly
Fire Ball Mail
Home in San Antone
Low and Lonely
Foggy River
Bringin' In the Georgia Mail
Blue Eyes Crying in the Rain

While the Blue Sky Boys were fighting for their country thousands of miles away, Acuff-Rose was precipitating changes in Nashville that would have profound effects on their lives and postwar careers. More new firms were competing to acquire and promote composed country songs that were becoming a prized commodity in Nashville's growing music industry. The situation was frustrating for Bill and Earl when they made new records for RCA following their discharge from the Army. Though their art was grounded in traditional songs, they were forced to adapt to the postwar environment by recording new ones of varying quality.

Fred Rose. Courtesy of John Rumble.

They earned modest royalties from a handful of original songs that Bill wrote, acquired, co-composed, or arranged. As he told historian Kinney Rorrer in 2006, if amateur songwriters sent him material it often needed melodies to fit written texts, *and then they wanted to claim absolute authorship. If you recorded one of their numbers they'd think they should make a million dollars.*

Larger record companies would pay a two-cent royalty per song. If it was your song and you had it copyrighted, they would only pay you one cent, whereas a publishing company would give you half of what they got. You would come out just as good [but] *with better publicity, so you were smarter to let some publishing company have it. The only thing, there were so many crooked publishing companies. I know two that owed me quite a bit of money and I don't know whatever happened to it.*

The Bolicks returned to record making in 1946 when RCA needed a cover version of the Bailes Brothers' "Dust on the Bible," first heard by large audiences in September 1944 after Johnnie and Walter Bailes left West Virginia to join the *Grand Ole Opry.* They recorded it for Columbia Records' budget label OKeh on February 17, 1945 and anticipated a timely release. Instead, they waited eighteen months while the OKeh brand was slowly phased out and releases by new country artists were postponed until 1946 and 1947, when they appeared on the full-priced Columbia label. "Dust on the Bible" was still unreleased when Bill and Earl covered it for RCA in Atlanta on September 30, 1946, on their first postwar record date. It was released two weeks after the Bailes disc in November and a third version by Wade Mainer on King appeared around the same time.

Steve (Stephen H.) Sholes (1911–1968) took charge of Victor's country catalog in 1945, when the Bolicks' old producer Frank Walker was hired away by MGM Pictures to create a phonograph records division. Sholes had worked his way up the RCA ladder since 1929 and inherited the company's country music operation as Bluebird was being phased out and new blues and country discs were selling at full price on RCA Victor. Sholes had business and personal ties with brothers Julian (1909–1974) and Jean (1910–1992) Aberbach, whose aggressive Hill and Range publishing company cultivated RCA as part of their strategy to acquire songs, song catalogs, and the allegiance of record executives, performers, and writers.

The controversial "Colonel" Tom Parker (1909–1997) became close to Sholes and Julian Aberbach when he assumed management of Eddy Arnold's career in 1945 after the singer signed with RCA. Arnold (1918–2008) became country music's leading artist in the late 1940s and got the pick of new Hill and Range songs. In return he steered promising material to the Aberbachs, including songs he opted to record himself. To keep Arnold loyal, Hill and Range created a new joint company with him and Parker, giving both a share of revenues from Hill and Range songs that Arnold recorded. Similar deals were created for Ernest Tubb, Hank Snow, Elvis Presley, and others, but not the Blue Sky Boys.

Their RCA sessions from 1946 through 1949 included eight Acuff-Rose songs, six from Hill and Range, and the rest from smaller houses. Steve Sholes then began to promote Hill and Range songs over others to RCA Victor country artists, a practice that irritated Bill. Arnold's success left Sholes little time for others, and there were few hits by anyone else on RCA before the 1950s. "Dust on the Bible" and "Kentucky" aside, the Blue

Bulletin 47-AA99 November 7, 1947

TO ALL RCA VICTOR RECORD DISTRIBUTORS

KENTUCKY

Reports coming into my desk indicate that the Blue Sky Boys' recording of KENTUCKY #20-2296 has, through popular demand - - - pushed its way up through the line of scrimmage - - passed the secondary by sheer power of customer appeal - - - and is now heading toward pay dirt.

If you don't have this star on your team of Best Sellers, it is suggested that you put him in the line-up. Give KENTUCKY a little interference in the way of a bulletin or promotion and I'm sure it will score for you.

Cordially,

D. J. Finn

D. J. FINN
General Sales Manager
Record Department

esc

cc: RM
RPM
CC2
GG2S

RADIO CORPORATION OF AMERICA • RCA Victor Division, Camden, N. J.
leads the way... IN RADIO... TELEVISION... TUBES... "VICTROLAS"*... RECORDS... ELECTRONICS
Printed in U. S. A. *Victrola Trade-Mark Reg. U. S. Pat. Off.

"Kentucky" endorsement, 1947. Courtesy of Alan Justice and Marshall Wyatt.

Sky Boys had few opportunities to record major songs and good reason to be unhappy with Sholes and RCA, starting with their first postwar record date.

We only did four numbers; "Speak to Me Little Darling" and "I Love Her More Now Mother's Old" were probably the best. RCA never gave us a fair shake. They never gave us any promotion, even in "Kentucky," which sold over half a million records in 1947. They never put anything in Billboard *about us, and I know that for a while we were next to Eddy Arnold in our field, and if you had known the way they pushed him, you could have understood why he was such a success.*

Bill had a point. *Billboard* judged 1940s country records in terms of jukebox appeal and invariably found the Blue Sky Boys wanting. Their reviews were anonymous, and condescending to both the artists and their audience:

Authentic hill chanting, with a male duo doing a heavily nasal, whining vocal on a so-so ballad ("I Cannot Take You Back Now") . . . *the boys' diction is unclear* (November 30, 1948).

Outdoorish with a vengeance. Boys are strictly from the hay-stacks, and for selling the tear-jerking tunes, there's enough cry in their vocal twangs to dampen any disk . . . It's the kind of singing and song that thrives in the prairie country, and if there is a juke box at the grange hall, they'll run themselves short of nickels in packing the machine for the Blue Sky Boys (November 4, 1944).

Billboard decided twice that new Blue Sky Boys records were "for the old folks at home" (December 7, 1946, and April 2, 1947), a stock phrase reserved for country music without honky-tonk appeal. As the 1940s came to an end, brother-style harmonies all but disappeared outside of bluegrass; in 1950 Bill and Earl would be the last brother duet to leave RCA.

I don't think Steve Sholes wanted to record us. I think Victor took us back because they didn't want anybody else to get us. Fred Rose came down to [Atlanta to] *see me about going with Columbia, and King Records sent a man down. They sent us such a contract that I couldn't even get a lawyer to decipher it. One way you read it, they were offering a fabulous royalty, and another way they were offering us practically nothing. I didn't understand it, so I took it over to WGST's lawyer and he said, "Anybody who would send me a contract like that, I wouldn't have anything to do with them."*

Now about that time the Carlisles were in Knoxville and Bill Carlisle would call me up and want us to go with King, and his brother Cliff would call and say go back with Victor. They had been with King and Cliff said

WEST VIRGINIA BROADCASTING CORP.

HAWLEY BUILDING
WHEELING, W. VA.

April 1, 1946

William A. Bolick
Route 4,
Box 325
Hickory, North Carolina

Dear Mr. Bolick

I was very disappointed when our plans fell through but I've been informed by your good friend, Pete, that you now have a pretty good set-up down South. I'd just like to wish you good luck in any venture you and the boys might undertake and perhaps sometime later we will be able to have you and the boys among our list of entertainers at W W V A.

Cordially yours

WEST VIRGINIA BROADCASTING CORP'N

Paul A. Myers
PAUL A. MYERS
Program Director

PAM/gfs

BASIC AMERICAN NETWORK

50,000 WATTS - SERVING EASTERN OHIO, WESTERN PENNSYLVANIA & WEST VIRGINIA

WWVA letter, April 1, 1946. Courtesy of Andy Merck, Bear Family Records.

that under no circumstances would he sign up with King if he were us, and he signed up with Victor himself. Frank Walker wanted us to go with MGM. We had worked under him and Dan Hornsby in 1940 and '41 [actually 1938–40]. *I knew Dan very well when he was an announcer at WGST, and he was pretty good friends with Frank.*

947 ☆ ☆ HILLBILLY ☆ ☆ 1948

tosalie Allen Melody Round-Up

ll hour live musical show featuring le Allen, the top female folk singer merica, her vocal trio and hillbilly . cowboy singer and featured instru- alist including fiddle and steel guitar. program maintains a western theme Rosalie and her group, a traveling tainment troupe which moves to to town in the west.
ability: Live talent, E. T.
Units: 30 minutes, 1 weekly
ence Appeal: juvenile, entire family
ested for: Afternoon, Evening
t Suitability: Home products, food- tuffs, soft drinks, cigarettes, clothing
ber of Artists: 8
ion Facilities: Transcriptions
itted by: Rosalie Allen Associates, 619 Broadway, Room 415, New York 19, N. Y.

ie Andrews Brothers With Uncle Elmer

Andrews Brothers, Jim and Floyd, e close-harmony balladning of simple ntain folk music was enjoyed for five on WSM's Grand Ole Opry, present rson a delightful, fast-moving, daily er-hour of songs of the hills and s. The Brothers sing in an unusually ing style, born of thirteen years ex- nce in radio as a duet. Comedy is hed on each program by a brief arance of Uncle Elmer Ledbetter. Thickety Creek. The program is an- ced by Lonny Moore, and Emceed by Andrews.
lability: E. T.
Units: 15 minutes, 5 weekly
ence Appeal: Entire family
Suggested for: Early morning
Client Suitability: Flour, Grain, Feed, Patent Medicine, Headache Powders, etc.
Number of Artists: 3
Audition Facilities: Transcriptions
Submitted by: WGAC, Augusta, Ga.

Blue Sky Boys

The popular Blue Sky Boys Trio, sings and plays those favorite Folk and Mountain songs. During a 30 day period this trio received 1443 letters and cards—averaging 66 pieces of mail per broadcast day, and this mail was postmarked from 175 towns throughout Georgia, Alabama, North and South Carolina. This group has two 15 minute program 5 days a week, and makes between 4 and 6 personal appearances each week. They also have been featured on RCA Victor Records for over a decade.
Availability: Live talent; E. T.
Time Units: 15 minutes, 5 weekly
Audience Appeal: Entire family
Suggested for: Morning; afternoon
Client Suitability: Farm products—household products—food products
Number of Artists: 3
Cost: On request
Audition Facilities: Transcriptions
Submitted by: WGST, Forsyth Bldg., Atlanta, Ga.

Brush Creek Follies

"Brush Creek Follies," a two-hour, all-star, radio-stage show; a smashing success of a barn dance, entering its tenth big season. The Brush Creek cast has been conscientiously built up as one of the country's finest groups of western and hill billy entertainers. Cast includes singers, comedians, vocal and instrumental units, and all sorts of teams. Available for full program or quarter-hour blocks.
Availability: Live talent
Time Units: Four 15-minute periods; 1 weekly
Audience Appeal: Entire family
Suggested for: Evening
Client Suitability: All types
Number of Artists: Approximately 40
Cost: Upon request
Audition Facilities: Transcriptions
Submitted by: KMBC, Pickwick Hotel, Kansas City 6, Mo.

Carolina Hayride

Colorful Hill-Billy Music and Variety Show, featuring WBT's roster of well-known hillbilly singers, together with specialists in sacred hymns, spirituals, westerns, and comedy. Has been broadcast from stage of Charlotte's Armory Auditorium for over a year to capacity audience from Charlotte and surrounding towns. Combining singing stars well-known throughout the southeast in a program format which has proved to have listener appeal.
Availability: Live talent
Time Units: 1 and one-half hours, 1 weekly
Audience Appeal: Entire family
Suggested for: Evening
Client Suitability: Has sold successfully for sponsors of all types—from Chesterfield to such offerings as Dr. LeGear, designed particularly for rural listeners.
Number of Artists: 30
Audition Facilities: Transcriptions
Submitted by: WBT and/or Radio Sales, Inc., N. Y., Wilder Bldg., Charlotte, N. C.

Cecil Brower's Western String Band

Cecil Brower's Western String Band has gained a large West Texas audience by featuring popular and old familiar music as well as western. The band's large audience has been proved by a recent give away of pictures of the members, who were formerly with Milton Brown's "Brownies" and the Light Crust Doughboys. Cecil Brower and Andy Schroder are featured on Andy's own hit composition "New Fort Worth Rag" which has just been released by Victor records.
Availability: Live talent
Time Units: 25 minutes, 6 weekly
Audience Appeal: Entire family
Suggested for: Morning; afternoon
Client Suitability: All types who desire a large audience
Number of Artists: 5
Audition Facilities: Transcriptions
Submitted by: KECK, Box 672, Odessa, Texas

Chow Time

Half-hour daily program at twelve o'clock noon. A fast moving, well-produced hill-billy show with the well-known KFH Ark Valley Boys, a hillbilly group featuring ten musicians. Show uses script. Has very high Hooper—highest noon time Hooper for last two years in the city. Open to two sponsors in fifteen minute sections.
Availability: Live talent
Time Units: Two 15-minute units; 5 weekly
Audience Appeal: Entire family

WGST electrical transcription series offer echoes Bill's claims. *Radio Daily* newsletter, 1947.

Though they renewed old ties with RCA and WGST, postwar entertainment realities forced them to learn by trial and error that new ways of doing things applied to broadcasting, too.

It seemed like people didn't want to inform you about things. It was just like starting all over again when we were kids and didn't know anybody. We should have hit the big stations when we had the opportunities. WWVA wanted us when we first came back from the war and offered us a good salary. We could have made enough selling songbooks alone because it was a very powerful station. Instead we went back to WGST because we knew we could make it there. We always had and, of course, they were anxious to get us back.

Immediately after we went back to WGST, WSB, a 50,000-watt station in Atlanta, tried to buy us away from WGST but we didn't take the offer. They had a Cross Roads Follies *show at noon, and I think that was about the time James and Martha Carson left WSB. But we drew a lot of mail at WGST and in May of 1947 the station reported that we received 1,443 letters and cards, averaging 66 pieces of mail per broadcast day, from Georgia, Alabama, North and South Carolina.*

We turned down things we should have taken. I let loyalty stand in the way and found out you can't do that. When we gave our word, even if it meant losing money, we usually kept it. When WSB wanted us, I couldn't bring myself to switch even though we could make more money there. I felt I owed WGST a certain amount of loyalty because I never asked for time on the air and got turned down. We stayed at WGST from March 25, 1946 until the early part of 1948.

On November 8, 1947, *Billboard* reported that Curly Parker had left the Blue Sky Boys for Connie B. Gay's Radio Ranchmen on WARL in Arlington, Virginia, near Washington, DC. In 2005 Bill told Walt Saunders that Curly left the Blue Sky Boys under a cloud, but he didn't elaborate. Joe Tyson substituted until Curly rejoined in January 1948, and a studio fiddler replaced him on the Bolicks' December 1947 RCA sessions in New York. Curly left for the last time in June 1949 while the Bolicks were at WCYB in Bristol, Virginia.

Goodbye to Atlanta, 1948

IN THE LATTER PART OF 1947, THE BLUE SKY BOYS GOT A TEMPTING offer from a respected Nashville promoter.

We had an opportunity to go on the Grand Ole Opry *one time. J. L. Frank, who was Roy Acuff's manager, wanted to take us up there. J. L. managed* [his son-in-law] *Pee Wee King and Roy Acuff, and he wanted to manage us. Whenever he would bring an act to Atlanta he would always hire us to play on the show for fifteen or twenty minutes. He knew that we were popular and it was cheaper to hire us than to buy spots* [commercial announcements] *on the radio.*

J. L. kind of liked me and we got to be pretty good friends. When he came to [Atlanta] *he would call me and say, "Bill, whatcha doin' this afternoon?" Well, if I didn't have a personal appearance or something, I'd go up to his hotel room and shoot the bull with him. He'd give me the lowdown on everybody in Nashville. He said, "Why don't you boys go up to Nashville? You've got no business on a station like WGST; you could make a lot of money* [at WSM]*." He said, "I tell you what I'll do. I'll get you on in Nashville and you can give me ten per cent for booking you. Or give me fifteen per cent and I'll manage records and everything for you. I can make you a lot of money."*

We were guest artists on the Prince Albert show on the NBC network part of the show one Saturday night [January 10] *in 1948, when Red Foley was master of ceremonies. We did "Kentucky" and "Sold Down the River." But I didn't know what to do because Nashville can make you or break you. If they gave you the right spot on the air you could make it easy, but if they threw you on after eleven o'clock, you could forget it.*

When they met again in Atlanta, J. L. tried once more to persuade the Blue Sky Boys to consider the *Opry.* He made a call to WSM program director Jack Stapp, who seconded Frank's invitation, but the Bolicks had accepted an offer to return to Raleigh and once more declined.

I had promised that we would take the job at Raleigh and, although I should have realized it then, I can see the mistakes now. Since we had promised to go to WNAO, I hesitated to go to Nashville, not knowing how our type of music might be accepted, although the Delmores had done pretty good up there in past years.

An additional factor was Earl's wife Gerry, who had family ties in Atlanta and strong reservations about living in Nashville. Bill himself thought there might be a "rough bunch" at WSM, and Earl agreed. They left WGST for the last time in February 1948 and wound up spending the rest of the year on WNAO in Raleigh, competing with WPTF where their old nemesis Graham Poyner still ruled. As they had with WGST, the Blue Sky Boys settled for less than a larger competitor could offer.

[WNAO] *was a new station which was owned by the* News and Observer, *a local newspaper. It was an AM and FM 5,000-watt station affiliated with ABC. We had been contacted by Dudley Tichenor, manager of the station, six months prior to the time the station opened. Frank Hardin, an announcer at WGST, had moved to a station in Denver where, I think, Mr. Tichenor was sales manager. Upon learning that Mr. Tichenor was leaving Denver to become manager of WNAO, Frank mentioned that we had worked in* [Raleigh] *with satisfying results. He told Mr. Tichenor he thought we would be a big boost to a new station, judging by our popularity at WGST.*

Mr. Tichenor contacted us and we worked out an agreement to be at WNAO when the station opened. We were to receive a $35 weekly salary, be able to advertise personal appearances, and sell songbooks, pictures, or anything of that nature without paying any of our proceeds to the station. Of course we would be bucking WPTF, a 50,000-watt station where we had worked before the war, but we didn't want to go back there.

So we went to WNAO and did pretty good, but things didn't work out the way we had planned. It had the nicest studios of any station I have ever worked in. We were given two programs daily, one in the morning and one around midday. [Eventually] *we had large crowds at personal appearances, but it took time to build our audiences* [since WNAO] *was a directional station and didn't cover as much territory as we had planned.*

*We had hardly gotten started when a polio epidemic hit that section of the country. Theaters and meeting places were closed, large gatherings were banned, and many of our personal appearances were canceled. It was some time before things returned to normal.**

*There were other factors also that caused us to decide to leave WNAO. I made a deal that no other country music act would be hired without our consent and we were getting along well when Lonzo and Oscar came down there. I don't know why they picked WNAO.***

Mr. Tichenor called me in and said, "You and I have a deal." I said, "That's right, you and I have a deal." He said, "Well, I'm as good as my word. It's not written, but I'll stick to the deal." I said, "Mr. Tichenor, you wouldn't have called me in unless you wanted them on the station, and I think that you think that the reason we're drawing this amount of mail is because we're the only act of this type on the station. Rather than have you feel this way, I would rather you bring them in under these conditions: that they charge the same admission price [as we do], *that they don't go out and book theaters and school houses for 50–50 when we're booking 75–25 per cent and, if any extra breaks come in by way of commercials or sponsors, we'll be given first chance at them. He said, "Yes, I'll promise you that, because I would like to bring them in."*

He brought them on the station but they didn't have the type of music that was popular in that part of the country. Sometime after that, I had a man booking dates for us at a school and someone asked, "Why is it you want 75 per cent of the door when this group from Nashville is offering to play for 50–50?"

---

* Devastating summer polio epidemics were commonplace before effective vaccines were widely distributed in 1954. In 1948 there were 2,516 cases and 143 deaths in North Carolina alone.

** They had been on the *Grand Ole Opry* with Eddy Arnold until parting company with him at the end of 1947. Their version of "I'm My Own Grandpa" was charting and they were seeking new employment.

Winding Down, 1949–51

IN DECEMBER 1948 OR THE EARLY PART OF 1949, WE RECEIVED WORD from Steve Sholes that he was planning to record Victor artists in Atlanta, Georgia, during the latter part of the month. We were to record on January 31 from 6 to 8 PM. Soon after arriving in Atlanta, we met with Mel Foree, a PR (public relations) man for Acuff-Rose. We knew Mel quite well, as he had visited a number of times when we were working over WGST. He told us he had several songs he would like us to consider recording at our forthcoming session. One was "Alabama" and the other was "The Little Paper Boy." "Alabama" was written by the Louvin Brothers and the other by Jim Anglin, a brother to Jack Anglin. Until this time, we had never heard of the Louvin Brothers. Mel had a portable phonograph and recordings of the two songs. He had previously talked with Steve Sholes and Steve wanted us to record them, especially "Alabama." He felt that because "Kentucky" had been successful, "Alabama" might prove to be a hit for us. Mel played the songs for us a number of times on the portable phonograph. Had he not done this, I feel we could have never learned the songs as quickly as we did. I never felt we did them justice as we had little time to learn them.

While trying to learn these two songs in Mel's hotel room, we told him we were planning to leave WNAO. He asked if we would be interested in working at WNOX in Knoxville, saying he knew Lowell Blanchard, who was manager of the station [and a popular music host], *and he would be glad to put in a word for us. Some entertainers playing over WNOX at that time were Maybelle Carter and her daughters, Chet Atkins, Homer and Jethro, Carl Story, and others.*

A bit later Mel called Blanchard. WNOX agreed to pay us seventy-five dollars if we would come by and play on [the Tennessee Barn Dance,] *their Saturday night program. As agreed, we played on the Saturday night jamboree. Lowell Blanchard seemed interested in us, but said there were a few matters he wanted to get straightened out and promised he would contact us within the next week or two.*

We went on to WCYB in Bristol [Virginia], *a 10,000-watt station with good coverage. When we returned to WNAO, we waited several weeks before giving them notice. Meantime, we expected to hear from Lowell Blanchard at WNOX since we felt certain he would hire us. Days passed and we heard nothing from him. It finally dawned on us that he had changed his mind and didn't want us working at WNOX. I have no idea why we never heard from him. Later, after we had been at WCYB for some time, I was told by some WNOX artists that some entertainers had objected to our coming there.*

When I turned in our resignation to Mr. Tichenor at WNAO, he appeared saddened to see us leave. Without our requesting it, he wrote us a very nice letter of recommendation. He stated that during our stay over half the mail the station received had been addressed to the Blue Sky Boys. He said, "more than 15,000 of our 30,000 pieces of fan mail have been addressed to your group since the station has been open," and if he had any idea that we would have left Raleigh he never would have let [Lonzo and Oscar] *come. He was very disappointed because they drew practically no fan mail at all even when they gave away free pictures. I still have this letter in my memorabilia. Very few station managers would have dared to include something of this nature in a letter of recommendation. We stayed at WNAO until March 12, 1949.*

We had heard of WCYB, a 10,000-watt station that had a noonday program known as Farm and Fun Time. *The Stanleys had turned down a program over WPTF to return there. We heard that Charlie Monroe was there, as were Flatt and Scruggs. We felt that if artists of their stature were there, WCYB must be a mecca for country musicians. We decided while we were in that part of the country that we would go by and see what they had to offer. We talked with Bill Lane, who was in charge. He knew of us and seemed anxious to have us there. Artists working over WCYB at that time were Curly King, Flatt and Scruggs, and the Stanleys. Charlie Monroe was no longer there.*

The station didn't pay a salary but we could advertise our personal appearances, sell songbooks, pictures, etc. Artists in return would pay five percent of net receipts from personal appearances—we knew of several other stations that worked on this basis. We told Bill Lane that we would let him know within the next three or four weeks. At that time, we had no thought of moving to WCYB, since we thought we would work at WNOX.

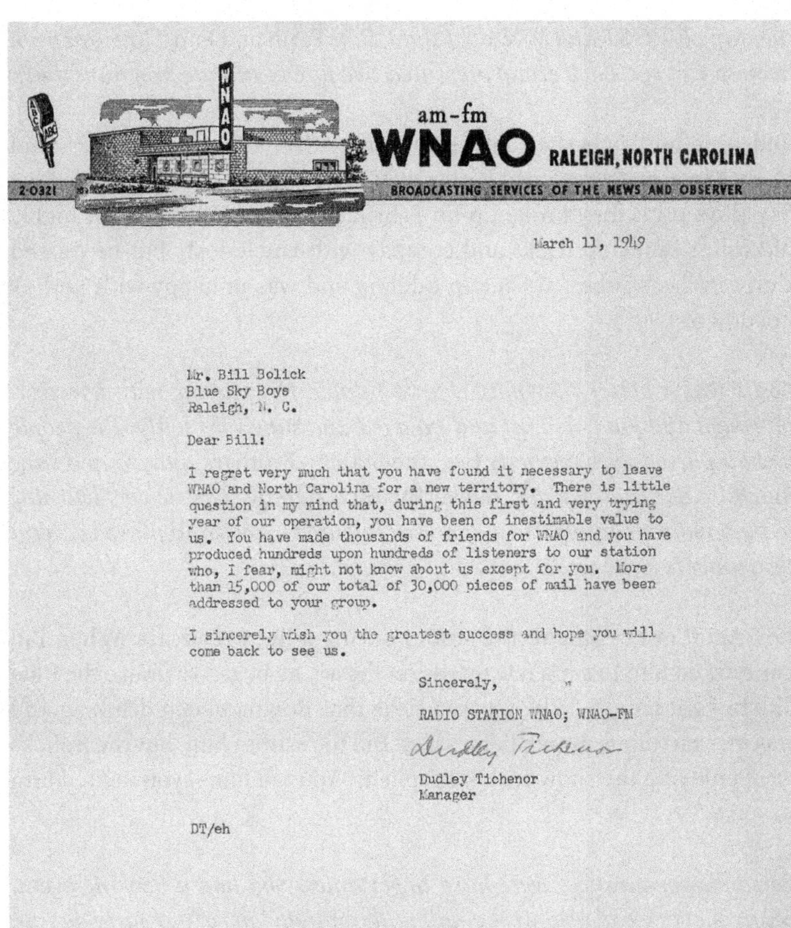

March 11, 1949

Mr. Bill Bolick
Blue Sky Boys
Raleigh, N. C.

Dear Bill:

I regret very much that you have found it necessary to leave WNAO and North Carolina for a new territory. There is little question in my mind that, during this first and very trying year of our operation, you have been of inestimable value to us. You have made thousands of friends for WNAO and you have produced hundreds upon hundreds of listeners to our station who, I fear, might not know about us except for you. More than 15,000 of our total of 30,000 pieces of mail have been addressed to your group.

I sincerely wish you the greatest success and hope you will come back to see us.

Sincerely,

RADIO STATION WNAO; WNAO-FM

Dudley Tichenor

Dudley Tichenor
Manager

DT/eh

WNAO letter March 11, 1949. Courtesy of Andy Merck, Bear Family Records.

It was probably one of the worst deals we ever had been offered. There were other radio stations that offered much better opportunities. WGST would have been pleased to have us back and WNAO would have been glad had we decided to stay. Either station would have paid us a weekly salary and required none of the proceeds from personal appearances.

We moved to WCYB in March 1949. It didn't take long for us to realize we hadn't made too wise a choice. It was one of the few stations we worked where I never met the manager or learned who owned the station. Bill Lane and the engineer were nice people and we enjoyed working with them [but otherwise] *I knew none of the staff. This seemed strange as we knew all the staff of WGST and WNAO. I think that* Farm and Fun Time *ran from noon to 1:30* PM. *Each group presented two fifteen-minute programs daily.*

Old-time fiddler Leslie Keith, formerly with the Stanley Brothers and Curly King bands, replaced Parker at WCYB and remained with the Blue Sky Boys until they broke up on February 17, 1951. Bill thought highly of Leslie's bullwhip tricks and comedy with Uncle Josh, but he missed Curly Parker's subdued backup fiddling and was unhappy with Leslie's hoedown style.

Leslie was a better showman than a fiddler. His playing with us was a bit rough and loud, as Earl and I played and sung very softly. The people he had played with formerly [i.e., the Stanley Brothers] *played and sang much louder than we did.* [Nevertheless,] *step by step, he was learning to play more smoothly. He was a very talented fellow, and played several instruments quite well.*

Roy Acuff once came to the studio during a live broadcast. When Bill Lane asked him to say a few words on the air, he began to praise the Blue Sky Boys at length. When it was clear that Roy had been drinking and was in a garrulous mood, Lane asked Bill to restrain him, but the Bolicks were enjoying the show and Bill replied, "You tell him—you invited him to speak!"

Personal appearances were hard to get unless you had a booking agent. Many places we played were small and reminded me of our early days in Georgia. Judging from what Leslie Keith told us, attendance at our appearances was as good or better as any other groups with whom he had worked. I found an entry in my notes that showed we had paid WCYB the sum of $390. This was the five percent we were to pay the station from our personal appearances. I'm certain that we made more than this one payment, but I could find no further information.

We left WCYB around the last of November 1949 or the early part of December, before winter began. I look back and wonder why we stayed there as long as we did. Perhaps we were in a rut and hesitated to make a move. I asked Bill Lane if we could have the transcriptions [made at WCYB]. *As with the Willys Jeep transcriptions made at WGST in 1946, I had no idea what we would do with them but I did feel that someday I might have a use for them.*

We moved to a thousand-watt station in Rome, Georgia, WROM. Earl's wife was from Atlanta and we thought it would be a nice place to stop off for a while. It was just a small station, but there was a nice bunch of people. We had the run of the station because they were tickled to get us. We had a program in the morning and one in the afternoon, approximately an hour a day on the air. That part of the country had been very good to us with personal appearances, and we usually had a good crowd. Show dates, however, were limited and, after we played there a while, I figured we ought to get away into another territory.

I wrote to KWKH in Shreveport and sent them a transcription. The manager of the station called me long distance, I talked to him for some time, and we went there in March or April of 1950. We weren't as well received as some other groups. It had the [Louisiana] Hayride *on Saturday nights with Johnnie and Jack, Zeke Clements, Red Sovine, the Rangers Quartet, the Wilburn Family (later the Wilburn Brothers), and Webb Pierce. No one was drawing real big crowds. That was about the cheapest station that I have ever worked on. It didn't even have ASCAP coverage. Our theme song, "Are You from Dixie," was ASCAP, and we had to change to something else.*

When we appeared on the Hayride, *we got little to no backing at all. Johnnie and Jack sang a lot of our songs but, when we would go on stage, promoters never whooped it up for us or anything like that. They'd say, "Here are the Blue Sky Boys," we'd play a number or so and get a little applause. Nobody would come out and keep clapping and jump five or six feet in the air and motion for the crowd to try to get us out again, like they did the rest of the groups.*

They wanted us to add two members to our group. We could play radio programs with just three, but they had a policy that we had to have five people when we made an appearance. I did add another fellow who was doing some booking for us, and we would let him play a fiddle tune on the stage. People enjoyed the program by the three of us more than if we had had half a dozen.

The union took four percent of your earnings and you had to pay each man if you got a sponsor. Most commercials were given to solo singers and a lot of groups had a hard time making it.

We left about August 1950 and came back to WNAO in Raleigh. Mr. Tichenor wasn't there anymore and they were losing listeners, especially with new stations going up. We did well while the tobacco season lasted and it's where we were when we decided to break up in early 1951.

Though Bill wanted to believe otherwise, when he admitted to being in a rut he implicitly acknowledged that the Blue Sky Boys' time was running out. After leaving WGST in Atlanta in 1948, their stays at other stations got shorter and shorter. By the time the brothers parted company in 1951, dazzling, rhinestone-sequined honky-tonk heroes like Lefty Frizzell, Carl Smith, Little Jimmy Dickens, Eddy Arnold, Hank Snow, Hank Williams, and Hank Thompson dominated country music, eclipsing Molly O'Day, Charlie Monroe, the Bailes Brothers, Wade Mainer, and Roy Acuff, who were no longer the major attractions they'd been a few years earlier.

Bill Monroe was an exception to the trend. In creating the genre later known as bluegrass, he learned how to coax big sounds and high-octane energy from acoustic instruments to compete with honky-tonk bands. He was further validated when ex–Blue Grass Boys Lester Flatt and Earl Scruggs, Mac Wiseman, and Jimmy Martin built popular bands of their own based on the Monroe formula. Bluegrass became the standard way to perform old-time music at the professional level, eclipsing other tradition-based styles as it became country music's primary alternative to honky-tonk. The Blue Sky Boys didn't much like bluegrass or view it as an option, but they might have been able to sustain a following by compromising with honky-tonk as the Louvin Brothers had, and as the Bolicks would eventually do themselves on a remarkable Starday LP in 1963.

Goodbye to RCA, 1950

BACK IN THE 1930S, WHEN ELI OBERSTEIN ROUTINELY DROPPED COMposer credits and altered titles on Bluebird records made for southern distribution, RCA could quietly avoid paying "mechanicals," licensing fees for the use of copyrighted music. In those days, most high-profile music publishers were clustered around Tin Pan Alley in lower Manhattan, either unaware or unconcerned that their songs could be heard royalty-free on jukeboxes and phonographs throughout much of the country.

The Bolicks and Oberstein liked each other and jointly produced outstanding records, but Bill Bolick found the retitled songs irritating and the brothers continued to perform them with their original titles, creating audience confusion that couldn't have done much to stimulate record sales. After Frank Walker replaced Oberstein in 1938, conventional titles reappeared on Bluebird labels, though composer credits were often still absent.

As we've seen, the Bolicks' final years at RCA from 1946 to 1950 were difficult. Bill preferred some newly composed songs to others, but most were routine and few were hits. His comment about "Speak to Me, Little Darling" from the first postwar Blue Sky Boys session revealed his displeasure with expediently chosen songs and mutual back scratching on the part of industry insiders.

Steve Sholes sent us this song and requested that we do it on our first recording session after World War II. He stated that he was asking this favor for a good friend of his, Murray Nash. Had we known at that time that we would only record four songs, it is doubtful that we would have learned it.

We never had any success with Victor after World War II, for the simple reason that they wanted us to add all kinds of instruments, rhythm guitar, drums, and this and that. I said if you do that you are taking away the sound of our music and I refused. They wanted us to get away from old *tearjerkers and sing some more modern stuff. Our contract read that we choose our songs mutually, but Sholes wanted to choose them all and he sent me a lot of sorry material. He used a lot of stuff from Hill and Range. I even signed a contract with them myself; they just hounded me until I finally gave in because Steve Sholes insisted. We collaborated with several other writers, but we didn't write most of our songs. Possibly fifteen or twenty songs is all. We wrote "I Love Her More Now Mother's Old," "Angel Mother," "You Branded Your Name on My Heart," "Behind These Prison Walls of Love," "Come to the Savior," and several others.**

I realized we couldn't sell like Eddy Arnold or Ernest Tubb but I said, "Where they sell a million, we can sell a quarter of a million and that's not bad. If you let us be the Blue Sky Boys you will give listeners a choice." Our first record, "Dust on the Bible," sold 200,000 or more. That's pretty doggone good for a group that hadn't recorded for six years. "Kentucky" sold about half a million, but we never got any publicity like Eddy Arnold. We must have done pretty good because RCA was interested in having us continue to record for them. Old-time record stores said we were continuous sellers. We didn't make an overnight hit but they could sell a record made two or three years earlier, just about as good as it did the first day it came out.

Conflict over one song put an end to the Blue Sky Boys' Victor tenure in 1950.

At our last recording session, Steve Sholes was peeved that we hadn't come prepared to record all the songs he had sent us. He got real upset because we didn't do one by Nick Kenny and he wouldn't allow us to record a song we preferred. Nick Kenny had a column in the New York Mirror *newspaper and was a very influential man, but the song just wasn't our type.*

Steve had some kind of deal worked out with Hill and Range. Practically all these numbers, "The Unfinished Rug," "Lord Be With Us, Amen," "The New Golden Rule," and several others he proposed [for the 1950 session] *were owned by Hill and Range. We were signed with them by that time and, when we recorded a number like that, they were supposed to give us two hundred dollars for each song in advance. We never received anything from them in that respect.*

He suggested that we add an electric guitar, which we refused to do. Ernie Newton, who played the bass, had a little wire brush. Whenever he

* Compositions claimed by the Bolicks are listed in "Sources for Blue Sky Boys Songs" in Appendix 1.

would pick, he would hit the wood on the bass and it would give it a kind of a drum effect as he picked it. I didn't care for that but Steve wanted to use it, so we used it on some numbers on the last session.

Steve said, "We're not getting anywhere. How about one you did a long time ago on the old Bluebird disc?" So we re-recorded "The Sunny Side of Life." As we were packing our instruments to leave, I told Earl that in all probability we would never record for RCA again.

Nick Kenny (1895–1975) was an influential columnist, poet, and lyricist who wrote several hit songs with his brother Charles, including "Gold Mine in the Sky," "Drop Me Off in Harlem," "Gone Fishin'," and "Love Letters in the Sand." Ernie Newton (1909–1976) was one of the most widely employed session bassists in Nashville in the 1940s and 50s, in part because the brush strokes on his upright bass sounded like a snare drum on records.

As Bill observed, Steve Sholes's popular-music background and publishing connections influenced choices he made as head of RCA's country music section. His favored artists included Eddy Arnold, Pee Wee King, Homer and Jethro, Hank Snow, Jim Reeves, the Browns, Elvis Presley, and others who successfully produced pop-flavored records. His job was to earn maximum profits for his employer, his friends, and himself, and he was happiest when his country records enjoyed crossover sales in the pop market. Sholes's counterpart at Columbia was Art Satherley (1889–1986), who was more hospitable to tradition-based artists like Bill Monroe, Roy Acuff, the Stanley Brothers, Wilma Lee and Stoney Cooper, Molly O'Day, the Bailes Brothers, and Bob Wills.

Earl and Bill owned all or part of a few titles placed with Acuff-Rose in 1946–47. Two Bolick originals from 1949 went to Hill and Range, who also controlled six of the eight songs from their last RCA session in 1950. Despite differences with Sholes, the Bolicks had always been receptive to current material, at least when Bill thought it could work for them.

A lot of people had the idea that the traditional stuff is the only songs we did, but we kept up with popular country music. In the 1930s, "The Last Letter" was a very popular song. After the war we sang "Searching for a Soldier's Grave" and songs like that. We tried to get Steve Sholes to let us do "Rainbow at Midnight" even though it was done by the Carlisles on King Records [and Ernest Tubb on Decca]. *With our style it could have been a big seller, but Texas Jim Robertson had recorded it* [for RCA, and

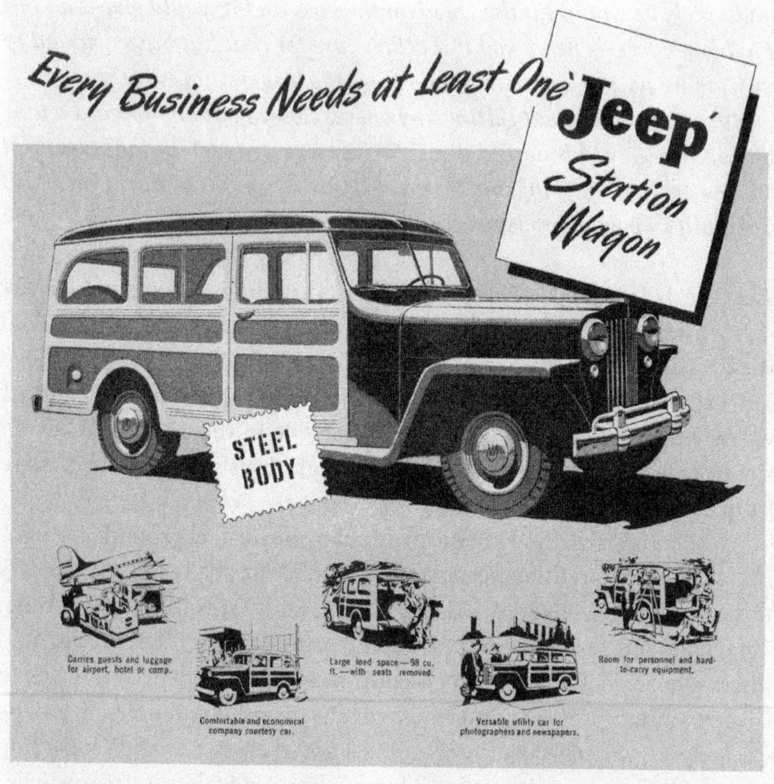

Willys Jeep station wagon, 1947.

Sholes] *didn't want any conflict there. Just because a song was popular, we didn't necessarily sing it, but if we felt it was a song we could rearrange and sing, then we did it.*

Their successful records of contemporary songs ranged from Karl and Harty's "I'm Just Here to Get My Baby Out of Jail" in 1936 to Eddie Noack's "Don't Trade Your Old Fashioned Sweetheart (For a Honky-Tonk Queen)" in 1963; an extended list would include "Why Not Confess," "Turn Your

Radio On," "Dust on the Bible," "Don't Say Goodbye If You Love Me," and "Behind These Prison Walls of Love." Their biggest hit, "Kentucky," was written by Karl Davis, who contributed several more songs to Hill and Range and the Blue Sky Boys discography between 1947 and 1950. The Bolicks themselves wrote, arranged or acquired a dozen new songs themselves, but they weren't composers by nature and thus relinquished a measure of control over what they could record.

If old music was no longer offered on new Blue Sky Boys records, it remained central to their live performances and WGST shows. Ruth Walker's earlier song lists from the Bolicks' 1939–40 broadcasts contain a balance of new and old hymns and secular songs, a short sequence with Uncle Josh (often tied in with sponsor products) and a dance tune, frequently performed to run out the clock as a fifteen-minute broadcast concluded. When they returned to WGST in 1946, the format stayed the same, and the shows rarely featured songs from their current RCA releases.

They soon acquired a congenial sponsor, Jack Briscoe, Inc., the Atlanta distributor for Willys Jeeps, whose wartime combat support vehicles had been modified for farm work and other civilian uses. In December 1946, Earl and Bill acquired a Jeep Station Wagon at fifty percent of its retail price for transportation to personal appearances, where they would promote it to audiences throughout the WGST area.

Mr. Briscoe was a nice fellow to work for. I used to stop in and talk with him every week or two. He was pleased with our work and felt the Willys Jeep people were also. On one of my visits, Mr. Briscoe told me that Willys Overland was making a station wagon that would be ready for the market in a short time. He told me that if we would use it for our personal appearances he would sell us one at cost, and it wasn't long until we took possession of a new Jeep station wagon. I think we were among the first people in Atlanta to get one. It was definitely an eye-catcher. It handled good and rode much better than we had ever expected. Until we left Atlanta in 1948, we used the station wagon on most of our appearances.

Tape recording technology was not yet available, and their fifteen-minute WGST shows were recorded live on sixteen-inch acetate discs for rebroadcast on additional Georgia stations. Bill saved a group of WGST shows from 1946 and 1947, and a second group from 1949, when he and Earl were at WCYB. The broadcasts often featured songs recorded before the war, even though the originals were long out of print. As Bill has noted, the Bolicks cooperated with Steve Sholes's demands for current material in their RCA sessions but elsewhere their postwar country songs were performed less frequently than traditional favorites.

Country music had broadened its appeal during World War II with "Pistol Packin' Mama," "Born to Lose," "San Antonio Rose," "There's a Star Spangled Banner Waving Somewhere," and other hits that enjoyed widespread popularity. Performers, songwriters, publishers, and broadcasters enjoyed the music's new visibility and sought to burnish its appeal by escaping the "hillbilly" label.

Bill Bolick heartily endorsed the effort. As late as 1990, country music historian Wayne Daniel called the Blue Sky Boys "by far the most popular hillbilly group to appear on WGST."* While appreciating the compliment, Bill would have politely objected to the adjective. In his introduction to a songbook, *Favorite Hymns and Folk Songs* (1947), he took exception to the word in a strong statement that defined the Blue Sky Boys' musical vision:

For quite a number of years we have tried to entertain our radio audience by singing and playing the Old-Time Songs. We have tried to sing them with the same spirit [in which] *we feel they were written. Some of these songs are hundreds of years old, and it is possible that no one knows their exact origin. Most people commonly refer to these songs as HILL-BILLY. We wish to take this opportunity to correct this misunderstanding. HILL-BILLY songs are usually the bum and hobo songs of the bar room and Honky-Tonk nature and do not carry the quality or character that you will find in the songs handed down to us by our Pioneer Ancestors.*

Today the word can be used affectionately to describe music with traditional roots and backwoods flavor, but in 1947 it still invoked stereotypical images of bearded barefoot hayseeds wearing overalls and smoking corncob pipes beneath worn straw hats. Earl Bolick's Uncle Josh was an affectionate stereotype, providing contrast with the Blue Sky Boys, who emphasized their personal distance from "hill-billy" by performing in conservative business suits. In 1949 the industry rebranded the category as "country and western" and later shortened it to "country," a neutral rubric Bill could accept.

---

* *Pickin' on Peachtree: A History of Country Music in Atlanta, Georgia* (Urbana and Chicago: University of Illinois Press, 1990), 155.

Sunset in the Blue Sky, 1950–74

ON SEPTEMBER 23, 1950, *BILLBOARD*'S JOHNNY SIPPEL REPORTED THAT "Earl Bolick, of the Blue Sky Boys (Victor), who recently moved to WNAO, Raleigh, N.C., is doing a daily d. j. slot. The Blue Sky Boys also do two half hour live shows daily." Nevertheless, Bill recalled:

We weren't doing very good there. We were drawing fan mail but it was hard to get personal appearances. Every time a [new] *local station sprang up it cut down on your listening audience. Unless we could move to a larger station like WWVA or WSM, our work was going to slow down.*

Finally Earl decided to toss in the towel, and the brothers separated on February 17, 1951. Earl's life became secure as he swapped music and life on the road for a day job, but Bill at age thirty-three found himself unexpectedly at the end of his career and uncertain about what to do next.

I had no idea that Earl had any idea of quitting, but I can understand his circumstances and I know it was the only way for him to be closer to his family. I didn't make any effort to persuade him to stay, because it was his decision to make. I wasn't expecting it and it shook me up so badly that I have never fully recovered from it or made any effort to form a group of my own, although entertaining was my whole life while we were performing together. I had a few contacts, a little money, and I could have gotten a good group together. I don't think it would have been as popular as the Blue Sky Boys, but you never know. I don't suppose I'll ever fully be satisfied trying to do anything else, although I have a fairly good job and make a decent living.

I went back to Hickory and attended Lenoir-Rhyne, a Lutheran liberal arts college. I went winter and summer and accumulated 114 semester hours, and I only needed 128 [to get] *my degree in business administration.*

LENOIR RHYNE COLLEGE
HICKORY, N. C.
OFFICE OF THE REGISTRAR

This Certifies, That William Anderson Bolick was admitted to
LENOIR RHYNE COLLEGE from Hickory High School

ADMISSION RECORD

SUBJECT	UNITS	COLLEGE CREDIT SEM. HOURS	SUBJECT	UNITS	COLLEGE CREDIT SEM. HOURS	SUBJECT	UNITS	COLLEGE CREDIT SEM. HOURS
English	4		Gen Science	1				
History	2		Biology	1				
Civics	1		Srench	2				
Algebra	2		Health	1				
Geometry	1		Mech Drawing	1				

RECORD AT LENOIR RHYNE

SESSION	COURSE	DESCRIPTION	NO. OF WEEKS	HOURS A WEEK REC.	HOURS A WEEK LAB.	RECORD 1ST SEM.	RECORD 2ND SEM.	RECORD SUMMER	CREDIT SEMESTER HOURS
1951 SS	Bible 4	Life of Christ	6	5				A	2
	Bible 5	Christian Missions	6	5				A	2
	Geography 2	World	6	8				A	3
1951-52	English 1-2	Rhetoric & Composition	36	3		B	A		6
	History 1-2	Found of Mod European Hist	36	3		B	B		6
	Mathematics 1A-2A	General	36	3		B	B		6
	Latin 1-2	First Year	36	3		B	B		6
	Biology 1-2	General	36	3	2	B	B		8
1952 SS	English 3	English Literature Survey	6	8				A	3
	Accounting 1-2	Principles	12	8				B/B	6
	Mathematics 1C-2C	Business	12	8				C/B	6
1952-53	English B	Business	18	3		A			3
	Economics 7	Business Administration	18	3		A			3
	Latin 3-4	History; Ovid	36	3		B	B		6
	Accounting 3-4	Cost; Income Tax	36	3		B	B		6
	Economics 9	Salesmanship	18	3		A			3
	Economics 1-2	Principles; Problems	36	3		B	A		6
	Economics 8	Office Management & Practice	18	3			A		3
	Economics 10	Business Law	18	3			A		3
	Public Spk 4	Debating	18	2			A		2
1953 SS	Government 3	State	6	8				B	3
	Secretarial Pr 1	Typing	6	8				F	-
	History 3	American Survey	6	8				B	3
1953-54	Accounting 5	Intermediate	18	3		B			3
	Bible 3A	Old Testament History	18	2		A			2
	Economics 3	Economic History of U S	18	3		A			3
	Government 2	Federal	18	3		B			3
	Philosophy 3	Christian Ethics	18	3		A			3
	Economics 5	Labor Problems	18	3		A			3
	Public Spk 3	Argumentation	18	2		A			2

Reason for Withdrawal Voluntary
Mr. Bolick is honorably dismissed and is entitled to return to this Institution.
DATE July 6, 1954 E. L. Setzer Registrar.
SCALE OF MARKING: A—100-95; B—94-87; C—86-78; D—77-70; E—Condition; F—Failure.

Lenoir-Rhyne College transcript, 1956. Courtesy of Alan Justice and Marshall Wyatt.

I've asked myself why I didn't finish, just like I asked myself why I didn't go on after Earl and I broke up.

Lenoir-Rhyne College in downtown Hickory was established in 1891 by the North Carolina Synod of the Evangelical Lutheran Church. Bill enrolled as a freshman under the G. I. Bill in the summer of 1951, eighteen years after receiving his high school diploma. He hit the ground running and managed to complete seven semester hours in Bible studies and geography by summer's end, earning all A's. He completed the 1953–54 academic year before leaving school, earning five more A's, two B's, and one C, in business mathematics. Given Bill's intellect and temperament, it's not surprising that he excelled academically, but his age and unique background meant that he had little in common with either students or faculty, and his recollections avoid any further mention of his college years.

As he approached graduation, Bill had no immediate career plans, and the lovely Ohio lady he'd courted long-distance for a decade was growing understandably impatient. Garland had earned a comfortable living as a mail carrier for more than thirty years and, when he learned about a job opening in Washington, encouraged Bill to take the Post Office exam. He passed easily and moved to Washington, DC, where he joined the Railway Mail Service and invited Doris to join him.

Doris: *I went there and got a job in November 1954. Before we were married, Bill lived with a couple up on Summit Place* [in Northeast Washington] *close to Rock Creek Park. We were married in* [Washington on February 19,] *1957 and lived in my third-floor apartment on Ontario Road until September, when Bill got transferred to Greensboro* [North Carolina] *and we moved there. I don't remember him having any instruments, but after we moved to Greensboro he did. Greensboro's not that far from Hickory. We lived at 2012 Todd Street until 1975, when we moved to a new house on some property that Bill's family owned at 1052 33d Street, SW, right next door* [to his parents].

Bill was really easygoing; he liked to entertain better than anything. He never really liked the job he had but he made a good living and he had a good retirement from it. For years he went to work at eleven o'clock at night and came home at seven in the morning. I didn't like it at first because I worked in the daytime—he'd no more than get home and then I'd have to go to work. He said to me one day, "If you think we can make it on what I make, you can quit tomorrow." And I quit! (telephone conversation, September 6, 2010)

Their marriage endured through Bill's final illness and death in 2008, for more than fifty years.

Earl's marriage to Gerry Bennett in 1946 produced two sons, William Steven and Joseph Alan. He quit the Blue Sky Boys in 1951, when his growing family needed more economic stability than music could provide, and a father who was home more often. Earl became a skilled machinist at Lockheed Aircraft in Marietta, where he prospered until his retirement in 1984, a year after Gerry's death. Today Steve Bolick remembers his father with love and affection, and offers some perspective:

Dad was quiet but he loved his family very much. He was very close to us and we were very close to him. He enjoyed the music when it was popular, enjoyed the traveling, and he enjoyed his second career just as much.

Mom could be the disciplinarian when she had to. Dad was quiet and only wanted to say something once. He'd say, "I don't want to have to repeat myself." He wasn't an outgoing individual; he was just the opposite of Uncle Josh. He was a calming person and always helpful. He wasn't overbearing or anything but when Dad spoke, everybody listened.

I didn't see him perform but, from what I understand, Josh was a character—very outgoing, very funny. People seemed to enjoy it and he enjoyed doing it. Maybe when he put on that costume he was Uncle Josh. Maybe Uncle Josh was part of him, so to speak.

He liked to listen to music but didn't follow it closely. Johnny Cash was one of his favorites, and he also liked Willie Nelson. Dad did teach me to play the guitar a little bit when I was nine, but I only play rarely. Dad didn't read music and neither do I. He had a great ear and could pick up on things. I still have his guitar and it's a highly treasured instrument. (telephone conversation, October 15, 2011, and email, December 9, 2012)

Earl's marriage and career kept him and his family in Tucker, where visits to and from Hickory were infrequent. Back there, three of Garland and Annie's other five children joined their parents, building new houses on the seven-acre plot where they'd grown up. Steve continues:

We didn't see Grandpa and Grandma Bolick more than once every two or three years. Grandaddy Bolick raised raspberries and, when I was very young—I couldn't have been more than five or six years old—we'd go out and pick them and eat them right off the vine. He grew muscadines, blackberries, strawberries, and raspberries. The house had an upstairs with ladder-type stairs, and we kids would sleep up there. I thought that was great, I thought that was super!

Folk Music and the Final Years, 1963–2008

WITH NO FURTHER PLANS TO MAKE MUSIC, BILL AND EARL WOUND up with jobs and marriages in towns three hundred miles apart. They rarely saw each other for the rest of their lives, even though their infrequent collaborations invariably produced great music.

Meanwhile, old-time country styles were becoming a fashionable part of the emerging folk revival in the north. In 1941 John Lomax produced a landmark five-disc Victor album called *Smoky Mountain Ballads.* It was the first attempt by a folklore specialist to reissue recordings made for regional consumption in the 1920s and 1930s, and redirect them to cosmopolitan audiences outside the South.

Smoky Mountain Ballads included songs recorded between 1930 and 1937 by the Mainers (together and separately), Arthur Smith, Uncle Dave Macon, the Monroe Brothers, the Dixon Brothers, and the Carter Family, artists whose old-fashioned rural sound and traditional material had a fresh appeal to sophisticated urban listeners who perceived them as exotic and authentic. Bill and Earl could have earned some useful name recognition from the set had they been included. John Lomax's biographer Nolan Porterfield suggests they were omitted "because, in John's estimation, they were too commercial or because John and Alan simply weren't familiar with the BSB."* Whatever the reason, it was a disservice to Bill and Earl, and it took another generation before the Blue Sky Boys were recognized in the folk music world.

Following *Smoky Mountain Ballads,* the Library of Congress began to publish record albums of field recordings collected and edited by the Lomaxes and others. These sets were available from the Library and copies went to libraries throughout the country, where curious listeners could experience the exotic sounds of backwoods and small-town America. For

* Email to me, July 16, 2012.

those preferring polished performances, Burl Ives, Susan Reed, John Jacob Niles, and others produced specialty albums of folk song interpretations with unobtrusive accompaniments. Josh White, Lead Belly, and Woody Guthrie followed with albums of their own, blending their southern roots with the progressive politics of the 1940s.

Folk song sets by country performers appeared in 1947 by two popular Kentucky country musicians: *Folk Songs of the Hills* by Merle Travis (Capitol) and *Kentucky Mountain Ballads* by Cousin Emmy (Decca). Neither album was a best seller but both were on major labels with national distribution, and they have influenced folk and country stylists for years. "Sixteen Tons" and "Dark as a Dungeon" were composed especially for the Travis album and his singular versions of "Nine Pound Hammer" and "I Am a Pilgrim" have been covered many times. "Ruby," a single from the Cousin Emmy sessions, became a career song for the Osborne Brothers nearly a decade later.

Had it occurred to the Bolicks, Steve Sholes, or RCA to produce a Blue Sky Boys folk song album, it would have played to their strengths, introduced them to new audiences, and popularized their unique vocal harmonies in folk music circles. They didn't perform or record outside the South until the 1960s, when knowledgeable aficionados persuaded them to work together again and perform for cosmopolitan folk music audiences for the first time.

As Bill makes clear in these pages, he was not a bluegrass fan. For him, it played a role in marginalizing the Bolicks' introspective style, almost from the time Bill Monroe's Blue Grass Boys joined the *Opry* in 1939. When Monroe added hot fiddle and jazzy bass to his assertive high-pitched vocals and driving mandolin, he infused old ingredients with new energy to create music that earned broad acceptance, especially after Earl Scruggs joined him in 1945, transforming the five-string banjo into a solo instrument and rivalling the virtuosity of his boss. Monroe-style bluegrass was aggressive, dynamic music that unintentionally upstaged the intimate, personal style of the Blue Sky Boys.

Nevertheless, bluegrass repertoire has always acknowledged the Blue Sky Boys with updated covers of their best-known songs, including "Why Not Confess," "The Knoxville Girl," "Katie Dear," "Kentucky," "Where the Soul Never Dies," "Sweet Allalee," "Midnight on the Stormy Deep," "Behind These Prison Walls of Love," and more. But such tributes didn't placate Bill, who didn't want the Blue Sky Boys to be classed as either hillbilly or bluegrass. He wasn't crazy about the Louvin Brothers, who nevertheless came closer than most to matching Bolick harmonies, though their vocal sound was aggressively high-pitched and bright compared to Bill and Earl's tasteful reticence. Charlie and Ira Louvin thought highly of the Blue Sky Boys and included five songs associated with them on their landmark 1956 collection *Tragic Songs of Life* (Capitol T769). The Everly Brothers revived five more on *Songs Our Daddy Taught Us* (Cadence CLP 3016), a 1958 collection of classic country duets dedicated to their legendary guitarist father Ike. Both records have rarely been out of print over the years.

Phil and Don Everly played their own acoustic guitars and string bass even on their pop hits. The Louvins, like the Bolicks, featured their own mandolin and guitar, though they updated their sound with a lead electric guitar that Bill disdained. Nonetheless he reluctantly came to terms with honky-tonk on the Blue Sky Boys' next records. In December 1961, the Cincinnati country singer, composer, and record retailer Jimmie Skinner persuaded Starday Records' Don Pierce to contact Bill with an offer to record the brothers again. Pierce had released a number of bluegrass singles and long-play records from 1957–61 and was expanding the Starday catalog to include new records by veteran performers like Stringbean, Charlie Monroe, Ola Belle and Alex Campbell, Lulu Belle and Scotty, Wayne Raney, Sam and Kirk McGee, Brother Oswald, and Lew Childre. Bill initially declined Pierce's invitation to make new records, agreeing instead to let him release excerpts from WGST transcriptions as *A Treasury of Rare Song Gems From the Past* (Starday SLP 205). The record was well received, especially by excited collectors who didn't know the transcriptions existed.

After the record was published, Martin Haerle, who worked for Starday, called and asked if there wasn't some way they could get us to do some recordings in person. I told Martin that I really didn't think that we could because it had been so long, twelve years. The only music I listened to was old-time groups I liked years ago, and not to any that were coming along at the time. I quit the mandolin and I didn't think Earl had played the guitar. But Martin was so insistent that I finally agreed to contact Earl.

We agreed to meet up at my father's in Hickory. I had a little tape recorder that we ran a few numbers over, and we recorded them. We realized that, with a little rehearsing, we still had practically the same sound and style that we did when we broke up in 1951. So we contacted Starday and told them we would do these albums.

The Starday engagement offered Bill and Earl the chance to become reacquainted, revisit youthful triumphs, and learn whether Blue Sky Boys music still had appeal. The catch was that Pierce wanted to produce a bluegrass record with

a Scruggs-type banjo on it, but I refused to have anything to do with that. It's taking away from our identification to call us bluegrass. A lot of bluegrass is similar to what we play, but I don't like to be identified as bluegrass.

Perhaps we have a little more feel for the songs we sing. Our singing is much slower, much softer, and our harmony is much better than bluegrass singing. Sometimes I have to raise the tenor real high and then drop it real low. In a lot of well-known acts, the lead and tenor run together, singing the same notes at the same pitch. I don't know any groups that have real close harmony to where it's hard to differentiate the lead from the tenor. I think that on a lot of our songs, it's difficult to do that.

Starday produced a lot of bluegrass in the early 1960s and correctly perceived that new recordings by the Blue Sky Boys would be a major event and prestigious addition to the catalog. Though conceding Bill's point, Don Pierce still wanted to test the waters by combining Blue Sky vocals with updated backing, and Starday producer Tommy Hill convinced Bill they could make successful records with a traditional/contemporary instrumental blend.

On the hymn album we only added a fiddle and soft bass. I think it's one of the best we ever recorded. [For the second one] *Tommy said to me, "I have some musicians I would like to add. I'll call them in; if you think they detract too much from your sound, we won't use them." Everybody wanted the Nashville Sound at that time, so I agreed to it. I wasn't crazy about adding all the other instruments, but they insisted that it would sell many more albums. Even with all the extra music, the* Together Again *album still has the Blue Sky Boys sound. I prefer that music than to have a bluegrass banjo in it.*

On August 28, 1963, Bill and Earl recorded *Precious Moments* (Starday SLP 269), a hymn collection with an all-acoustic fiddle, mandolin, guitar, and bass ensemble that recaptured the sound of their 1940s records. On August 29, Hill added rhythm guitar, steel guitar, piano, and drums for a second LP, *Together Again* (Starday SLP 257), whose title was taken from a current Buck Owens hit.

Though Bill later publicly disparaged the record, the results vindicated Tommy Hill's judgment and convinced him that the Blue Sky Boys could blend successfully with appropriately discreet modern country instrumentation. Despite artificial echo, their voices never sounded better and the backups were sympathetic. Drums and piano were subdued and Pete Drake's steel guitar was played with taste, polish, and restraint. Tommy Vaden's responsive fiddling embellished Bolick harmonies with lovely obbligatos that neither Leslie Keith nor Curly Parker matched on the old records. Both Starday LPs proved that Earl and Bill still had the magic touch.

In 1964 the folklorist Archie Green annotated an LP reissue of their 1930s Bluebird sides, *The Blue Sky Boys* (RCA Camden CAL 797), and organized a milestone concert on November 17, 1964, at the University of Illinois in Champaign. It was the first time the Bolicks performed for a folk music audience, and they weren't confident about what was expected of them or how well old country and gospel songs would be received by university intellectuals. Bill thought it ironic that they couldn't perform at schools in the South unless they either rented an auditorium or split proceeds with the school. If he thought about the baccalaureate he'd nearly earned ten years earlier, he'd have wondered what the Lenoir-Rhyne College back in Hickory would make of the celebration of his and Earl's artistry on a major academic campus less than seven hundred miles away. Arhoolie Records' Tom Diamant recalls the event:

That was some evening. Archie Green was the one who put that together. He was the faculty advisor to the Folk Song Club. Archie had written the notes to that RCA Camden reissue I devoured as a teenager, so it was a thrill to see them live. They performed with a music stand with lyrics, since they couldn't remember all the words. I remember the audience treating the song "Don't Trade" as more of a joke (I think you can hear laughter on the recording) than a serious song. I was learning mandolin at the time and remember being amazed at Bill's smooth playing. The shocking moment of the evening was at the reception after the show. I was in a group talking with Bill and he was standing there drinking a beer! I thought it strange that someone who sang such songs would drink. I guess I didn't know much back then.
(email, September 9, 2011)

Starday LP cover, *Together Again*, 1963. Courtesy of Alan Justice and Marshall Wyatt.

As the concert neared its end, Bill wanted to be sure his audience understood what the Blue Sky Boys were all about. Archie Green appreciated Bill's eloquence and encouraged him to speak informally from the stage. By then, he felt relaxed enough to joke about their recent Starday and Camden records with a humorous sales pitch. In disparaging the honky-tonk instrumentation of *Together Again*, he elicited laughter from his audience and ensured their agreement with his feelings about country music and authenticity:

If Earl will give me a hand, I would like to show you these albums. We have a copy of each of them and, if you haven't gotten yours, we hope that you will do that in the very near future. In fact, if we sell a half a dozen of these, we might be enticed to actually get back into the business!

This album here is one that we did last August [1963] *for Starday, in the Starday studios in Nashville, Tennessee, and it contains some of the numbers that we did for you tonight: "Kentucky," "Just Because," "In the Pines," "Don't Trade"—that beautiful number that we did for you* [laughter]*—and our theme song "Are You From Dixie?," "Why Not Confess"(really, we do have some old-timers here), "Wednesday Night Waltz," "Little Paper Boy," and so on and so forth!*

Now I am not going to say pro or con, for or against this album [laughter]. *Now just let me explain to you. You see . . . (Earl says he wants a little explanation also). On this album you'll find a lot of instruments that, although I have nothing against them, anyone who likes them is perfectly all right with me. But we did these numbers at the request of Starday. In making a compromise, we did one album the way we wanted and one album the way they wanted. Although on this album* [Together Again] *you'll find a number of good songs, it does have a modern background to it. In it you will find drums* [laughter]. *In it you will also find an electric hot guitar and in it you will also find an electric steel or Hawaiian guitar and, above all, you will find a honky-tonk piano. You don't want to miss that!*

Now this album [Precious Moments] *was made entirely of hymns, and we do have some mighty fine numbers. We have a few of the numbers that we did for you tonight, "Whispering Hope" and "Beautiful," "Precious Moments," "Why Should You Be Troubled and Sad," "God Is Still on the Throne," "Radio Station S-A-V-E-D," and quite a few other selections. Now we have as a background on this only a fiddle and a bass, the mandolin, and the guitar. We used to play* [with a fiddle] *quite often on our personal appearances and we usually always had a fiddle player with us on our radio programs, so we felt kindly at home with that. But it is a little bit different from the latest release that's been put out by RCA Victor on the Camden label. There's the Camden album that I'll tell you about in just a few moments. But if you do like hymns I'm sure that you will enjoy that album of hymns. Now this, well, maybe I should cover this picture here, actually this picture was taken so many years ago that I don't even like to remember it. This picture was actually taken in 1947.*

When Starday contacted me about making some recordings, I told them we had been disbanded for almost twelve years and the only thing I had available was a number of radio transcriptions that were made for the Willys Overland people over a network of stations in Georgia back in 1946 and 1947. We made a number of radio transcriptions then, full

Capitol LP cover, *Presenting the Blue Sky Boys*, 1965. Courtesy of Alan Justice and Marshall Wyatt.

fifteen-minute radio programs including, of course, all our commercials and even a little chat with Uncle Josh.

I managed to get twenty-five or thirty of those old transcriptions, and I wrote to Mr. Pierce at Starday Records that, if there were any selections he thought he might be able to use, that he could use them if he cared to do so. They chose quite a number and included them on this album. It was released before Earl and I made the two albums which I was telling you about a moment ago. But it does have some very fine numbers on it and these are actually the old-time songs.

Bill followed with some entertaining recollections of record making in the days before tape, and before most of his audience was born:

I would like to tell you about this Blue Sky Boys RCA Camden album. This contains some of the first recordings we ever done. They were [recorded directly] *on a big thick piece of wax, an inch and a half or two inches thick and maybe twelve inches around. They took a soft camel hair brush, brushed the shavings off, and wrapped* [the wax disc master] *carefully and put it in a trunk. These were sent back to Camden to be processed. You had to handle these wax masters very gently because if you didn't they* [would easily] *get damaged.*

Back then they didn't take too many pains, especially with so-called hillbilly artists. We were rushed through all the selections we did. Sometimes we did only one take. At times we thought we were only running through them to time them, and then the recording director would say, "That's it, boys, it sounds good to me." One take was it; they didn't want you messing up too many big waxes.

If their enthusiastic university reception didn't persuade Bill and Earl to abandon their day jobs, it nevertheless validated their art, made them comfortable with non-country audiences and let them know they still mattered. When *Saturday Review* weighed in on the RCA Camden set, an anonymous reviewer claimed that "the Bolicks were, quite probably, the finest harmonizing duo ever recorded. Their renditions are incomparable, their guitar and mandolin playing is delightful, and their songs are rich in tradition."*

Folklorists Ed Kahn and D. K. Wilgus persuaded them to appear at a UCLA (University of California at Los Angeles) Folk Festival on May 14–16, 1965, followed by a Capitol Records session on May 18. *Presenting the Blue Sky Boys* (Capitol ST 2483) featured traditional material they hoped would be favorably received in folk circles. It presented the Bolicks as they'd sounded at the dawn of their career, two voices miked closely with spare guitar, mandolin, and a barely audible bass. Even though it was a superb record, things didn't work out. According to Bill, "Ken Nelson promised to put the album in their record club and give us advertising, but I understand that they just printed a few thousand copies and let it go at that."

Arguably it's the collection RCA should have produced back in the 1940s at the dawn of the folk revival, when it would have been unique and influential. Instead, as it turned out, pitching their music to folk fans in

---

* *Saturday Review,* March 13, 1965, p. 134. The late Charles Wolfe quoted from it, mistakenly dating it to 1946 (*Classic Country,* Routledge, 2001), p. 98.

1965 distanced the Blue Sky Boys from country music without creating an impact in the folk world, whose fans by then preferred the professionally produced folk/pop/rock of Judy Collins, Bob Dylan, and Peter, Paul and Mary over traditional music. Had the Capitol record included country songs, it might have reached the same receptive audience Don Pierce and Starday had targeted in 1963. Instead, as Bill ruefully noted, it was released without fanfare and quietly went out of print. The John Edwards Memorial Foundation at UCLA reissued it in a limited, extensively annotated collectors' edition in 1974. After that, *Presenting the Blue Sky Boys* remained in eclipse until it was reissued on compact disc by Arhoolie Records in 2012.

Though Bill and Earl were venerated by knowledgeable fans at campus appearances and folk festivals, broader demand for their music was clearly not forthcoming. If they were too commercial for John Lomax in 1941, they were too refined for folk audiences a generation later. Their last northern appearance was at a New York Folk Festival at Carnegie Hall on June 18 and 20, 1965. After performing in Atlanta's Municipal Auditorium and a few miles south of Hickory in Cat Square, the Blue Sky Boys retired once more, returning to their homes, families, and livelihoods.

In 1967 Bill wrote about his life and art in a remarkably candid article for the folk journal *Sing Out!* His hope of returning to music hadn't materialized and he was experiencing a midlife struggle with career choices he'd made. Bill also let the privacy curtain slip a bit, revealing that relations between the brothers weren't always smooth.

I'm with what used to be the old Railway Mail Service, a terminal that distributes mail for North Carolina in Greensboro. I've vowed for years to get away from there, but I don't know what else I'd be qualified to do, and now I'm forty-nine. I'm quite exhausted after working there eight hours at night; it's hard work, heavy. I lift a lot of sacks and handle heavy mail, magazines, stuff like that. I don't have a desk job; it's plain old hard back-breaking work.

Earl works for Lockheed at Marietta, Georgia. He's a machinist, but I'm not sure just what kind of machine he operates. He's done very well there. Actually, we are similar in very few respects. I'm a person who worries about things; he takes life as it comes. He's usually quiet, and I do the talking. I don't remember that he learned even one song and taught it to me. Every song that we sang, so far as I remember, I learned and then taught to Earl. I think he's very good, but he never seemed to take the interest that I did. He wasn't too interested in practicing, and I suppose that's one reason we broke up. I don't think he'd mind my mentioning this, but that's the way things were. He doesn't have my interest in collecting records or the old-time songs. He has a tape recorder and possibly a portable phonograph, but other than that I don't think he takes much interest even now. When we get together I suggest the songs we are to do.

Earl Bolick had little to say to outsiders about the Blue Sky Boys, and his reticence over the years allowed Bill to make statements that have mostly gone unchallenged. For the record, Steven Bolick recalled his father saying tersely that "It was either Bill's way or no way." Bill aired a few more grievances for *Sing Out!*:

I was so disgusted with the business that I hardly picked up an instrument except in recent years, since Earl and I have accepted invitations to appear at the University of Illinois, at UCLA, at the New York Folk Festival, and at the Atlanta Municipal Auditorium. The objections I have with the folk festivals is that they build some acts up too much—not that I have any objection to entertainment or variation, but I think they mix in too much entertainment and don't devote enough time to songs. It's difficult for us to compete with acts that go out and pull jokes and make a lot of noise. The people seem to find a soft duet of our type strange. We have very few minutes to introduce our singing to people who possibly never heard it before. We're not out there to put on a show, we're not entertainers now. The old audiences expected a show and a comedian, but the main reason they came out was to hear you play and sing the old-time songs. They wanted to see how you did them in person. They listened. People today, they don't seem to listen.

If I had it to do over, I don't think I'd go back into the entertainment business, knowing what I do now. Had things worked out like I wanted them to, like I'd envisioned them and tried to get them to, and had I not had so many disappointments, I would. I don't honestly know what I'd do if I had it all to do over. That would be hard to say, I've made so many mistakes. It would possibly take several days to run all those up.

The failure of the Blue Sky Boys to make an impact at mid-1960s folk festivals unfortunately fueled Bill's bleak assessment of his life and career. The unhurried, understated performances that worked in 1930s southern schoolhouses were no longer possible in a world where music had become commodified and the word "folk" had become marketing shorthand for any acoustic, string-based pop music. By then, both Earl and Bill were heavily invested in families and careers with job security, health insurance, retirement, and other perquisites they could hardly do without, so they inevitably abandoned music again. Seven years later, the combined efforts of a college professor and a country music promoter persuaded them to come out of retirement and perform at bluegrass festivals and a southern campus. Once more, the Bolicks initially were reluctant:

I would say no later than the first of the year [1974] *I told David Whisnant, who was trying to get us to play at Duke University, that I wouldn't play another date if someone were to lay ten thousand dollars in my hand, and at that time I really meant it. But I guess it wasn't over a month later until I let Carlton Haney talk me into it. Carlton has a way about him that you can hardly say no to. He just kept on and I finally promised him that if Earl would agree to it, we would play at some of his festivals that summer. So then I felt I owed it to David Whisnant to make the appearance at Duke in April.*

The Bolicks were as good as their word, and they performed at Duke on April 19, 1974. Carlton Haney (1928–2011) was a tireless impresario with a long record of bluegrass and country events, whose enthusiasm for the music he promoted was unrestrained. He gave the Blue Sky Boys a place of honor alongside Maybelle Carter, Charlie Monroe, and the Lilly Brothers at his 1974 Memorial Day Weekend First Traditional Grass Music Festival, at Blue Grass Park in Camp Springs, near Carlton's Reidsville, North Carolina, home. On stage, Bill Bolick introduced himself and Earl, repeating a few familiar tropes and signifying a little in the direction of folk and bluegrass.

One of our purposes for appearing here at this festival is to introduce and bring back to you some of the songs that were sung in the 1930s and '40s. It seems as if you don't hear these songs much anymore and we would like to keep them alive. If you do hear them, it's really not in the old-time style. They're kind of jazzed up a bit or played a little faster, and sometimes it's hard to even recognize them.

People ask us why we sing so many tragic songs. Well, I guess if you'll just remember, those of you who do remember the '30s and '40s, those were pretty tough years and, I'll tell you, you didn't have too much to be happy about back then. A lot of the songs we sang were mother songs. Nowadays people don't think much about singing mother songs. A song of this type which we might also include as a hymn, although it wasn't used much in church but rather in brush arbor meetings and camp meetings, is "If I Could Hear My Mother Pray Again."

When I sing a song I kind of relive the song as I'm singing it. That's just like if you're watching a movie, and it looks like there's nothing but a bunch of people up there acting a part, then that movie's not going to be interesting to you. I try to put a feeling into the music that I think should be there, and think that's something that is missing in a lot of music today.

This makes only the second time we've played together in nine years, and by that I don't mean we have practiced by ourselves because we haven't. We kind of hung up the mandolin and guitar on the wall and didn't do any singing or playing at all, so we want to thank Carlton Haney and David Whisnant for getting us interested again in coming back and trying to sing a few of these old songs for you.

Their warm reception at Camp Springs briefly reactivated the Blue Sky Boys. Bluegrass historian Fred Bartenstein produced the event with Carlton Haney:

My memory was that the Bolicks were received with respect and appreciation. It is true that Piedmont-region locals born since the 1940s would have had no exposure to the Blue Sky Boys unless they tapped into the folk revival's awareness of the group (few did). The folkies and knowledgeable outsiders were amazed that the Bolicks still performed, and that their skills had hardly diminished. As I recall, [bluegrass performers] *Everett and Bea Lilly were particularly excited to meet and hear their heroes.*

It was pretty ambitious for Carlton to put this lineup up against Ralph Stanley's McClure Festival the same weekend, and in North Carolina. A site nearer Washington [DC] *would have made more sense. As I recall, the Blue Sky Boys' best reception that summer was at the Gettysburg, Pennsylvania festival.* (email, September 30, 2011)

Bill Monroe biographer Richard D. Smith has warm memories of the Bolicks at another Haney event that summer, and he echoes Bill's sentiments about sharing the stage with louder music:

I was a happy Yankee tooling around the southern bluegrass festival circuit in my MGB sports car, just big enough to carry me, my mandolin, a tent and miscellaneous camping gear. One of the best shows at which I landed was Carlton Haney's Berryville, Virginia Bluegrass Festival in July 1974. The Blue Sky Boys were on the bill. I'd discovered The Original and Great: Early Authentic Country Recordings (1964, RCA Camden) *at the only record store in Princeton, N. J., that consistently carried bluegrass and old-timey albums, and they'd had me from the first instrumental pulsings and wistful harmonies of "Are You from Dixie?"*

Unfortunately the Bolicks went on after a loud, bright, banjo-driven bluegrass band. The audience clearly wasn't adjusting to their softer, gentler duo sound. It was sad to watch the wonderful Blue Sky Boys lose the audience and play to the murmur of distracted conversations. But then Bill Bolick announced, "Maybe some of you have seen the movie 'Paper Moon.' Well, the Blue Sky Boys' music is featured in that film and we'd like to play it for you now."

Director Peter Bogdanovich had used their original recording of "The Banks of the Ohio" on the soundtrack, and Bill's mention of the hit movie attracted attention. The audience tuned into the Bolicks' rendition—and, increasingly, to everything else they played. At the end of their set the crowd rose in a heartfelt standing ovation and called them back for an encore. It was a chills-and-tears moment, knowing I was witnessing a genuine triumph of their later career. And it was made possible because both director Bogdanovich and promoter Haney had showcased, with true appreciation, the music of the Blue Sky Boys. (email, March 3, 2016)

The Gettysburg Bluegrass Festival was on August 17–18, 1974, and Carlton's Original Bluegrass Festival was back in Camp Springs over Labor Day weekend. After a final reunion at a Duke University concert in April 1975, the Blue Sky Boys never performed in public again. In May, Rounder Records brought them to Starday's Nashville studio for an LP of songs they'd sung in the past but not recorded commercially. *The Blue Sky Boys* (Rounder 0052) appeared in 1976, along with a thoughtfully produced RCA reissue edited by Doug Green.

By then, Earl's career at Lockheed was flourishing and he had little reason to regret leaving music behind. He remained close to his career, family, and home until he died of heart failure in 1998. Once, Charlie Louvin sought Earl out:

Publicity shot, 1975 Rounder session, Nashville, TN. Courtesy of Alan Justice.

I'd never met either one of [the Blue Sky Boys] *and I wanted to, so when I was passing through Atlanta one time I knocked on* [Earl's] *door, introduced myself, and he welcomed me into his home. Then, after we'd sat and talked for a while, I made the mistake of asking, "How's your brother Bill?" He got this kind of funny look on his face and said, "Well, I see we've run out of things to talk about." I knew it was time to move on then.**

---

* Charlie Louvin. *Satan Is Real: The Ballad of the Louvin Brothers.* New York: Itbooks, 2012, p. 212.

The Blue Sky Boys, 1936. Courtesy of Alan Justice and Marshall Wyatt.

Bill, however, never stopped missing the music and would have welcomed occasions to perform again. When asked about bringing the Blue Sky Boys to England, he replied:

> *I don't think* [Earl] *could be persuaded to ever entertain again. He has refused to entertain at all during the last ten years, even though we have been offered quite a number of lucrative proposals including a tour of Japan, World's Fair, colleges and universities . . . If he is agreeable, I would certainly be glad to reconsider my decision, but I must say to you truthfully, I don't think he will do it.* (letter to John Dodds in England, January 4, 1985)

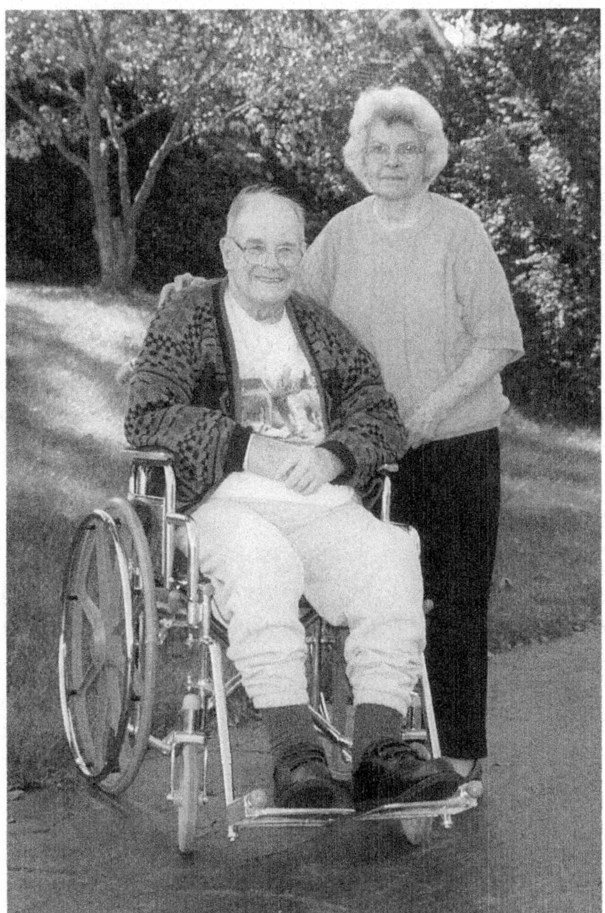

Bill (in wheelchair) and Doris Bolick, ca. 2007. Courtesy of Charles Travis.

Bill worked at the US Postal Service in Greensboro, North Carolina until he retired and built a new house with Doris on the Bolick family estate in Hickory. As a lively raconteur, he was frequently the subject of interviews and radio tributes. He remained an eloquent spokesman for the Blue Sky Boys' art for the rest of his long life, both in correspondence with fans and in the forthright interviews and personal writings that form a significant portion of this book.

Around 1988, Bill was diagnosed with spastic paraparesis, a hereditary degenerative nerve disease in his lower limbs. In 2004, he was further diagnosed with lung cancer, although he'd never smoked. Bill was ninety when he died in his sleep on March 13, 2008. Subsequently Doris Bolick sold their home in Hickory and returned to Bellaire, Ohio, where she passed away on May 19, 2017.

In 1973 Bill Bolick prepared an essay called "I Always Liked the Type of Music That I Play," that appeared with a 1974 reissue of the 1965 Capitol LP, and is embedded in a compact disc reissue of *Presenting the Blue Sky Boys* (Arhoolie CD 9063). Bill concluded with these words:

We might sing this or that song for a while. Then we would sing the new songs we would learn, and they seemed just as popular as the others had been. I always liked the type of music that I play. It has always been a very deep part of my life. There is nothing I would have liked better than to have continued it up to this very day, had things just turned out a little differently.

In 2005 he told Walt Saunders:

I'll tell you how I would like to be remembered. I would like to hear people say, "Now that is pure and true country music. That is the way it should be played and sung."

APPENDIX 1

Blue Sky Boys Songs: An Annotated List

The following annotated list covers titles on surviving studio records made for publication and broadcast by the Blue Sky Boys between 1936 and 1975. Copper Creek has published six compact discs of excerpts from sixteen-inch program transcription discs made at WGST (Atlanta) in 1946–47 and WCYB (Bristol, Virginia) in 1949. For the discography, Copper Creek's Gary Reid generously supplied all titles and indicated those on compact disc. Many of Bill Bolick's discussions of individual songs come from Gary's interviews. Bill's comments appear in italics, and I've noted 78 rpm discs (excluding those by the Blue Sky Boys) that were in his personal collection.

In organizing entries I normally default to a published song's original title when known. In the 1930s producer Eli Oberstein routinely altered titles to avoid royalty payments on copyrighted songs. It was a practice unique to Eli and RCA, and Bill's comments about it alternate between irritation and resignation. In other cases titles have evolved over time as old songs entered tradition and acquired multiple identifications. In cases where I've substituted title headings for those appearing on Blue Sky Boys records, the latter are noted with a *see* reference. I've overlooked minor variations that don't disturb the alphabetic sequence.

Songs are fungible and negotiable properties, and record label composer credits rarely differentiate between copyright ownership and actual composition. Songs cited here are credited with composers of record even when identifications are inconclusive or clearly spurious. Many songs once in the public domain have been copyrighted, re-copyrighted, and bear credits substituting owner names for actual composers. Others have been published more than once by different claimants, and still others are too old or obscure to be traced to their origins with certainty. Traditional ballads and other songs with narrative content have been collected and indexed by G. Malcolm Laws Jr. in *American Balladry from British Broadsides* (1957) and *Native American Balladry*, rev. ed. (1964). The Blue Sky Boys recorded variants of five songs found in Francis James Child's *The English and Scottish Popular Ballads* (1882–98). Songs appearing in these collections are cited.

In 1973 an entire issue of the *Journal of Country Music* (Volume IV, No. 4) was devoted to a diary of songs performed by the Blue Sky Boys from May 9, 1939, through May 9, 1940, on daily fifteen-minute shows from WGST (Atlanta) and WPTF (Raleigh), maintained by a loyal listener, Ruth Walker of Greensboro, Georgia. Although her list is a valuable document, the shows themselves do not survive. Titles known only from her entries are not always clear and are omitted here.

Annotations for recently composed songs the Bolicks recorded for RCA in 1946–50 and Starday (1963) are often brief or nonexistent. With a handful of exceptions, songs from this era were the product of professional writers and few enjoyed an afterlife. Bill assessed them candidly: "Songs that we recorded postwar weren't necessarily our most popular or ones we liked best. They were songs that as far as we knew had never previously been recorded, or we felt that our style was so much different that it wouldn't hurt us if they had been recorded." Other professionally composed songs reach back to the mid-nineteenth century, and Bill sometimes had no comments to make on them either. A list of sources for Blue Sky Boys songs follows this song list.

Lists of Blue Sky Boys songs recorded by other artists that follow each entry are selective. The citations include early versions, later ones that Bill and Earl probably knew, and significant later ones. Entries normally include original record numbers, selected appearances on further labels, and current or recently available compact discs. The abbreviation ARC stands for American Record Corporation, whose 1930s releases appeared with identical catalog numbers on Melotone, Perfect, Oriole, and other chain-store labels after 1935. Conqueror was a Sears and Roebuck house label that used an independent numbered series. For further information, see:

Guthrie T. Meade, Jr., Dick Spottswood, and Douglas S. Meade, *Country Music Sources.* Chapel Hill: University of North Carolina Press, 2002.
Praguefrank.com, an online country music discography site.
Tony Russell, *Country Music Records, a Discography, 1921–1942.* New York: Oxford University Press, 2004.

The following compact disc sets include broadcast excerpts and virtually all published Blue Sky recordings except for 1963 home recordings collected on County 752, which have yet to appear on compact disc.

Sunny Side of Life, Bear Family BCD 15951 EK (RCA studio tracks, 1936–50)
A Treasury of Rare Song Gems From the Past, Gusto GT7-0695-2 (1947/49 radio transcriptions)
Are You from Dixie, Gusto GT7-0549 (Starday sessions, 1963)
The Blue Sky Boys in Concert, Rounder 11536 (1964)
Presenting The Blue Sky Boys, Capitol ST2483, Arhoolie CD 9063 (1965)
The Blue Sky Boys, Rounder 0052 (1975)

Several others, drawn from radio transcriptions made at WGST (Atlanta) and WCYB (Bristol) are no longer in print:

On Radio, Volumes 1–4, Copper Creek CCCD-0120, 0121, 0145, 0146 (WGST radio transcriptions, 1946–47)
Farm and Fun Time Favorites, Volumes 1–2, Copper Creek CCCD-0125, 0126 (WCYB radio transcriptions, 1949)

At this writing, a new collection is in preparation:

Rare Radio Transcriptions, Patuxent CD-280

RECORDINGS

The ABC Song (Esther Glosson)

We learned this song from Ray and Ina Patterson, who came to visit when we were broadcasting over WNAO in 1948. We had them as guests on several programs. To the best of my knowledge, they sent us their recording of it in 1947. We termed this a religious song but always considered it a novelty number. It was different from other spelling songs we knew and we drew better than average fan mail with it.

"I'm S-A-V-E-D" and "The B-I-B-L-E" are other Blue Sky Boys songs with spelling themes.

Blue Sky Boys, WCYB (Bristol, VA, 1949), Copper Creek CCCD-0125

I'M S-A-V-E-D

Some folks jump up and down all night and D-A-N-C-E,
While others go to church to show their brand new H-A-T
And on their faces they put great gobs of P-A-I-N-T;
And then they'll have the brass to say they're S-A-V-E-D.

CHORUS:

It's G-L-O-R-Y to know that I'm S-A-V-E-D,
I'm H-A-P-P-Y because I'm F-R-double-E;
I once was B-O-U-N-D with the chains of S-I-N,
But it's V-I-C-T-O-R-Y to know I've Christ within.

I know some girls in this town who are so N-I-C-E;
They do their hair in the latest style just B-O-B-B-E-D;
They go to parties every night and drink W-I-N-E;
And then they'll have the nerve to say they're S-A-V-E-D.

I've seen some boys lean back and puff their S-M-O-K-E,
While others chew and spit out all their J-U-I-C-E;
They play their cards and shoot their guns and drink their P-O-P,
And then they'll have the brass to say they're S-A-V-E-D.

I know a man, I think his name is B-R-O-W-N;
He prays for prohibition and he votes for G-I-N.
He helps to put the poison in his neighbors C-U-P,
And then he'll have the brass to say he's S-A-V-E-D.

THE A-B-C SONG

A is for anyone who's not afraid to die;
B is for blood, we mean to hold it high.
C is for Christ who saves our souls from hell;
D is for the Devil, the one we know so well.
E is for the enemy who tries to obsess;
F is for the fountain—into it you must get;
G is for the Gospel—we preach it very plain;
H is for Heaven—come get aboard this train.
I is for the ignorant, so many folks do seem;
J is for Jesus who did our souls redeem.
K is for the kingdom that we must try to win;
L is for the Lamb of God who was for sinners slain.
M is for the many who find they are too late;
N is for the narrow way that leads to heaven's gate.
O is like eternity for it has no end;
P is for the promise unto us He did send.
Q is for the queer folks who say there is no hell;
R is for the righteous, the truth they will not sell.
S is for salvation—it lifts us from our strife;
T is for the trumpet that will bring the dead to life.
U is for unity, we have it in our band;
V is for victory that will help the weak to stand.
W is for work that we must not forsake;
X is for the crossroads—you'll know which one to take.
Y is for you and I hope that you will know
That Z is for that zig-zag road that leads to pain and woe.

Courtesy of Lester S. Levy Collection of Sheet Music, Sheridan Libraries, Johns Hopkins University.

After the Ball (Charles K. Harris, 1897)

This landmark song laid a career foundation for a Tin Pan Alley pioneer. Harris (1867–1930) had been a bellhop, pawnbroker, and banjo instructor before composing and self-publishing this song, and opening a songwriting office in Milwaukee. It became an immediate hit and enduring standard, and he moved his office to New York around 1895. Other Harris hits that became country classics include:

I Love You Best of All (1893)
There'll Come a Time (1895)
Break the News to Mother (1897)
'Mid the Green Fields of Virginia (1898)
Filipino Baby (originally "Ma Filipino Babe") (1898)
Hello, Central, Give Me Heaven (1901)

Harris himself sang "After the Ball" in a 1929 one-reeler, viewable on Youtube. The Bolicks also recorded "There'll Come a Time."

George Gaskin, Edison unnumbered cylinder (1892–93)
Vernon Dalhart, Brunswick 2925, Columbia 15030-D, Edison 51610 (three versions, all 1925)
Darby & Tarlton, Columbia 15254-D, Bear Family BCD 15764 (1928)
Bradley Kincaid, Gennett 7081 (1929), Vocalion 5474 (1931) (two versions)
Bill Bolick, Rounder 0236, 11536 (1964)

Alabama (Ira Louvin-Charlie Louvin)

This song was written by the Louvin Brothers. We had never heard of the Louvins or the song until Mel Foree of Acuff-Rose Publications brought it to us. I can't remember if we recorded it the same day we learned it or the following day. I wish we could have had more time to see what different arrangements we could have worked out.

Louvin Brothers, Apollo 202 (1947), Decca 46182 (1949), Capitol T769 (1955) (all three versions on Bear Family BCD 15561)
Blue Sky Boys, RCA Victor 21-0075, Bear Family BCD 15951 (1949)
Blue Sky Boys, WCYB (Bristol, VA, 1949), Copper Creek CCCD-0126
Bailey Brothers, Rich-R'-Tone 446 (1949)

Amazing Grace (John Newton-words, arr. William Walker)

It astounds me that this song wasn't well known until [the 1970s, though] *it has been available in almost any hymnal or religious songbook you can find. I can't tell you when we learned this song but I knew it as far back as I can remember. I can recall hearing my father singing it early on Sunday mornings. He would sing the same song over and over. I can almost hear my mother saying, "Let's sing another song, Daddy." He would change to another song for a short time but would soon be back singing the same song. When he sang "Amazing Grace" and "Angel Band," he usually sang them in long meter style. I can't recall ever hearing anyone else sing that way. My father was a very religious man and didn't kid about his religion or sacred songs; however, he once told me that people used to say that Grace was a drunk's wife who referred to her as Amazing Grace. I noticed in some of my songbooks the song has as many as five or six verses. We usually sang only four. This song was written by John Newton. Without doubt it is one of the oldest hymns we sang.*

John Newton (1725–1807) worked on English slave ships, experienced a spiritual conversion in 1757, and became an abolitionist before he was ordained by the Church of England in 1764. "Amazing Grace" first appeared in *Olney Hymns* (1779), edited by Rev. Newton and the poet William Cowper. It was set to the tune "New Britain" by William Walker in the first edition of *Southern Harmony* (1835).

Wisdom Sisters, Columbia 15090-D (1926)
Denson-Parris Sacred Harp Singers, "New Britain," Bluebird B-5597 (1934)
Blue Sky Boys, WCYB (Bristol, VA, 1949), Copper Creek CCCD-0126
Pipes and Drums and the Military Band of the Royal Scots Dragoon Guards, RCA 2191 (1972)
Aretha Franklin, Atlantic 2-906, Rhino 75627 (1972)
Jim & Jesse, Old Dominion 498-12 (1979)

Angel Mother (Hugh Anglyn, arr. Bill Bolick, 1947)

Blue Sky Boys, RCA Victor 20-2900, Bear Family BCD 15951 (1947)
Shorty Morris, Mercury 6159 (1948, in the Bolick collection)
Jim & Jesse, Epic BN 26204, Bear Family BCD 15716 (1966)

Answer to 'The Prisoner's Dream' (Karl Davis-Harty Taylor-Patrick McAdory, 1936)

We hadn't planned to do this selection at the session. When we recorded "The Prisoner's Dream," Eli Oberstein wanted to know if we knew the answer to it. We informed him that we did and he asked us to record it. To the best of my knowledge, this is the only particular number Eli ever asked us to record. We usually chose the songs ourselves and Eli agreed with our choices. It was never as popular for us as the original "Prisoner's Dream" that was written by the same authors, [though] *we did receive requests for it on our radio programs. This song was written by Karl and Harty and Pat McAdory, and sent to us by the M.M. Cole Publishing Company of Chicago.*

Patrick McAdory was the pen name of Frank Johnson, who also wrote songs in collaboration with Doc Hopkins.

Karl & Harty, ARC 7-05-60 (1937, in the Bolick collection)
Blue Sky Boys, Bluebird B-7411, Montgomery Ward M-7469, Bear Family BCD 15951 (1938)
Blue Sky Boys, WGST Program 17, September 24, 1946
Blue Sky Boys, WGST Program 41, October 8, 1946, Copper Creek CCCD-0145

Are You Building on the Rock? (Barney E. Warren, 1897)

Rev. Warren was a prolific hymn composer and minister in the Church of God (Anderson, Indiana), to which the Bolick family belonged. The Blue Sky Boys recorded several of his hymns, including "The Blood of Jesus" and his setting of "Farther Along."

Blue Sky Boys, WGST unnumbered program transcription, December 19, 1946

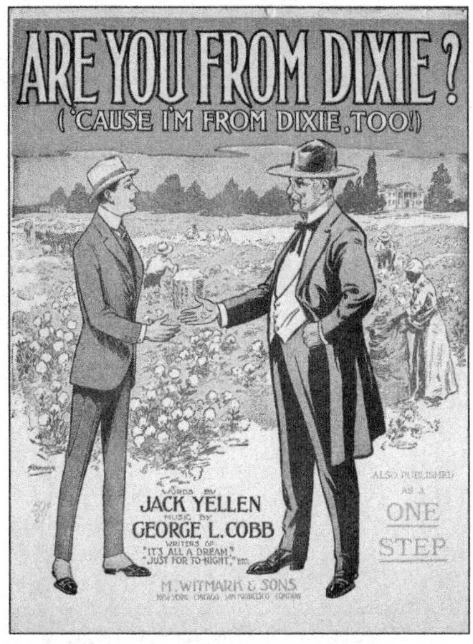

Courtesy of Lester S. Levy Collection of Sheet Music, Sheridan Libraries, Johns Hopkins University.

Are You from Dixie? (Jack Yellen-words, George L. Cobb-music, 1915)

Our theme song was "Are You from Dixie." It was a peppy little tune to come on the air with and it appealed to people in the South. We started using it when we returned to WGST in 1938 and used it whenever we could until we quit radio in 1951.

We learned it from a neighbor, Lloyd Price, who lived down the road about half a mile. He was a disabled World War I veteran, the son of a Lutheran minister, and he knew many songs we had never heard. He loved for Earl and me to come down to his house. Lloyd would sing bass, I would sing harmony and Earl would sing lead. That's the way we figured out our kind of trio; it was more like a quartet.

The prolific Jack Yellen (1892–1991) wrote lyrics to popular songs from the 1910s through the 1960s. His other notable collaboration with George L. Cobb (1886–1942) was "Alabama Jubilee," also from 1915.

Irving Kaufman & Billy Murray, Victor 17942 (1915)
Ernest Thompson, Columbia 130-D (1924)
Poplin-Woods Tennessee String Band, Victor V-40080, Bear Family BCD 16094 (1928)
Blue Sky Boys, Bluebird B-8294, Montgomery Ward M-8410, Bear Family BCD 15951 (1938)
Grandpa Jones, King 847 (1947)
Jerry Reed, RCA Victor 74-0211, LSP-4204 (1969)

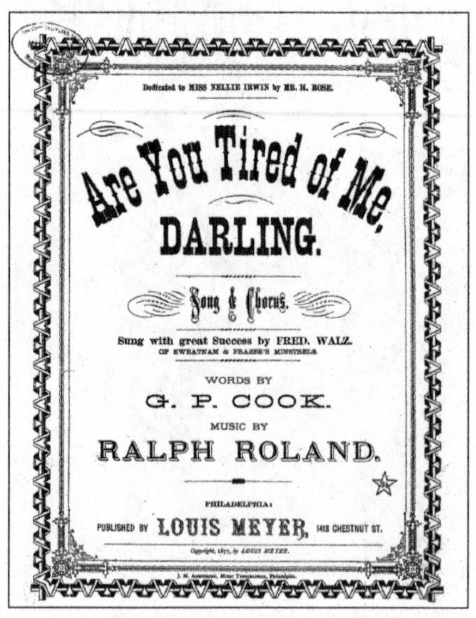

Courtesy of Library of Congress, Music Division.

Are You Tired of Me, My Darling?
(G. P. Cook-words, Ralph Roland-music, 1877)

This is one of the first songs Earl and I ever sang together. Mac and Bob were the first artists I ever heard sing this song and we learned it from their early songbook. It proved to be popular with our radio audiences.

Mac & Bob's WLS Book of Songs (1931), 32

Lester McFarland & Robert A. Gardner, Brunswick 109 (1926)
Carter Family, Bluebird B-5956, Montgomery Ward M-4946, Bear Family BCD 15865 (1934)
Blue Sky Boys, WGST Program 28, October 9, 1946, Copper Creek CCCD-0146
Nanci Griffith, Elektra 61464-2 (1993)

As Long As I Live (Roy Acuff)

I'm certain this song was sent to us by Acuff-Rose. We never sang it prior to World War II. We thought it sounded better as a trio and that's the way we always sang it.

"As Long As I Live" is one of twenty-one songs that Jim Anglin wrote and sold outright to Roy Acuff in 1943 for fifteen dollars each. They were credited to Acuff and several became early hits for the Acuff-Rose music publishing house, established in Nashville in 1942. Jim was the brother of Jack Anglin of Johnnie and Jack, and he composed many of their songs, including some with their collaboration. Both the Bailes Brothers and Blue Sky Boys performed "As Long As I Live" as a vocal trio, something neither did often with secular songs.

Bailes Brothers, Columbia 36932, Bear Family BCD 15973 (1945)
Blue Sky Boys, WGST Program 6, September 9, 1946
Blue Sky Boys, WGST Program 38, October 23, 1946
Blue Sky Boys, WGST Program 137, March 11, 1947, Copper Creek CCCD-0121

Asleep in the Briny Deep (Doc Hopkins)

> *Way out here on the ocean we do not call it the sad sea waves but the briny deep. Isn't it a kind of awful name? It made me shiver when I first heard it. It was Mr. Stevens said it when we were all going to our state-rooms that first night. "Well," he said, "there's no doubt but we're launched, for good or bad, out on the briny deep."*
>
> —LETTER 6 FROM BESSIE MAYNARD TO HER DOLL, ON BOARD THE STEAMSHIP MAINE, OCTOBER 1880, IN *HARPER'S YOUNG PEOPLE 1881*, NOVEMBER 30, 1880, P. 74

Ms. Maynard and other references place the ominous "briny deep" conceit in the 1880s. Though this song is usually attributed to Doc Hopkins, it probably dates from that era.

Blue Sky Boys, Montgomery Ward M-7568, Bear Family BCD 15951 (1938)
Doc Hopkins, M.M. Cole Program No. 50 (ca. 1946, 16" electrical transcription), B.A.C.M. CD D 08
Mac Martin & Ed Brozi, Patuxent CD-207 (1970)

Baby Mine *See* Going Round This World, Baby Mine

Barbara Allen (Child 84)

"But above all, my dear Mrs. Knipp with whom I sang; and in perfect pleasure I was to hear her sing, and especially her little Scotch song of Barbary Allen." — Samuel Pepys's diary, January 2, 1666.

Royal Dadmun, Victor 45310 (1922), 4023 (1927) (two versions)
Bradley Kincaid, Silvertone 5186, 8217 (1927), Conqueror 7982 (1930) (two versions)
Merle Travis, Capitol G109, T891, T2662, Bear Family BCD 15636, BCD 17355 (1946)
Lilly Brothers & Don Stover, Folkways FW 2433, Smithsonian Folkways CD 40158 (1962)
Everly Brothers, Cadence CLP-3016, Ace CH75, Bear Family BCD 17355 (1958)
Bill Bolick, University of Illinois concert, 1964 (Rounder, unreleased)

Beautiful (Barney E. Warren, 1897)

This is one of the prettiest songs we tried to sing; we knew it as far back as I can remember. It was in the First Church of God hymnbook where we attended church when we were boys. Before Red Hicks joined us in 1938, we sang it as a duet; here [1949] *we sing it as a trio. This song was written by Barney E. Warren of Springfield, Ohio. I wrote to him in 1946 or '47 asking permission to put several of his songs in our songbook. He answered me with a very nice letter. I think he was in his eighties at that time.*

Barney Elliott Warren (1867–1951) was a minister in the Church of God and a prolific composer, who edited songbooks and hymnals for the Gospel Trumpet Company of Anderson, Indiana, from 1888 to 1940. "Beautiful" appears in the Church of God hymnal *Reformation Glory* (1923).

Garland Brothers & Grinstead, Columbia 15679-D (1928)

No. 147.
Beautiful.
Copyright, 1911, by J. A. Lee.
B. E. W.
B. E. Warren.
1. Beautiful robes so white, Beautiful land of light, Beautiful home so bright, Where there shall come no night; Beautiful crown I'll wear, Shining with stars o'er there, Yonder in mansions fair, Gath-er us there.....
2. Beautiful thought to me, We shall for-ev-er be Thine in e-ter-ni - ty, When from this world we're free; Free from its toil and care, Heavenly joys to share, Let me cross over there; This is my pray'r....
3. Beautiful things on high, O-ver in yonder sky, Thus I shall leave this shore, Counting my treas-ures o'er; Where we shall never die, Carry me by and by, Nev-er to sor-row more, Heav-en - ly store.....
Chorus.
Beau-ti - ful robes,.............. Beau-ti - ful land,.......... Beau-ti-ful home,.......... Beautiful band,..........
Beau-ti-ful robes of white, Beautiful land of light, Beautiful home so bright, Beautiful band of might,
Beau-ti-ful crown,................ Shining so fair,...................
Beau-ti-ful, beau-ti-ful crown, Shining, yes, shin-ing so fair,
Beau-ti - ful man - sion bright, Gath-er us there...............
Beau-ti-ful mansion bright, Gath-er us there, yes, gath-er us there.

Blue Sky Boys, WCYB (Bristol, VA, 1949), Copper Creek CCCD-0126
Blue Sky Boys, County 752 (1963)
Blue Sky Boys, Starday SLP-269, Gusto GT7-0549 (1963)
Blue Sky Boys, Rounder 11536 (1964)
Bill Clifton & Jimmy Gaudreau, Elf CD-103 (1991)

Beautiful, Beautiful Brown Eyes

I am not certain when or how we learned this song. I'm inclined to think the words were sent to us by one of our radio listeners. People did this quite often, [though] *many times the words weren't quite correct. After World War II, Fiddling Arthur Smith told me he had written the song.*

"Beautiful Brown Eyes" is usually attributed to Arthur Smith and Alton Delmore.

Arthur Smith Trio, Bluebird B-7221, Montgomery Ward M-7343 (1937)
Blue Sky Boys, Bluebird B-7755, Montgomery Ward M-7470, Bear Family BCD 15951 (1938)
Roy Acuff, Vocalion 05163, Conqueror 9579, Bear Family BCD 17300 (1939)
Rosemary Clooney, Columbia 39212 (1950)

A Beautiful Life (William M. Golden, 1918)

This song was well known by the time Earl and I started broadcasting. Because of the part the bass singer takes in this song, we never sang it until "Red" Hicks joined us in 1938. Earl always sings bass in the trios. Several country groups have recorded this selection [and it] *can be found in a number of old-time religious songbooks. It was written by William M. Golden and has always been one of my favorite religious songs.*

Offering no details, an online note cites a claim that William Matthew Golden (1878–1934) "wrote most of his songs while serving an eight-year sentence in the state penitentiary."

Smith's Sacred Singers, Columbia 15671-D (1927)
Chuck Wagon Gang, Vocalion 04342, Bear Family BCD 17348 (1936)
Monroe Brothers, Bluebird B-7562, Montgomery Ward M-7450, Bear Family BCD 16399 (1938)
Wade Mainer, "Life's Evenin' Sun," Bluebird B-B-8007, Montgomery Ward M-7559, JSP 77124 (1938)

Byron Parker and his Mountaineers, Bluebird B-8476, Montgomery Ward M-8722, Old Homestead OHCD 4169 (1940)
Blue Sky Boys, audition disc, 1941
Blue Sky Boys, WGST Program 24, October 3, 1946, Copper Creek CCCD-0146
Bill Monroe, Decca DL 8769, Bear Family BCD 15423 (1958)
Jimmy Martin, Decca DL 75226, Bear Family BCD 15705 (1962)

Behind These Prison Walls of Love (Hazel Hope Jarrard-Bill Bolick, 1947)

I did write the melody to the song and re-arranged some of the words. I estimate that I wrote, helped write, and put all the music to at least sixty or seventy songs, many of which were never published and many that we never even sang.

Blue Sky Boys, RCA Victor 20-3307, Bear Family BCD 15951 (1947)
Country Gentlemen, Folkways FA 2410, Smithsonian Folkways CD 40022 (1961)
Blue Sky Boys, Gusto GT7-0549 (1963)
Peter Rowan, Sugar Hill CD-3791 (1991)

The B-I-B-L-E (Karl Davis-Harty Taylor)

As well as I can remember, this was sent to us by M.M. Cole Publishers of Chicago.

"I'm S-A-V-E-D" and "The ABC Song" are other Blue Sky Boys songs with spelling themes.

Karl & Harty, Capitol 415 (1947, in the Bolick collection)
Blue Sky Boys, WCYB (Bristol, VA, 1949), Copper Creek CCCD-0126

The Blood of Jesus (Barney E. Warren, 1902)

ALL THINGS ARE CLEANSED WITH BLOOD, AND WITHOUT SHEDDING OF BLOOD THERE IS NO FORGIVENESS. —HEBREWS 9:22

This song was taken from a hymnbook used by the First Church of God. Our family attended this church. It was written by Barney E. Warren who I think was one of the founders of this denomination. My father sang it around the house, usually on Sunday mornings. It was one of our most popular hymns.

See note to "Beautiful."

Blue Sky Boys, *Folk Songs and Hymns*, 18

Blue Sky Boys, "Nothing But the Blood of Jesus," WGST Program 11, September 16, 1946
Blue Sky Boys, WGST Program 140, March 14, 1947, Copper Creek CCCD-0120 (1947)

Boat of Life (George Jones-Burt Stephen)

George Jones, Starday 256, SLP-101, Mercury MG 20462 (1956)
Blue Sky Boys, Starday SLP-269, Gusto GT7-0549 (1963)

Bring Back My Blue Eyed Boy to Me

I can't recall when we learned this song, although I remember singing it in the thirties. It's quite possible we learned it from hearing the Carters sing it.

Carl Sandburg, *The American Songbag* (Harcourt, 1927), "Go Bring Me Back My Blue-Eyed Boy"

Carter Family, Victor V-40190, Bear Family BCD 15865 (1929)
Blue Sky Boys, WGST Program 11, September 16, 1946
Blue Sky Boys, WGST Program 51, November 11, 1946, Copper Creek CCCD-0145
Lilly Brothers & Don Stover, Event E-4272, Rebel CD-1688 (1956–57)
Bill Clifton, Starday 561, SLP-146, Bear Family BCD 16425 (1961)

Bring Back My Wandering Boy
See Somebody's Boy Is Homeless Tonight

Brown Eyes

This is a spinoff from "Those Dark Eyes" (1865), credited to Armand (Armand Edward Blackmar) of New Orleans. Bill told Charles Wolfe that he learned it in 1932 from the West Virginia radio personality Buddy Starcher, when the latter was working at WSOC in Gastonia, North Carolina.

Bill Cox, Banner 33094, Conqueror 8330 (1933)
Wade Mainer-Zeke Morris, Bluebird B-6347, Montgomery Ward M-4713, JSP 77118 (1936)
Dixon Brothers, "Dark Eyes," Bluebird B-6809, Montgomery Ward M-7173, Bear Family BCD 16817 (1936)
Blue Sky Boys, Bluebird B-8693, Montgomery Ward M-8848, Bear Family BCD 15951 (1940)
Maddox Brothers & Rose, 4-Star 1238, 1288, Arhoolie CD-391 (1947)
Ray & Ina Patterson, "Those Brown Eyes," Gold Star 1370 (1949)
Benny Cain, "Angry Brown Eyes," Adelphi 47 (1956)

Bury Me Beneath the Willow

I have heard bits of this song almost as long as I can remember. I have no idea who composed it or when we first started singing it.

Henry Whitter, "Weeping Willow Tree," OKeh 40187 (1923)
Carter Family, Victor 21074, Bear Family BCD 15865 (1929)
Carter Family, "Answer to The Weeping Willow," Decca 5254, Montgomery Ward 8004, Bear Family BCD 15865 (1936)
Monroe Brothers, "Weeping Willow Tree," Bluebird B-7093, Montgomery Ward M-7145, Bear Family BCD 16399 (1937)
Blue Sky Boys, WGST Program 33, October 16, 1946, Copper Creek CCCD-0121

The Butcher's Boy (Laws P24)

I think my daddy told me that his mother used to sing "The Butcher's Boy." I had heard it in a different tune than Earl and I sing it. I don't think I'd ever heard "Mary of the Wild Moor" or "The Butcher's Boy" sung as a duet. We took songs that were difficult for duets to sing and made them into harmony numbers.

Bill told Charles Wolfe that he didn't like the minor key melody his father sang, so he composed a new one.

Kelly Harrell, Victor 19563 (1925), Victor 20242 (1926) (two versions)
Buell Kazee, Brunswick 213, 437, Smithsonian Folkways CD 40090 (1927)
Blue Sky Boys, Bluebird B-8482, Montgomery Ward M-8668, Bear Family BCD 15951 (1940), Rounder 11536 (1964) (two versions)

Can't You Hear That Night Bird Crying?

This is a song I connect with Lute Isenhour although I can't say I learned it from him. If memory serves me correctly, we pieced this song together from songs we both knew. I'm pretty certain our version is almost identical to the way Lute and I sang it.

See also "Don't This Road Look Rough and Rocky." Two verses here roughly correspond to that song, which adds a chorus.

Murphy Brothers Harp Band, "Little Bunch of Roses," Columbia 15646-D, Yazoo 2031 (1930)
Blue Sky Boys, Bluebird B-6854, Montgomery Ward M-7162, Bear Family BCD 15951 (1936)

The Chapel in the Hills (Karl Davis-Harty Taylor, 1947)

This song was sent to us by Steve Sholes, who wanted us to record it.

Blue Sky Boys, RCA Victor 20-3158, Bear Family BCD 15951 (1947)
Blue Sky Boys, WCYB (Bristol, VA, 1949), Copper Creek CCCD-0126

Cindy *See* Get Along Home, Cindy

Come to the Saviour (Thomas D. Lynn-Bill and Earl Bolick, 1947)

Like "Dust on the Bible," this appealing hymn was recorded by both the Bailes Brothers and Blue Sky Boys.

Blue Sky Boys, *Favorite Hymns and Folk Songs*, 7

Blue Sky Boys, RCA Victor 20-3055, Bear Family BCD 15951 (1947)
Bailes Brothers, Columbia 20529, Bear Family BCD 15973 (1947)
Blue Sky Boys, WCYB (Bristol, VA, 1949)

Companions Draw Nigh (Rev. Sanford Miller Brown, 1892)

This is another song our father helped us with. The book this song was taken from contained notes regarding the theme. As well as I can recall, this boy was fatally injured while working with a construction crew far from home. Realizing he was dying, he asked that someone pray for him or read to him from the Bible. No one could be found with a Bible or anyone that knew how to pray.

Rev. Brown included "Companions Draw Nigh" in his *Songs of Zion* (1892). James D. Vaughan re-titled it "Dying from Home, and Lost" in *Crowning Praises* (1911) and added the story that Bill recalled:

Two young men, who had been brought up together in a distant state, came to Kansas City to get a start in the world. They were employed in laboring on one of the piers of the great railroad bridge over the Missouri River. An accident occurred in which several men were injured. Among them was one of the young men, who was fatally crushed. He was taken into one of the tents in which the laborers were living and, being conscious, he was told by the physicians that he could live only a few hours. He requested his companions to pray with him, and stated that he was not prepared to die. His friend assured him that he did not pray for himself, and was not fit to pray for a dying man. Then he asked that a song might be sung, but was again assured by his friends that they knew no song appropriate to an occasion like that. Finally he begged that a Bible might be brought, and a few verses read to him before he died. The tents and cabins were searched, but there was not a copy of the Word of God to be found, and so among his last words the dying man exclaimed: "And is it possible that away from home and without a prayer, a song, or a verse of Scripture, I am to be ushered into the presence of God unprepared?" —Vance Randolph, *Ozark Folksongs,* University of Illinois, 1980, 429.

Blue Sky Boys, "The Dying Boy's Prayer," Bluebird B-6621, Montgomery Ward M-7017, Bear Family BCD 15951 (1936)
Wade Mainer, "Companions Draw Nigh," Bluebird B-7384, Montgomery Ward M-7306, JSP 77118 (1937)
Louvin Brothers, "Dying from Home and Lost," Capitol T1277, Bear Family BCD 15561 (1958)

The Convict and the Rose (Ballard MacDonald-Robert A. King, 1925)

This was a successful early attempt by Tin Pan Alley writers to create a song for the country music market. Vernon Dalhart recorded it ten times for various companies between 1925 and 1928. Ballard MacDonald also composed "Rose of Washington Square," "Beautiful Ohio," "Back Home in Indiana," and other pop hits in the 1910s and 1920s.

Vernon Dalhart, Victor 19770 (1925)
Bob Wills, Vocalion 04755, Conqueror 9226, Bear Family BCD 15933 (1938)

Blue Sky Boys, Bluebird B-8522, Montgomery Ward M-8415, Bear Family BCD 15951 (1939)
Hank Snow, Thesaurus transcription 1660, Bear Family BCD 15488 (1950)
Country Gentlemen, Rebel REB-CD-4002, CD-7508 (1965)

Corrina, Corrina

Bo Carter (Armenter Chatmon, 1893–1964) of Bolton, Mississippi, recorded early versions of this as Bo Chatman, and with the Jackson Blue Boys. This was one of the few blues in the Blue Sky Boys' repertoire; they also sang "Midnight Special" on their 1965 record date, and brought part of its title verse to "Corrina, Corrina."

Charlie McCoy & Bo Chatman, Brunswick 7080, Vocalion 02701 (1928)
Jackson Blue Boys, "Sweet Alberta," Columbia 14397-D (1928)
Cab Calloway, Banner 32378, Perfect 15551, JSP 908 (1931)
Milton Brown, "Where You Been So Long, Corrine," Bluebird B-5808, Montgomery Ward M-4755, OJL TXR 1 (1934)
Wingy Manone, Bluebird B-10266 (1939)
Bob Wills, OKeh 06530, Columbia 37428, Bear Family BCD 15933 (1940)
Joe Turner, Decca 8563, 48062, 29924 (1941), Atlantic 1088 (1956)
Blue Sky Boys, "Corina, Corina," Capitol T2483, ST2483, Arhoolie CD-9063 (1965)
Merle Haggard, Capitol ST451, Bear Family BCD 16782 (1970)

Cotton Mill Colic (David McCarn)

I learned that from Lute Isenhour before Earl and I ever started singing together. I had it down in my [note] *book and, when we went out to California and played on a folk festival at UCLA, Ed Kahn wanted to know if we'd record for Capitol and I said sure. I let him pick out all of the numbers for that Capitol album. Some of those songs we hadn't sung in years.*

David McCarn (1905–1964) was a mill hand in Gastonia, North Carolina, a few miles south of the Bolicks in Hickory. Workers there struck in 1929 when attempts to organize a union were frustrated. Strikers were killed when National Guard troops assisted local police and vigilantes in suppressing the movement. The satirical "Cotton Mill Colic" was part of the fallout and McCarn recorded it twice more with new sets of lyrics.

David McCarn, Victor V-40274, Old Hat CD-1007 (1930)
Blue Sky Boys, Capitol T2483, ST2483, Arhoolie CD 9063 (1965)

The Cross on the Hill (Deke Mason-Tex Jackson, 1947)

"The Cross on the Hill" is a war tune that Steve sent us. I didn't care to do a lot of war songs and neither did Earl. We had a lot of trouble with Steve over a few he insisted we do that were written by cronies or companies he was affiliated with. One was something about English Rose, a girl left back in England when a soldier came home after the war. We didn't particularly like it. A woman was the head of the music company, and she came to one of our sessions in New York and exerted through Steve quite a bit of pressure on us to do it, but we resisted.

Blue Sky Boys, RCA Victor 20-3307, Bear Family BCD 15951 (1947)

Crying Holy Unto the Lord

This is one of several popular spirituals recorded by the Norfolk Jubilee Quartet in the 1920s that were later adopted by the Carter Family, Monroe Brothers, and country and bluegrass groups.

Norfolk Jubilee Quartet, Paramount 12217 (1924)
Carter Family, "On the Rock Where Moses Stood," Victor 23513, Bluebird B-6055, Bear Family BCD 15865 (1930)
Bill Monroe, "Cryin' Holy Unto My Lord," Bluebird B-8611, Montgomery Ward M-8862, Bear Family BCD 16399 (1940)
Blue Sky Boys, WGST Program 43, October 30, 1946
Clyde Moody, Wango LP-102, Rebel CD-1672 (1962)

Curly Headed Baby *See* She's My Curly Headed Baby

Darling, Think of What You've Done (Karl Davis-Harty Taylor, 1936)

This version is Karl and Harty's arrangement of an old song of undetermined origin. Lute Isenhour and I sang this with almost identical lyrics, but somewhat different melody. When Earl and I received this edition from M.M. Cole, it seemed we could attain better harmony singing it this way. I feel our [1946] *recording is somewhat better than the original, as the recording equipment was probably more improved and our voices were more mature.* [On the 1937 version] *Eli Oberstein changed the title.*

This is a variation of "East Virginia Blues," with a tune and verses in common with "Greenback Dollar."

Karl & Harty, "Darling, Think What You've Done," ARC 7-01-53 (1936)
Blue Sky Boys, "What Have You Done?" Bluebird B-7173, Montgomery Ward M-7324, Bear Family BCD 15951 (1937)
Morris Brothers, "Darling, Think What You Have Done," Bluebird B-7967 (1938)
Blue Sky Boys, WGST Program 5, September 6, 1946, Copper Creek CCCD-0146

Death Is Only a Dream (Rev. C. W. Ray-words, A. J. Buchanan-music, 1892)

My father helped Earl and I learn this song. It was in one of the religious songbooks he purchased at an old-time singing school. We usually sang it as a trio, as we felt it gave a little more feeling to the song. A religious song sung as a trio was the opening selection on most of our radio programs. Few acts sang as many religious songs as we did.

This appears in *Living Songs for the Sunday School,* Methodist Episcopal Church South (Nashville, TN, 1892).

Edward W. Clayborn (The Guitar Evangelist), Vocalion 1096 (1927)
Blue Sky Boys, WGST Program 33, October 16, 1946, Copper Creek CCCD-0145
Stanley Brothers, Rich-R'-Tone 466, Rounder 11661-1110-2 (1947)

The Death of Little Joe (V. E. Marston, 1866)

Charles E. Nabell, "Little Joe," OKeh 40418 (1925)
Carter Family, "Darling Little Joe," RCA Victor CNV-102, Bear Family BCD 15865 (1934)
Monroe Brothers, "Little Joe," Bluebird B-7598, Montgomery Ward M-7451, Bear Family BCD 16399 (1938)
Carter Family, "Little Joe," Decca 5632, Montgomery Ward 8068, Bear Family BCD 15865 (1938)
Blue Sky Boys, "Little Joe," WCYB (Bristol, VA, 1949)
Bill Monroe, "Little Joe," Decca 74080, Bear Family BCD 15529 (1960)

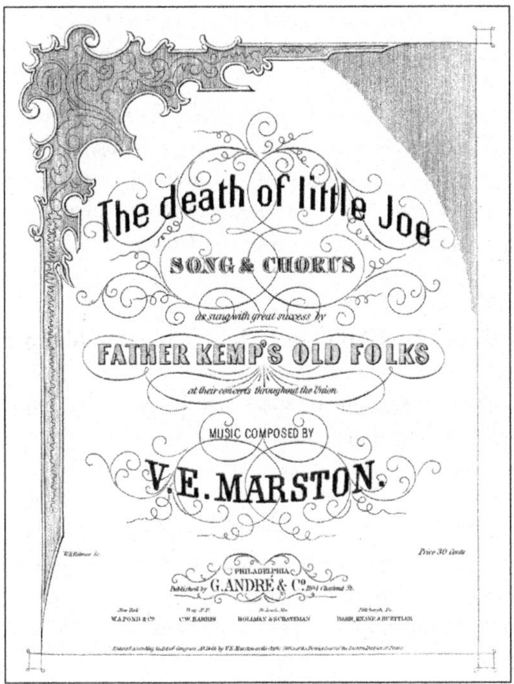

Courtesy of Lester S. Levy Collection of Sheet Music, Sheridan Libraries, Johns Hopkins University.

Didn't They Crucify My Lord?

I learned this from Lute Isenhour. He and I sang it frequently when we were working for the Crazy Water Crystals Company over WWNC, Asheville, NC, back in early 1935. Earl and I sing it a little differently from the way Lute and I sang it, but it is essentially the same. I'm very flat on my tenor. I don't know why, because it was an easy song for us to sing. On a lot of numbers we were so rushed that we only did one take, and a lot of times they didn't even play them back to us.

See note to "Crying Holy Unto the Lord," to which this is related.

Norfolk Jubilee Quartette, "He Just Hung His Head and Died," Paramount 12734, 13155, Champion 50005 (1927)
Bessemer Melody Boys, Victor 23252 (1930)
Blue Sky Boys, Bluebird B-6764, Montgomery Ward M-7160, Bear Family BCD 15951 (1936)
T. Texas Tyler, 4-Star ET-22 (ca. 1950)
Hylo Brown & the Lonesome Pine Fiddlers, "They Crucified My Lord," Starday SLP 220 (1963)
Gram Parsons, Sierra Briar SRS-8702 (1960s)

Don't Let Your Sweet Love Die (Clarke Van Ness-Zeke Manners)

Roy Hall & the Blue Ridge Entertainers, Bluebird B-8656 (1940)
Mac Wiseman, Dot 1158, Bear Family BCD 15976 (1953)
Blue Sky Boys, County 752, Gusto GT7-0549 (1963, two versions)
Del McCoury, Grassound GSD-102, Rebel CD-1709 (1971)
Jimmy Martin, Gusto GT-0077, GT-3302-2 (1980)

Don't Say Goodbye If You Love Me (Bonnie Dodd-Jimmie Davis)

Bonnie Dodd (1914–1984) from Arkansas also wrote "Be Careful of Stones That You Throw" and "I Dreamed of an Old Love Affair." She played steel guitar in Tex Ritter's band and recorded with him in 1945.

Jimmie Davis, Decca 5270, Bear Family BCD 15943 (1936)
Anglin Twins, "Don't Say Goodbye When You Go," Vocalion 02963 (1937)
Morris Brothers, Bluebird B-8136 (1938)
Blue Sky Boys, Bluebird B-8829, Montgomery Ward M-8849, Bear Family BCD 15951 (1940)
Luke Gordon, L&C LP-0014, World Artists WACD-101 (1955)
Jim & Jesse, Epic BN 26031, Bear Family BCD 15716 (1962)

Don't Take the Light (From My Dark Cell) (Calvin Van Pelt-Bill Bolick, 1947)

Blue Sky Boys, RCA Victor 20-2755, Bear Family BCD 15951 (1947)

Don't This Road Look Rough and Rocky? (Lester Flatt-Earl Scruggs, 1954)

This song is like "Can't You Hear That Night Bird Crying?" with an added chorus. It appeared around 1939 in a Holden Brothers song pamphlet in Bill's possession.

Charles Lundy & his Virginia Valley Boys, "Lover's Farewell," Mercury 6129 (1948)
Lester Flatt & Earl Scruggs, Columbia 21334, Bear Family BCD 15472 (1954)
Blue Sky Boys, Rounder 0052 (1975)

Don't Trade (Eddie Noack)

A number here that is more or less entirely out of our line, although it does have a plaintive tune to it. It's a song that more or less, I guess you might say, is sung by a lot of the present-day so-called folk singers. We changed it a little bit and we hope it sounds a little bit differently than what most of 'em sing.

Eddie Noack (1930–1978) was a Texas singer and Starday artist whose song was pitched to Bill and Earl by Don Pierce. Bill's quote was a humorous apology to his audience at the University of Illinois in 1964 when he sought to maintain the distance between the Blue Sky Boys and honky-tonk.

Eddie Noack, Starday 159, Bear Family BCD 17142 (1954)
Ernest Tubb, "Don't Trade Your Old Fashioned Sweetheart (For a Honky-Tonk Queen)," Decca DL 78834, Bear Family BCD 15688 (1958)
Blue Sky Boys, Starday SLP-257, Gusto GT7-0549 (1963)
Blue Sky Boys, Rounder 0236, 11536 (1964)

Down Home Rag (Wilbur C. Sweatman, 1911)

One of the ragtime's greatest hits found homes in both country music and dixieland jazz.

Europe's Society Orchestra, Victor 35359 (1913)
Wilbur C. Sweatman, Emerson 5163, 7161, Jazz Oracle BDW8046 (1916)
Frank Welling & John McGee, "Beech Fork Special," Banner 32593, Conqueror 7976, Perfect 12893 (1931)
Benny Goodman and His Orchestra, Columbia 3033-D (1935)
Blue Sky Boys, WGST program transcription (unnumbered), December 19, 1946

Down on the Banks of the Ohio (Laws F5)

I have no idea where I learned this song but I do recall rearranging parts of it, as the version I had of it didn't appear too clear in places.

The Blue Sky Boys version appeared in the soundtrack of the 1973 film *Paper Moon*. The Monroe Brothers' record was made six days after the Bolicks' but not released until late in 1937.

Blue Sky Boys, *Favorite Hymns and Folk Songs*, 24

Patterson's Piedmont Log Rollers, Victor 35874 (1927)
G.B. Grayson & Henry Whitter, "I'll Never Be Yours," Gennett 6373, County CD-3517 (1927)
Blue Sky Boys, Bluebird B-6480, Montgomery Ward M-5033, Bear Family BCD 15951 (1936)
Monroe Brothers, "On the Banks of the Ohio," Bluebird B-7385, Montgomery Ward M-7010, Bear Family BCD 16399 (1936)
Johnny Cash, "The Banks of the Ohio," Columbia CS 8952, Bear Family BCD 15588 (1963)
Porter Wagoner, "Banks of the Ohio," RCA Victor AHL1-3210 (1976)
Alison Krauss, "The Banks of the Ohio," Rounder 11661-0526-2 (2002)

Drifting Too Far from the Shore (Charles E. Moody, 1923)

This was taught to us by Mr. J. W. Fincher. It was popular for the Monroe Brothers and he felt we should learn it. He taught us this song and "What Would You Give in Exchange for Your Soul?" in one session. Back in those days if we were interested in a song it would take only a short time to learn it.

Monroe Brothers, Bluebird B-6363, Montgomery Ward M-4746, Bear Family BCD 16399 (1936)
Blue Sky Boys, WGST Program 31, October 14, 1946, Copper Creek CCCD-0121
Stanley Brothers, Columbia CK 86747, Copper Creek CCCD-5513 (two versions, 1956), Rebel SLP-1487 (1962)
Country Gentlemen, Folkways FA 2409, Smithsonian Folkways CD 40004 (1960)

Drop Your Net (Tommy "Butterball" Paige)

Butterball Paige played electric lead guitar for Ernest Tubb from 1947 to 1949.

Blue Sky Boys, RCA Victor 21-0370, Bear Family BCD 15951 (1950)

Dust on the Bible (Walter and Johnnie Bailes, 1944)

Blue Sky Boys, *Favorite Hymns and Folk Songs*, 12

"Dust on the Bible" probably did 200,000 units or more. Had it not been for that, I doubt that RCA would have made any more recordings by us.

The Bailes Brothers brought it to the Opry in 1944, recorded it in February 1945, and waited until November 1946 for Columbia Records to release it. Steve Sholes at RCA recorded the Blue Sky Boys version on September 30, 1946, placing the word RUSH next to the entry on the recording log. It was on the market in three or four weeks, only slightly later than the Bailes original. Both sold briskly and producer Sholes kept the Bolicks on RCA Victor despite a condescending review on December 7, 1946, by an anonymous *Billboard* writer who was unaware that Bill and Earl had been RCA artists for a decade: "*Strictly backwoods and with a heavy outdoor twang in their song, the Blue Sky Boys, a twosome new to the label, appeal to the rocking chair brigade. . . . All within hearing to find salvation for the soul in* Dust on the Bible."

Billboard had already awarded the same verdict to the Bailes Brothers original on November 23, 1946: "*Swell for the rocking chair brigade, but they don't spend nickels.*"

Bailes Brothers, Columbia 37154, Bear Family BCD 15973 (1945)
Blue Sky Boys, WGST Program 12, September 17, 1946, Gusto GT7-0695-2
Blue Sky Boys, WGST program transcription (unnumbered), December 19, 1946
Wade Mainer, King 574, Gusto GT2-0957-2 (1946)
Kitty Wells, Decca 78858, Bear Family BCD 15638 (1958)
Wanda Jackson, Third Man TMR 031 (2010)

The Dying Boy's Prayer *See* Companions Draw Nigh

The Dying Mother (Miss Nona Lawson-words, C. M. Tate-music, ca. 1882)

This is a song we learned from Ray and Ina Patterson. The original Carter Family recorded a similar song called "The Dying Mother." However, the lyrics and melody are somewhat different from those used by Ray and Ina.

Frank & James McCravy, "Prepare to Meet Your Mother," Victor V-40151 (1929)
Carter Family, Conqueror 9569, Bear Family BCD 15865 (1940)
Blue Sky Boys, "One Cold Winter's Eve," RCA Victor 21-0156, Bear Family BCD 15951 (1949)
Blue Sky Boys, "One Cold Winter's Eve," WCYB (Bristol, VA, 1949), Copper Creek CCCD-0125

The East Bound Train (James Thornton, 1896)

Mac and Bob were the first artists I can remember hearing sing this song. I am quite certain we learned it from one of their early songbooks.

Mac & Bob's WLS Book of Songs (1931), p. 17

Dock Walsh, Columbia 15047-D (1926)
Lester McFarland & Robert A. Gardner, Brunswick 169, Vocalion 5174 (1927)
Blue Sky Boys, Bluebird B-8552, Montgomery Ward M-8670, Bear Family BCD 15951 (1940)
Blue Sky Boys, WGST Program 24, October 3, 1946
Blue Sky Boys, WGST Program 49, November 7, 1946, Copper Creek CCCD-0146
Slim Martin, Versatile VLP 701 (1960s)
Mac Wiseman, Hamilton HLP-12167, Bear Family BCD 16736 (1966), Wrinkled WR-8336 (2014)
Ray & Ina Patterson, County 708 (1966)
Gibson Brothers, "Eastbound Train," Sugar Hill CD-3986 (2003), Rounder 11661 35986 02 (2014)

An Empty Mansion (C. A. Luttrell-Mrs. J. B. Karnes, 1939)

IN MY FATHER'S HOUSE ARE MANY MANSIONS. IF IT WERE NOT SO, I WOULD HAVE TOLD YOU. I GO TO PREPARE A PLACE FOR YOU. —JOHN 14:2

Blue Sky Boys, *Favorite Hymns and Folk Songs*, 6

J.B. Whitmire's Blue Sky Trio, Bluebird B-8344, Montgomery Ward M-8506 (1939)
Chuck Wagon Gang, Vocalion 05536, Bear Family BCD 17348 (1940)
Blue Sky Boys, WGST Program 1, September 2, 1946
Bailes Brothers, King 985, Bear Family BCD 17132 (1946)
Grandpa Jones, Monument SLP 18041, Bear Family BCD 15788 (1965)

Fair Eyed Ellen *See* The Jealous Lover

Farther Along
(Rev. W. B. Stevens(?)-words, arr. Barney Elliott Warren, 1911)

JESUS ANSWERED AND SAID UNTO HIM, "WHAT I DO THOU KNOWEST NOT NOW, BUT THOU SHALT KNOW HEREAFTER." —JOHN 13:7

We learned this from one of the songbooks sent to us by the Stamps-Baxter Music Company of Dallas. We always sang it as a trio, probably first over the air in 1938 when Red Hicks joined us, and received a number of requests for it. It was usually sung by quartets and I don't think many country groups sang it in those days. Our type of trio singing was different from most trios even back then. We sang lead, tenor, and bass, instead of using a baritone.

When gospel song publisher J. R. (Jesse Randolph) Baxter copyrighted the hymn in 1937, he recalled a 1911 meeting with one Rev. W. A. Fletcher on a train trip. Baxter is said to have bought the poem from him for two dollars, and it appeared in *Select Hymns for Christian Worship,* edited by Barney E. Warren in 1911. In 1940 the Blue Sky Boys used the melody for "In the Hills of Roane County," and Roy Acuff borrowed it for "The Precious Jewel," recorded on the same date as "Farther Along."

Stamps Quartet, Vocalion 04236 (1938)
Wade Mainer, Bluebird B-8023, Montgomery Ward M-7560, JSP 77124 (1938)

Roy Acuff, OKeh 05766, Conqueror 9433, 9667, Bear Family BCD 17300 (1940)

Blue Sky Boys, WGST Program 5, September 6, 1946, Copper Creek CCCD-0145

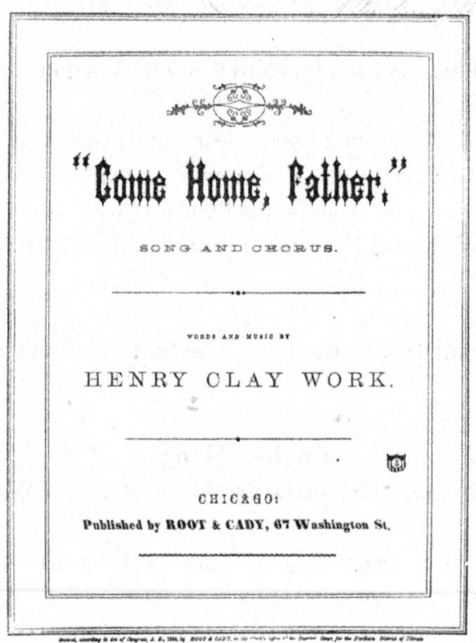

Courtesy of the Lester S. Levy Collection of Sheet Music, Sheridan Libraries, Johns Hopkins University.

Father, Dear Father, Come Home (Come Home, Father) (Henry Clay Work, 1864)

The original sheet music preface states:

> 'Tis the song of little Mary, standing at the bar-room door
> While the shameful midnight revel rages wildly as before

Henry Clay Work (1832–1884) was one of the most prominent songwriters of his day. Several of his hits, including "Kingdom Coming" (aka "The Year of Jubilo," 1862), "Marching Through Georgia" (1864), "Come Home, Father" (1864), and "Grandfather's Clock" (1876), became twentieth-century country standards. Work's melody of "The Ship That Never Returned" (1865) was recycled for "The Wreck of the Old 97," following a 1903 train disaster.

Peerless Quartet, Victor 19716 (1925)

Bela Lam & His Greene County Singers, "Poor Little Bennie," OKeh 45136 (1927)
Blue Sky Boys, Bluebird B-8522, Montgomery Ward M-8415, Bear Family BCD 15951 (1939)

The Fox

I had sung it as a solo [to a different melody]. *Then I found this version in a Burl Ives songbook, and the tune was easier to harmonize to.*

Joe Hickerson writes:

> "The Fox" ("Old Daddy Fox," etc.) seems to have a venerable history in England and is widespread in North American folksong collections. The online "Traditional Ballad Index" cites many examples and adds the following: "The earliest version of this piece appears to have been a Middle English poem found in British Museum MS. Royal 19.B.iv, and is thought to date from the fifteenth century. About as old is a strange version in Cambridge MS. Ee.1.12 with an extended prologue about the fox's raids but with lyrics closer to most modern versions. It is reasonable to assume that this and perhaps even the British Museum text are rewritings of documents still older. It should perhaps be noted that foxes are asocial animals; the males do not take part in raising the young." (email, December 16, 2010)

Burl Ives, Asch 345, Stinson 345 (ca. 1939), Decca 23506 (1946) (two versions)
Blue Sky Boys, Rounder 0236, 11536 (1964)

Garden in the Sky (Louisiana Lou, 1946)

Louisiana Lou, a.k.a. Eva Mae Greenwood or Eva Conn, performed on radio throughout the Midwest in the 1930s and 40s.

Blue Sky Boys, RCA Victor 20-2570, Bear Family BCD 15951 (1947)
Don Reno & Red Smiley, King LP 932, Gusto GT7-2209-2 (1962)
Ted Lundy, Bob Paisley & the Southern Mountain Boys, GHP LP-909 (1972)
James King, Rounder 0303 (1993)

Gathering Buds
(James Rowe-words, James D. Vaughan-music, 1921)

This song can be found in many of the old-time religious books printed by various publishers. A note beneath the title states the theme was suggested by W. W. Bates.

English-born Rowe (1865–1933) and music publisher Vaughan collaborated on popular hymns for over two decades. Online biographies claim that Rowe emigrated in 1890 and worked on railroads in New York for ten years before becoming an inspector for the Hudson River Humane Society. He then worked for music publishers in Texas and Tennessee, and later moved to Vermont to work with his daughter, an artist, writing verses for greeting cards.

Judie & Julie, Bluebird B-8386, Montgomery Ward M-8445 (1939)
Blue Sky Boys, WGST Program 29, October 10, 1946, Copper Creek CCCD-0120
Cope Brothers, Federal 10007, Audio Lab AL 1504 (1947)
Doc Watson, Sugar Hill CD 3779 (1990)

Gathering Shells from the Seashore
(Will L. Thompson, 1874)

Carter Family, "Happiest Days of All," Victor 23701, Bear Family BCD 15865 (1932)

Blue Sky Boys, "Gathering Up the Shells from the Seashore," County 752 (1963)

Get Along Home, Cindy

This can be an instrumental piece or song. I sang the verses and then changed to tenor on the chorus. There are many verses but we only had time to do a few.

Samantha Bumgarner & Eva Davis, "Cindy in the Meadows," Columbia 167-D, J2K 65816 (1924); reissued on Diva 6010-G, Harmony 5097-H, and Velvet Tone 7036-V, all as Gardner & David
Uncle Dave Macon, "Whoop 'Em Up, Cindy," Vocalion 15323, 5099, Bear Family BCD 15976 (1926)
Bascom Lamar Lunsford, Brunswick 228 (1928, in the Bolick collection)
Lulu Belle & Scotty, ARC 6-03-59, Conqueror 8594 (1935)
J.E. Mainer's Mountaineers, "Kiss Me Cindy," Bluebird B-7289, Montgomery Ward M-7305, JSP 77118 (1937)
Blue Sky Boys, WGST Program 45, November 1, 1946, Copper Creek CCCD-0121

Getting Ready to Leave This World (Luther G. Presley, 1937)

Luther Presley (1887–1974) composed "Waiting for the Boys," "Dreaming of a Little Cabin," and wrote new lyrics for "When the Saints Go Marching In" around 1937.

Chuck Wagon Gang, OKeh 05782, Bear Family BCD 17348 (1940)
Blue Sky Boys, WGST Program 20, September 27, 1946
Blue Sky Boys, WCYB (Bristol, VA, 1949)
Lewis Family, Canaan CAS-9820 (1977)

Give Me My Roses Now (James Rowe-words, R. H. Cornelius-music, 1925)

See note to "Gathering Buds."

Carter Family, "Give Me the Roses While I Live," Victor 23821, Montgomery Ward M-7356, Bear Family BCD 15865 (1933)
Blue Sky Boys, Bluebird B-8308, Montgomery Ward M-8411, Bear Family BCD 15951 (1939)

Masters Family, Mercury 6131 (1948)
Ray & Ina Patterson, "Give Me the Roses While I Live," County 708 (1966)
Ferlin Husky, King KSCD-0300 (ca. 1977)

God Is Still on the Throne (Bill and Earl Bolick)

Blue Sky Boys, Starday SLP-269, Gusto GT7-0549 (1963)

God Sent My Little Girl (Karl Davis-Harty Taylor, 1936)

This was written to celebrate the birth of Karl Davis's daughter Diana Jean in 1934.

Blue Sky Boys, Bluebird B-8339, Montgomery Ward M-8412, Bear Family BCD 15951 (1939)
Carter Sisters & Mother Maybelle, RCA Victor 21-0372, B.A.C.M. CD D 176 (1949)

Going Round This World, Baby Mine

Leslie [Keith] *does this number as well as anyone I've heard.* [He] *told me he could play the old-time banjo but didn't own one. I loaned him mine and was surprised at how well he played it.*

This song is related to "Differences" (p. 125) and "The Sailor's Wife" (p. 255) in *The Collected Songs of Charles Mackay* (London: G. Routledge & Co., 1859). "The Sailor's Wife" was set to music by Archibald Johnston and published in 1875. It was first published as "Baby Mine" in 1878.

I've a letter from thy sire, baby mine, baby mine
I could read and never tire, baby mine, baby mine
He is sailing o'er the sea, he is coming back to me
He is coming back to me, baby mine

Dick Burnett called it "Going Round the World" in a song booklet published around 1913. Songs like "Sam Hall," "Froggie Went A-Courtin'," "Sugar Babe," "Crawdad Song," "Going Back to Jericho," "Stand by Me," "Old Age Pension Check," "Wondrous Love," and "Ain't It Grand to Be a Christian" are structurally similar.

Elizabeth Spencer, "Baby Mine," Edison Amberol 1103, Edison Blue Amberol 2383 (ca. 1911)

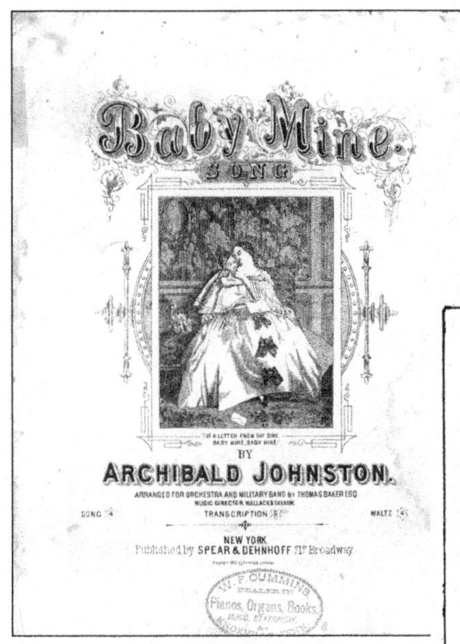

Courtesy of the Lester S. Levy Collection of Sheet Music, Sheridan Libraries, Johns Hopkins University.

GOING AROUND THE WORLD

I'm going across the ocean friend of mine,
I'm going across the ocean friend of mine
I'm going across the ocean if I don't change my notion.
I'm going around the world friend of mine
I'll write my girl a letter friend of mine
I'll write my girl a letter friend of mine
I'll write my girl a letter friend of mine and I'll write my girl a letter and I'll tell her that she'd better
For I'm going around the world friend of mine.
Oh! Come and sit by me girl O mine
Come and sit down by me girl O mine.
Come and sit down by me, say you love no one but me, and we'll go around this world friend O mine
Oh, give to me your hand girl 'O mine,
Oh! give to me your hand girl 'O mine,
Oh! give to me your hand, Say you love no other man, And we'll go around the world, Girl 'O mine.
I may cross the sea girl of mine
I may cross the sea girl of mine.
I may cross the sea.
Oh! come and go with me, I'm going around the world girl of mine
I'm going around the world friend of mine
I'm going around the world friend of mine
I've been around the world, with a banjo picking girl, I've been around the world friend of mine
—: Composed By
R. D. BURNETT
Monticello, Ky.

Sophie Braslau, "Baby Mine," Victor 64810 (1918)
Emry Arthur, "Going Around the World," Vocalion 5230 (1928)
Coon Creek Girls, "Banjo Pickin' Girl," Vocalion 04413, County CD-3533 (1938)
Blue Sky Boys, WCYB (Bristol, VA, 1949), Copper Creek CCCD-0126

Golden Slippers (James A. Bland, 1879)

This song is familiar to most country artists but no one seems to sing it anymore. We usually started our program with it if we chose to sing it. If it was to be an instrumental, we put it at the last of the program.

Courtesy of Lester S. Levy Collection of Sheet Music, Sheridan Libraries, Johns Hopkins University.

James Alan Bland (1854–1911) was a New York–born African American minstrel star who performed from the 1860s to the end of the century. His other successes included "In the Evening by the Moonlight" and "Carry Me Back to Old Virginny." Both romanticized pre–Civil War southern plantation life. Curly and Ruel Parker performed it as a fiddle duet on an October 9, 1946, Blue Sky Boys broadcast.

Harry C. Browne, Columbia A2116 (1916)
Vernon Dalhart & Carson Robison, Victor 20539 (1927)
Blue Sky Boys, WCYB (Bristol, VA, 1949), Copper Creek CCCD-0125

Goodbye Maggie (C. B. Coolidge, 1891)
Annie Dear, I'm Called Away (Harry Hunter-John Guest, ca. 1891)

This was taken from the WLS Barn Dance book that was sent to us by M.M. Cole. As well as I can remember, someone from the WLS Barn Dance used to sing it occasionally. I'm not certain if it was Mac and Bob or Karl and Harty.

Jack Mathis, "Annie Dear I'm Called Away," Columbia 15450-D (1929)
Monroe Brothers, "Goodbye Maggie," Bluebird B-7508, Montgomery Ward M-7447, Bear Family BCD 16399 (1938)
Blue Sky Boys, "Goodbye Maggie," Program 6, September 9, 1946, Copper Creek CCCD-0121
Blue Sky Boys, "Goodbye Maggie," WCYB (Bristol, VA, 1949)

Great Grand Dad
(Lowell Otus Reese-words, Romaine Lowdermilk-music, 1925)

This comic celebration of frontier hardships first appeared as a poem in the *Saturday Evening Post* on February 28, 1925. An Arizona cattle rancher, Romaine Lowdermilk, later worked it into a song and passed it on to John I. White, a cowboy singer on WOR in New York starting in 1927. In *Git Along, Little Dogies* (University of Illinois, 1975), White said it was popular enough to inspire an answer song, "Great Grandma," to answer a complaint that the original "had not done right by the other side of the family."

John I. White, Banner 6561 (1929)
Blue Sky Boys, WGST Program 20, September 27, 1946, Library of Congress LBC-10
Bo Diddley, "The Great Grandfather," Checker 924, Hip-O Select B0009231-02 (1958)
Lulu Belle & Scotty, "Great Grandad and Great Grandma," Mar-Lu 8903 (1950s)

Green Grow the Lilacs

This old Scots-Irish song is sometimes called "Green Grows the Laurel." It was the title song in a 1931 Broadway production that included Tex Ritter (1905–1974), and it was identified with him thereafter. Its complex history reputedly includes soldiers singing it during the Mexican-American War in the 1840s, where natives called them "green-grows" or "gringos."

Georgia Dell, "Keep Your Love Letters, I'll Keep Mine," Bluebird B-7914, Montgomery Ward M-7749 (1938)
Tex Ritter, Capitol Transcription G-24, Bear Family BCD 16239 (1945)
Tex Ritter, Capitol 206, 15259, Bear Family BCD 16260 (1945)
Maddox Brothers & Rose, Columbia 21099, Bear Family BCD 15850 (1952)
Tex Ritter, Capitol 3589 (1956), Capitol T1623, ST1623 (1961) (two versions)
Blue Sky Boys, Rounder 0052 (1975)

Greenback Dollar
See I Don't Want Your Greenback Dollar

Hang Out the Front Door Key (Benjamin Hapgood Burt, 1908)

One of the Blue Sky Boys' few comic songs and a rare feature for Bill's solo voice. The original includes a third verse that Bill omits:

Now Percy stays at home, he wouldn't dare to roam
He leaves the boys alone when work is through
He beats it home for fair to see if wifey's there
When he goes out, he takes her too
Now all the sporting's done by Percy's younger son
He's never home 'til one, two, three, or four
He makes the poor old man look like an also ran
Since Percy Junior's had the floor
When he calls up father every night at home
This is what he sings across the telephone:

Hang out the front door key, Dad, hang out the front door key
I won't be home till three, Dad, don't you sit up for me
I'm with some poor sick friends, Dad, just like you used to be
Cheer up and smile, I'll be home in a while, so hang out the front door key

George Lashwood, Zonophone 39 (recorded in London, 1908)
Shelton Brothers, Decca 5099 (1935, in the Bolick collection)
Lew Childre, ARC 6-06-51 (1936), Old Homestead OCHS-132 (1940s) (two versions)
Blue Sky Boys, Bluebird B-8110, Montgomery Ward M-7567, Bear Family BCD 15951 (1938)
Little John & Cherokee Sue, Cozy 290 (1950)

Have No Desire to Roam *See* The Hills of Home

Have You Seen My Daddy Here?
(Wallace Fowler-Russ Hull-Ida de Milo Lammers, 1944)

Blue Sky Boys, *Folk Songs and Hymns,* 26

The sheet music calls this a "companion song to 'Mommy, Please Stay Home With Me.'" The latter was one side of Eddy Arnold's first record in 1944, and credited to him, Wally Fowler, and J. G. Hall. Both songs scold irresponsible parents for neglecting their children.

Blue Sky Boys, RCA Victor 20-2151, Bear Family BCD 15951 (1946)

Heaven Holds All to Me (Tillit S. Teddlie, ca. 1915)

It was written by Tillit S. Teddlie [1885–1987] *who wrote "Sunny Side of Life." This song was taken from the hymnal* Reformation Glory *that was used by the First Church of God in Hickory. This is the church that Earl and I attended when we were boys. I'm sure my father helped us learn it. It was fairly popular for us.*

According to an online anecdote, Teddlie revisited his boyhood farm after growing up, and found it abandoned and in shambles. He sat against a tree and wrote on a blank page in a pocket Bible:

Earth holds no treasures but perish with using, however precious they be
Yet there's a country to which I am going; Heaven holds all to me

Blue Sky Boys, "Heaven Holds All for Me," Bluebird B-7803, Montgomery Ward M-7472, Bear Family BCD 15951 (1938)
Blue Sky Boys, Program 37, October 22, 1946, Copper Creek CCCD-0145

Her Mansion Is Higher than Mine (Albert E. Brumley, 1942)

Blue Sky Boys, WGST Christmas broadcast, December 19, 1946.
Al Brumley (Albert E. Brumley, Jr.), Memory Valley MV 1986 (1970s)
Blackwood Brothers, Artco LPG-106, 1973
Mac Wiseman, "Mother's Mansion Is Higher Than Mine," Wise MAC W-108-2, Music Mill 50108, 50115 (2001)

The Hills of Home (James Rowe-words, James D. Vaughan-music, 1914)

This song we definitely learned from our father. I located it in several of the old-time gospel songbooks that I have. Other than my father, I have never heard anyone else sing it.

See note to "Gathering Buds."

Blue Sky Boys, "Have No Desire to Roam," Bluebird B-7348, Montgomery Ward M-7326, Bear Family BCD 15951 (1937)
Tennessee Ramblers, Bluebird B-8176 (1939)

The Hills of Roane County *See* In the Hills of Roane County

The Holiness Mother (Karl Davis-Harty Taylor, 1936)

This was sent to us by M.M. Cole. Most mother songs we sang were requested often.

Blue Sky Boys, "Mother Went Her Holiness Way," Bluebird B-7984, Bear Family BCD 15951 (1938)
Karl & Harty, OKeh 05640 (1940)
Blue Sky Boys, WGST Program 3, September 4, 1946, Copper Creek CCD-0120

Hop Light Ladies *See* Miss McLeod's Reel

The House Where We Were Wed (Will Carleton, 1873 / Karl Davis-Harty Taylor, 1936)

This was one of the many songs sent to us by M.M. Cole. This, in my opinion, was one of the finer [Karl and Harty] *songs. I feel* [our 1946] *recording is as good or better than the original.*

The poem is from Will Carleton's *Farm Ballads* (1873), still in print. All versions below use the first three of its four verses.

Karl & Harty, ARC 7-04-57 (1936)
Blue Sky Boys, Bluebird B-8308, Montgomery Ward M-8411, Bear Family BCD 15951 (1939)
Blue Sky Boys, WGST Program 19, September 26, 1946, Copper Creek CCCD-0146
Blue Sky Boys, WCYB (Bristol, VA, 1949)
Ray & Ina Patterson, County 708 (1966)

How Beautiful Heaven Must Be (Mrs. A.S. (Cordie) Bridgewater-words, Andy P. Bland-music, ca. 1920)

Prairie Ramblers, ARC 6-11-70, Vocalion 03115, Conqueror 8726, Columbia 20209, 37610 (1936)
Monroe Brothers, "We Read of a Place Called Heaven," Bluebird B-6676, Montgomery Ward M-7087, Bear Family BCD 16399 (1936)
Blue Sky Boys, WGST program transcription (unnumbered), December 19, 1946

Hymns My Mother Sang (B. B. Edmiston, 1924)

I'm almost certain we learned this song by hearing Karl and Harty sing it.

Karl & Harty, ARC 7-05-60 (1936, in the Bolick collection)
Blue Sky Boys, Bluebird B-7311, Montgomery Ward M-7326, Bear Family BCD 15951 (1937)

I Believe It for My Mother Told Me So (Paul Dresser, 1887)

We called this song "I Believe It for My Mother Told Me So." Eli Oberstein shortened it [to "I Believe It"]. *It was taken from the Mac and Bob songbook.* [Before] *we received it, we had no idea that Mac and Bob were blind as it was never mentioned on the radio. They were usually introduced as Mac and Bob, the Knoxville Boys. It is one of the first songs* [Earl and I] *ever sang together.*

Paul Dresser (1857–1906) is best remembered for "On the Banks of the Wabash" (1897), and he was the older brother of novelist Theodore Dreiser. The Bolicks also recorded his "Just Tell Them That You Saw Me."

Mac & Bob's WLS Book of Songs (1931), 50

Delmore Brothers, Bluebird B-5857, Montgomery Ward M-4552 (1935)
Blue Sky Boys, "I Believe It," Bluebird B-6808, Montgomery Ward M-7085, Bear Family BCD 15951 (1936)
Blue Sky Boys, WGST Program 30, October 11, 1946, Copper Creek CCCD-0121
Ray & Ina Patterson, County 737 (1973)

I Cannot Take You Back Now (Bill and Earl Bolick, 1947)

Blue Sky Boys, RCA Victor 20-3158, Bear Family BCD 15951 (1947)
Blue Sky Boys, WCYB (Bristol, VA, 1949)

I Don't Want Your Greenback Dollar

We usually sang several more verses than this version [1965, below] *but most of the songs we did on* [the Capitol] *album were so long, we cut this one a bit short.*

Greenback dollars were special currency printed in 1861 when the Lincoln administration was unable to secure bank loans to support the Civil War. When it ended, Confederate money was worthless, and southerners had to adopt the currency of their conquerors. Calling the bills "greenbacks," they accepted them with reluctance.

Clarence (Tom) Ashley mentored Roy Acuff when they worked in medicine shows together in the early 1930s. Each made popular records of the song; cover and answer versions by J.E. Mainer's Mountaineers, the Callahan Brothers, and others followed.

Davis & Nelson, QRS R.9014, Paramount 3188, Broadway 8243 (1929)
Ashley & Foster, "Greenback Dollar," Vocalion 02554, Conqueror 9112 (1933)
Dixon Brothers, "Greenback Dollar, Part 2," Bluebird B-6462, Montgomery Ward M-5025, Bear Family BCD 16817, JSP 77113 (1936, in the Bolick collection)
Roy Acuff, "New Greenback Dollar," Vocalion 03255, Columbia 37614, 20213, Bear Family BCD 17300 (1936)
Blue Sky Boys, Capitol T2483, ST2483, Arhoolie CD-9063 (1965)

I Dreamed I Searched Heaven for You (Mary Ethel Weiss-James D. Vaughan, 1931)

I never really considered this a true hymn but it is a religious song, found in old-time religious songbooks. Earl and I sang it from our first to our last radio programs.

Karl & Harty, Melotone M13085, Conqueror 8310 (1934)
Bill Carlisle's Kentucky Boys, Decca 5724 (1939)
Blue Sky Boys, WGST Program 23, October 2, 1946
Blue Sky Boys, WCYB (Bristol, VA, 1949), Copper Creek CCCD-0125
Kitty Wells, Decca DL 8858, Bear Family BCD 15638 (1958)

I Have Found a Friend *See* The Lily of the Valley

I Have Found the Way (Rev. L. E. Green-Adger M. Pace, 1920s)

This song can be found in old-time religious songbooks but usually not in hymnals. We first learned it in the thirties. I don't remember how popular it was with our radio audiences but, as I have stated on numerous occasions, over half our written requests were for songs of a religious nature.

Smith's Sacred Singers, Columbia 15749-D (1929)
Monroe Brothers, Bluebird B-6932, Montgomery Ward M-8454, Bear Family BCD 16399 (1937)
Blue Sky Boys, WGST Program 16, September 23, 1946, Copper Creek CCCD-0145
Gibson Brothers, Rounder 11661 35986 02 (2014)

I Love Her More, Now Mother's Old (Bill & Earl Bolick, 1946)

That is my number — I wrote that one.

Blue Sky Boys, *Folk Songs and Hymns*, 30

Blue Sky Boys, RCA Victor 20-2151, Bear Family BCD 15951 (1946)

I Need the Prayers (Of Those I Love)
(J. E. Rankin, ca. 1878/James D. Vaughan, 1908)

This song can be found in many old-time gospel songbooks. It appeared in many Vaughan publications.

Karl & Harty, ARC 6-10-54, Conqueror 8660 (1936)
Blue Sky Boys, Bluebird B-7803, Montgomery Ward M-7472, Bear Family BCD 15951 (1938)
Blue Sky Boys, audition disc, November 20, 1939
Blue Sky Boys, WGST program transcription (unnumbered), December 19, 1946
Blue Sky Boys, WCYB (Bristol, VA, 1949)
Don Reno & Red Smiley, King 693, 853, Gusto GT4-0955-2 (1959)

I Never Will Marry (Laws K17)

This old song has a number of variations, and has been known in England and Ireland since at least the nineteenth century.

Carter Family, Bluebird B-8350, Montgomery Ward M-7356, Bear Family BCD 15865 (1933)
Bailey Brothers, "I Will Never Marry," Rich-R'-Tone 449 (1949)
Carter Sisters & Mother Maybelle, Columbia 20974, B.A.C.M. CD D 176 (1952)
Country Gentlemen, Starday 434, 3510-2-2 (1958)
The Weavers, Vanguard VSD 2022 (1958)
Hank Snow & Anita Carter, RCA Victor LSP 2580, Bear Family BCD 16414 (1962)
Blue Sky Boys, County 752 (1963)

I Told the Stars About You
(Thomas Burton-Lester McFarland, 1931)

Mac & Bob's WLS Book of Songs (1931), 20

Mac & Bob (Lester McFarland & Robert A. Gardner), Banner 32692, Conqueror 8137, Old Homestead OHCD-4158 (1933)
Blue Sky Boys, "Last Night While Standing by My Window," Bluebird B-7878, Bear Family BCD 15951 (1938)
Blue Sky Boys, audition disc, November 20, 1939
Bailey Brothers, Canary 006 (1952)

Don Reno & Bill Harrell, "I Told," King KSD-1033, Gusto GT7-2176-2 (1967)
Warrior River Boys, Rounder 11661-0270-2 (1989)

I Wish I Had Died in My Cradle (Lew Brown-words, Max C. Friedman-music, 1926)

The first person I ever heard sing this was Jimmie Davis. We thought it would make a good duet and always sang it that way.

Max Charles Friedman (1893–1962) claimed two more hits, "Sioux City Sue" (as Ray Freedman, 1945) and "Rock Around the Clock" (1954).

Gene Austin, Victor 21833 (1928)
Max Friedman, OKeh 45316 (1929)
Lester McFarland & Robert A. Gardner, Brunswick 307 (1929)
Jimmie Davis, "I Wish I Had Never Seen Sunshine," Decca 5231, 46004, Bear Family BCD 15943 (1936)
Blue Sky Boys, "I Wish I Had Never Seen Sunshine," WCYB (Bristol, VA, 1949), Copper Creek CCCD-0126
Tommy Collins, Capitol 3591, Bear Family BCD 15577 (1956)

If I Could Hear My Mother Pray Again (James Rowe-words, James D. Vaughan-music, 1922)

Bill told Rounder Records' Ken Irwin that this was the first song he could remember. See note to "Gathering Buds."

A.C. Forehand, "Mother's Prayer," Victor 20547, Yazoo 2073 (1927)
Callahan Family, Banner 33243, Conqueror 8404, Old Homestead OHCD-4031 (1934)
Blue Sky Boys, WGST Program 22, October 1, 1946
Blue Sky Boys, WCYB (Bristol, VA, 1949)
Mac Wiseman, Dot DLP 25373, Bear Family BCD 15976 (1960)
Blue Sky Boys, Rounder 11536 (1964)

I'll Be Listening (Virgil. O. Stamps-J. B. Coats, 1937)

This song was sent to us by the Stamps-Baxter Company of Dallas.

J.B. Whitmire's Blue Sky Trio, "I'll Be List'ning," Bluebird B-7550, Montgomery Ward M-7721 (1937)

Blue Sky Boys, WGST Program 26, October 7, 1946, Copper Creek CCCD-0121

Jim & Jesse, Kentucky 547 (as Virginia Trio, 1951), Old Dominion OD-498-15 (1995) (two versions)

I'll Be No Stranger There (J. S. Alcon-A. B. Sebren)

This is a song we learned from one of our Stamps-Baxter books. [They were] *very good about sending us religious material.*

Chuck Wagon Gang, OKeh 06596, Conqueror 9882, Bear Family BCD 17348 (1941)

Blue Sky Boys, WCYB (Bristol, VA, 1949), Copper Creek CCCD-0125

Sauceman Brothers, Rich-R'-Tone 701 (1950)

Paul Williams, Rebel CD-1804 (2004)

I'll Be with You When the Roses Bloom Again (Will D. Cobb-words, Gus Edwards-music, 1901)

I can't recall when we first learned the song. A parody was recorded back in the twenties by an Earl Shirkey who did a peculiar yodel with it. Other than Mac and Bob, I can't recall hearing anyone else sing it.

Harry Macdonough, Edison 7942 (1901), 8276 (1902), Columbia 357 (1903), Victor 1097 (1903) (four versions)

Lester McFarland & Robert A. Gardner, "When the Roses Bloom Again," Brunswick 111, Vocalion 5027 (1926, in the Bolick collection)

Earl Shirkey & Roy Harper, "When the Roses Bloom Again for the Bootlegger" (parody), Columbia 15326-D (1928)

Blue Sky Boys, "When the Roses Bloom Again," WGST Program 26, October 7, 1946, Copper Creek CCCD-0145

Mac Wiseman, "When the Roses Bloom Again," Dot 1266, Bear Family BCD 15976 (1954)

Johnny Cash, "When the Roses Bloom Again," Columbia CS 8952, Bear Family BCD 15588 (1963)

I'll Meet You in the Morning (Albert E. Brumley, 1936)

Albert E. Brumley (1905–1977) was one of the most successful hymn composers of his era. "If We Never Meet Again" and "Turn Your Radio On" were recorded by the

Blue Sky Boys. "Did You Ever Go Sailing," "Jesus, Hold My Hand," "I'll Fly Away," "If We Never Meet Again," "Dreaming of a Little Cabin," and "He Set Me Free" are among his other perennials.

J. B. Whitmire's Blue Sky Trio, Bluebird B-7132, Montgomery Ward M-7718 (1937)
Whitey & Hogan, Decca 5838 (1940)
Blue Sky Boys, WGST Program 34, October 17, 1946
Bill Monroe, Decca DL8769, Bear Family BCD 15423 (1958)

I'll Take My Saviour by the Hand (Whitey-Hogan [i.e. Roy Grant and Arval Hogan], 1947)

Blue Sky Boys, RCA Victor 20-3055, Bear Family BCD 15951 (1947)

I'll Wear a White Flower for You (Dorsey Dixon)

The Dixon Brothers (Dorsey and Howard) were mill workers in East Rockingham, North Carolina, who performed on the Crazy Barn Dance at WBT (1934–35) and WPTF (1935–36).

"I'll Wear a White Flower for You, Mother Dear" by Rev. Charles M. Fillmore (1912) appeared as a Mother's Day song in the collection *Special Days in the Sunday School* by Marion Lawrance (Revell, 1916). Dorsey Dixon may have incorporated some changes, since these versions differ somewhat from the original.

Dixon Brothers, "White Flower for You," Bluebird B-6630, Montgomery Ward M-7014, JSP 77113, Bear Family BCD 16817 (1936)
Alex Campbell, Olabelle & Deacon, "White Flower," New River 1034, Starday SLP 214 (ca. 1962)
Blue Sky Boys, County 752 (1963)

I'm Glad (I'm Glad He's Gone and Left You) (Famous Lashua-Bill Boyd, 1944)

Blue Sky Boys, *Folk Songs and Hymns,* 25

Blue Sky Boys, RCA Victor 20-2380, Bear Family BCD 15951 (1947)

I'm Going Home This Evening (Karl Davis-Harty Taylor-Patrick McAdory, 1936)

This was sent to us by M.M. Cole. When we sang it, we always introduced it by the correct title.

Bill refers to Eli Oberstein's altered title "Within the Circle," disguising the use of a copyrighted song. Blue Sky fans wanting to buy "I'm Going Home This Evening" in a record shop would understandably have been confused.

Karl & Harty, ARC 7-04-57, Conqueror 8833 (1936)
Blue Sky Boys, "Within the Circle," Bluebird B-7113, Montgomery Ward M-7325, Bear Family BCD 15951 (1937)
Blue Sky Boys, WGST Program 4, September 5, 1946

I'm Going to Write to Heaven (Chuck Harding-Cousin Joe Maphis, 1944)

This song was sent to us by Country Music Publishers of Chicago. [New] *publishing companies came into existence immediately after World War II and we received music from a large number of them. All wanted us to record their songs and often offered lucrative deals. Many were what I called "war songs." This type of song was popular immediately after the war but the desire to hear them soon faded away.*

Blue Sky Boys, *Folk Songs and Hymns,* 22

Blue Sky Boys, RCA Victor 20-2296, Bear Family BCD 15951 (1947)
Blue Sky Boys, WCYB (Bristol, VA, 1949), Copper Creek CCCD-0125

I'm Just Here to Get My Baby Out of Jail (Karl Davis-Harty Taylor, 1936)

This song is attributed to Karl Davis and it's very probable that he is the author. However, I cannot say that we learned this song from Karl and Harty. Back when Earl and I started singing together, few entertainers gave much thought to who composed a song. I was a collector of country and folk songs even before I learned to play an instrument. If I heard a song I liked I usually committed it to memory. It seemed I had heard this song neither on record nor radio. It was one of the first that Earl and I ever sang together. I am sure no other group in this section of the country sang it until we started singing it in 1935 over WWNC. It was one of our most requested numbers both at WWNC and later at WGST. When we suggested it at our first session, Eli Oberstein was reluctant to let us do it as he told us he had let Wade [Mainer] *and Zeke* [Morris] *do it and he didn't want to run into conflict. Having convinced him that we were instrumental in popularizing the song he let us do it. However, a number of other songs from our first session were released before this was made available.*

The Blue Sky Boys' first release, "Sunny Side of Life"/"Where the Soul Never Dies" (Bluebird B-6457), was an immediate best-seller, and Oberstein wisely delayed releasing "I'm Just Here to Get My Baby Out of Jail." Karl Davis wrote it in 1934 after visiting a Madison, Wisconsin, jail with a pastor associated with WLS. The Mainer-Morris record was published with an altered title and made only a moderate impact, but the Bolicks' version became a career hit and country standard.

Karl & Harty, Banner 33118, Conqueror 8310 (1934)
Wade Mainer & Zeke Morris, "Mother Came to Get Her Boy from Jail," Bluebird B-6383, Montgomery Ward M-4718, JSP 77118 (1936)
Blue Sky Boys, Bluebird B-6621, Montgomery Ward M-7017, Bear Family BCD 15951, BCD 17355 (1936)
Blue Sky Boys, WGTS Program 20, September 27, 1946
Hank Snow, Thesaurus 1618, Bear Family BCD 15488 (1950), RCA Victor LSP 1861, Bear Family BCD 15476 (1958) (two versions)
Everly Brothers, Cadence CLP-3016, Ace CH75, Bear Family BCD 17355 (1958)

I'm S-A-V-E-D

This is more or less a hymn, although it wasn't usually sung by the congregation. I think we picked this number up at some of the old-time singing conventions or brush arbor meetings we used to attend.

"The B-I-B-L-E" and "The ABC Song" are other Blue Sky Boys songs with spelling themes.

Gid Tanner, "S-A-V-E-D," Columbia 15097-D (1926)
Ernest V. Stoneman, "The Religious Critic," OKeh 45051, 5-String 5SPH 001 (1926)
Karl Davis, ARC 6-10-54, Conqueror 8664 (1935)
Blue Sky Boys, Bluebird B-8401, Montgomery Ward M-8666, Bear Family BCD 15951 (1940)
Blue Sky Boys, WCYB (Bristol, VA, 1949)
Blue Sky Boys, "I'm Saved," Rounder 0236, 11536 (1964)

I'm Troubled, I'm Troubled

Earl and I learned this by hearing our mother sing it. I always thought she had a good voice for old-time songs but she never sang very much. She knew "Single Girl, Married Girl," "Bonnie Blue Eyes," and others; however, she never seemed to know many verses. We gave the song this title as she sang this verse more than any other. As time went by we added a verse here and there and soon sang it as a full-length song.

Blue Sky Boys, *Folk Songs and Hymns,* 20

The Bolick family's music normally didn't intersect with the blues, but Annie Bolick's "troubled in mind" refrain in this song recalls the Richard M. Jones blues "Trouble in Mind" that became a country standard following Bertha "Chippie" Hill's popular record in 1926.

Carolina Tar Heels, "I'm Going to Georgia," Victor 20544 (1927)
Blue Sky Boys, Bluebird B-6538, Montgomery Ward M-7016, Bear Family BCD 15951 (1936)
Blue Sky Boys, WCYB (Bristol, VA, 1949), Copper Creek CCCD-0125
Gibson Brothers, Rounder 11661 35986 02 (2014)

I've Found a Friend *See* The Lily of the Valley

If We Never Meet Again (Albert E. Brumley, 1945)

See note to "I'll Meet You in the Morning."

Charlie Monroe, RCA 20-2961, Bear Family BCD 16808 (1947)
Chuck Wagon Gang, Columbia 20537, Bear Family BCD 17348 (1948)
Blue Sky Boys, WCYB (Bristol, VA, 1949)
Elvis Presley, RCA LSP 2328 (1960)
Johnny Cash, Columbia CS 8522, Bear Family BCD 15562 (1961)

In My Little Home in Tennessee (Carson J. Robison, 1926)

I learned this song from Lute Isenhour.

Vernon Dalhart (as Al Craver), "My Little Home in Tennessee," Columbia 15056-D (1925)
Vernon Dalhart, Victor 19918 (1925), Edison 51670 (1925), Brunswick 102, Vocalion 15284 (1926) (three versions)

Blue Sky Boys, Bluebird B-8143, Montgomery Ward M-7327, Bear Family BCD 15951 (1937)

Mac Wiseman, "My Little Home in Tennessee," Dot 1194, Bear Family BCD 15976 (1953)

In the Hills of Roane County

I don't remember exactly where we learned this tune. Later we found out there was no town by the name of [Spencer] *in Tennessee.*

In 1986 Bill Bolick told Ken Irwin that he learned this song from Curly Parker in 1940.

Willis Mayberry was a black railroad section hand who killed his brother-in-law Tom Galbraith around 1883 in Kingston (Roane County), Tennessee. He stood trial but escaped and fled. He was captured in Knoxville in 1909 and sent back to Kingston, where he was retried and given a life sentence for his old crime. He wrote this song in the Tennessee State Penitentiary in Nashville and taught it to a fellow inmate, Booger Gilbreath (no relation to Tom Galbraith), who performed the song after his release.*

Familiar versions use the melody of "Farther Along," as does Roy Acuff's "The Precious Jewel" (1940). Grandpa Jones learned an earlier and longer version called "Willis Mayberry" from Andy Patterson and Warren Caplinger in the 1930s, adding that the pair met as assistant warden and inmate respectively at Tennessee's Brushy Mountain State Penitentiary in the 1920s. "Spencer" is an apparent misreading of Kingston, where Mayberry's trial was held.

Andy Patterson & Warren Caplinger, "Willis Mabry," Gennett unissued (1929, 1930) (two versions)

Blue Sky Boys, Bluebird B-8693, Montgomery Ward M-8848, Bear Family BCD 15951 (1940)

Blue Sky Boys, audition disc, 1941

Cope Brothers, King 670 (1947)

Jimmie Osborne, "The Hills of Roan County," King 1231 (1953)

Bill Monroe, "Roane County Prison," Decca DL 8731, Bear Family BCD 15423 (1957)

---

* Charles K. Wolfe, "Old Cumberland Land: The Musical Legacy of the Upper Cumberland," in *Rural Life and Culture in the Upper Cumberland*, edited by Michael E. Birdwell and W. Calvin Dickinson. University Press of Kentucky, 2004, 274–83. Dick Spottswood, "In the Hills of Roane County: The Story and the Song," *Bluegrass Unlimited*, vol. 50, no. 9 (March 2016): 46–47

Grandpa Jones, "Willis Mayberry," Monument SLP 18021, Bear Family BCD 15788 (1962)
Hylo Brown, "Roane County Prisoner," Starday SLP-204, SLP-207, 0124-2 (1962)
Paul Williams, Mountain Home MH 1502-2 (2014)

In the Pines *See* The Longest Train I Ever Saw

It Was Midnight on the Stormy Deep *See* Midnight on the Stormy Sea

Jack O' Diamonds

This song has many different versions. We didn't sing it often as we couldn't devote that much time to one song on a fifteen-minute radio program.

Bill learned the poem from a book his father ordered from an ad in the magazine *Youth's Companion.* Along with "Rye Whiskey," "Poor Rebel Soldier," and "Drunkard's Hiccoughs," "Jack O' Diamonds" is part of an extended family of songs with mix-and-match verses that show up under these and other titles.

Ben Jarrell, Herwin 75561 (as Jackson Young), Old Hat CD-1006 (1927)
Tex Ritter, "Rye Whiskey," Bear Family BCD 16260 (1932), Banner 32735, Conqueror 8144 (1933), Capitol 40084 (1945) (all three versions on Bear Family BCD 16260)
J.E. Mainer, "Drunkard's Hiccoughs," Bluebird B-8400, Montgomery Ward M-7881, JSP 77124 (1939)
Tex Ritter, Capitol F4217, T1292, ST1292 (1959)
Blue Sky Boys, Capitol T2483, ST2483, Arhoolie CD 9063 (1965)
Tommy Jarrell, County 723, CD-2734 (1971)

The Jealous Lover (Laws F1)

I have heard variations of this song as long as I can remember, but can't recall just how or when we adapted this version.

Vernon Dalhart, "The Jealous Lover of Lone Green Valley," Victor 19951 (1925), Edison 51749 (1926), Brunswick 143 (1927) (three versions)
David Miller, "Sweet Floetta," Gennett 6333, Challenge 386 (as Dan Kutter) (1927)

Blue Sky Boys, "Fair Eyed Ellen," Bluebird B-6808, Montgomery Ward M-7161, Bear Family BCD 15951 (1936)
Stanley Brothers, Rebel CD-2003 (1947), Rich-R'-Tone 435, Rounder CD 1110 (1948) (two versions)

Just a Little Talk with Jesus (Rev. Cleavant Derricks, 1937)

This was a very popular spiritual. We found it in one of many songbooks sent to us by Stamps-Baxter. The bass is essential in this selection, and I feel Earl does a good job with it. We probably started singing this in 1938 when Red Hicks joined us.

Blue Sky Boys, *Favorite Hymns and Folk Songs*, 8

Rev. Derricks (1910–1977), from Chattanooga, Tennessee, was a Baptist preacher and prominent choir director who also composed "We'll Soon Be Done with Troubles and Trials" and "When God Dips His Love in My Heart." "Just a Little Talk with Jesus" first appeared in *Harbor Bells No. 6* (1937).

Stamps Quartet, Vocalion 04329 (1938)
Blue Sky Boys, WGST Program 4, September 5, 1946
Bill Monroe, Bluegrass Classics 80 (1948)
Blue Sky Boys, WCYB (Bristol, VA, 1949), Copper Creek CCCD-0126
Stanley Brothers, Mercury 70718, Bear Family BCD 15681 (1955)
Reverend Cleavant Derricks and Family, Canaan CAS-9778 (1975)
Bill Monroe, MCA MCAD-10017, Bear Family BCD 16637 (1990)

Just a Strand from a Yellow Curl (J. Everett Buskirk, 1939)

We never knew this song until Curly Parker joined us. He had previously worked with the Holden Brothers who sang it frequently.

Ivan Tribe writes" "I'm almost sure that 'Strand from a Yellow Curl' came from the Buskirk Family. The song, called 'Treasures in Heaven,' appears on page 7 in *Old Fashioned Songs as sung by The Buskirk Family*, Folio *No. 1*, sub-titled *Original Hill Songs and Sacred Numbers*. At the bottom of the page is this citation: 'Copyright 1939 by J. Everett Buskirk.' He was the father of the clan." (email, July 12, 2011)

Blue Sky Boys, WGST Program 28, October 9, 1946, Copper Creek CCCD-0120
Mac Wiseman, Capitol T1800, ST1800, Bear Family BCD 15976 (1962)
Lester Flatt & Mac Wiseman, RCA LSP 4688, Bear Family BCD 15975 (1971)
Blue Sky Boys, Rounder 0052 (1975)

Just Because (Hubert A. Nelson-James D. Touchstone, 1929)

"Just Because" echoes the chord changes of "Washington and Lee Swing" (1910), as do "The Dummy Song" (1925), "I Saw Your Face in the Moon" (1936), and the traditional hymn "Meeting in the Air."

Nelstone's Hawaiians, Victor V-40273 (1929)
Lone Star Cowboys, Bluebird B-6052, RCA 8417-2 (1933)
Shelton Brothers, Decca 5100, 46008 (1935)
Frankie Yankovic, Columbia 38072 (1947)
Elvis Presley, RCA Victor LPM 1254, 82876-61205-2 (1954)
Blue Sky Boys, County 752 (1963)

Just One Way to the Pearly Gate (James Rowe-words, James D. Vaughan-music, 1920)

This is one of the first songs Earl and I sang together.

See note to "Gathering Buds."

Uncle Dave Macon, Bluebird B-5926, Bear Family BCD 15978 (1935)
Wade Mainer-Zeke Morris-Homer Sherrill, Bluebird B-6784, Montgomery Ward M-7132, JSP 77118 (1936)
Monroe Brothers, "The Old Crossroad," Bluebird B-6676, Montgomery Ward M-7087, Bear Family BCD 16399 (1936)
Blue Sky Boys, "Just One Way to the Gate," WGST Program 12, September 17, 1946, Copper Creek CCCD-0145
Blue Sky Boys, "Just One Way to the Gate," WGST Program 35, October 17, 1946

Just Tell Them That You Saw Me (Paul Dresser, 1895)

Bradley Kincaid is the first person I ever heard sing this. The only copy I can find is in a songbook published by Lonnie "Red" Anderson when he was broadcasting over WCKY in Covington, Kentucky, in the early thirties. I never heard of him until we went to Atlanta in 1936. At that time Red and his group were working for WSB on the Cross Road Follies.

Paul Dresser also wrote "I Believe It for My Mother Told Me So" (see entry).

George J. Gaskin, Edison 1565 (1895), Berliner 187 (1896)
Vernon Dalhart, Gennett 3143 (1925), Gennett 6512 (1928) (two versions)

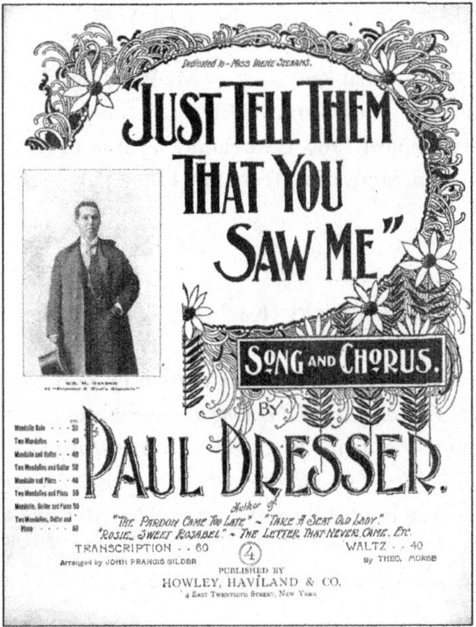

Courtesy of Lester S. Levy Collection of Sheet Music, Sheridan Libraries, Johns Hopkins University.

Uncle Dave Macon, Vocalion 15324, 5100, Bear Family BCD 15978 (1926)
Clayton McMichen's Georgia Wildcats, Decca 5765 (1939)
Blue Sky Boys, WCYB (Bristol, VA, 1949), Copper Creek CCCD-0125
Mac Wiseman, Dot DLP-25213, Bear Family BCD 15976 (1959)

Katie Dear (Laws G21, M4)

This was one of the first songs Lute Isenhour and I ever sang together. In later years, my mother told me I almost drove her up the walls singing the song so incessantly around the house. I suppose this was when I was first learning it.

Laws G21 ("Silver Dagger") and M4 ("Drowsy Sleeper") are variations of "Katie Dear," and the "go ask your mother" sequence is sometimes attached to "East Virginia Blues." Bill and Earl's version is close to the Callahan Brothers, as are those by the Louvin Brothers and Country Gentlemen.

Blue Sky Boys, *Favorite Hymns and Folk Songs*, 28

B.F. Shelton, "Oh Molly Dear," Victor V-40107, Bear Family BCD 16094 (1927)
Callahan Brothers, Banner 33103, Conqueror 9145 (1934)

Blue Sky Boys, Bluebird B-7661, Montgomery Ward M-7468, Bear Family BCD 15951 (1938)
Carter Family, "Who's That Knocking on My Window," Decca 5612, Montgomery Ward 8071, Bear Family BCD 15865 (1938)
Louvin Brothers, Capitol T769, Bear Family BCD 15561 (1956)
Country Gentlemen, Stereo Spectrum SDLP-613, Rebel SLP-1494, CD-7508 (1963)

Kentucky (Karl Davis, 1941)

This was sent to us by Steve Sholes. It was written by Karl Davis of the Karl and Harty team. I had never considered this song as one we could sing as Karl and Harty had sung it with somewhat of a calypso beat. I was surprised that Steve sent us a song of this type but I felt we should at least try to sing it. I reached the conclusion that if we would change the tempo and play a different mandolin style, we could work it into a suitable song. "Kentucky" [became] *the best-selling recording we ever made. Curly Parker played very good fiddle back-up and his efforts greatly helped.*

Karl & Harty, OKeh 06163, Columbia 38139, Bear Family BCD 17355 (1941, in the Bolick collection)
Blue Sky Boys, RCA Victor 20-2296, Bear Family BCD 15951 (1947)
Blue Sky Boys, WCYB (Bristol, VA, 1949), Copper Creek CCCD-0125
Louvin Brothers, Capitol T769, Bear Family BCD 15561 (1956)
Everly Brothers, Cadence CLP-3016, Ace CH75, Bear Family BCD 17355 (1958)
Carl Butler & Pearl, Columbia CS 8925 (1963)
Blue Sky Boys, Starday SLP-257, Gusto GT7-0549 (1963)
Osborne Brothers, Decca 74602, Bear Family BCD 15598 (1964)
Blue Sky Boys, Rounder 11536 (1964)

Kicking Mule (Billy Carter, 1879)

Carter (1834-1912) from New Orleans was a popular entertainer and banjo player who worked in minstrelsy up to a few years before his death.

Bradley Kincaid, "Let That Mule Go Aunk! Aunk!" Gennett 6944, Champion 15787 (as Dan Hughey), Supertone 9471 (1929)
Blue Sky Boys, audition disc (for WPTF, Raleigh, NC), November 20, 1939

Kneel at the Cross (Charles Ernest Moody, 1924)

Ernest Moody (1891–1977) wrote "Drifting Too Far from the Shore" (1923) and made lively string band records with the Georgia Yellow Hammers from 1927 to 1929. See the note to "Picture on the Wall" (1927), a song later made famous by the Carter Family.

Chuck Wagon Gang, ARC 7-04-37, Conqueror 8836, Bear Family BCD 17348 (1936)
Blue Sky Boys, Bluebird B-8843, Montgomery Ward M-8847, Bear Family BCD 15951 (1940)
Blue Sky Boys, WCYB (Bristol, VA, 1949)
Louvin Brothers, Rounder CD 1030 (1952), Capitol ST1834, Bear Family BCD 15561 (1961) (two versions)
Rose Maddox, Capitol T1437, ST1437, Bear Family BCD 15743 (1960)
Jim & Jesse, Epic BN 26107, Bear Family BCD 15716 (1964)
John Jackson, Arhoolie F1035, CD471 (1967)

The Knoxville Girl (Laws P35)

This is one of the first songs Earl and I sang together before we began singing over radio. It is in a songbook that Crazy Water Crystal Company allowed us to publish in 1936 when we were the Blue Ridge Hill Billies over WGST. I remember changing a few words and the structure of the song from its original version. I can usually tell if later artists that recorded the song use our version.

Blue Sky Boys, *Favorite Hymns and Folk Songs*, 32 (Story of the Knoxville Girl)

Old versions of this ballad were called "The Wexford Girl" (Ireland) and "Oxford Girl" (England). A broadside version from 1796 exists, but the song is older. The Blue Sky Boys record inspired numerous covers and it is one of the most popular ballads in country music.

Lester McFarland & Robert A. Gardner, Brunswick 110, Vocalion 5121 (1926)
Carter Family, "Never Let the Devil Get the Upper Hand of You," Decca 5479, Montgomery Ward 8027, Bear Family BCD 15865 (1937)
Blue Sky Boys, "Story of the Knoxville Girl," Bluebird B-7755, Montgomery Ward M-7327, Bear Family BCD 15951 (1937)
Cope Brothers, King 589 (1947)
Louvin Brothers, Capitol T769, Bear Family BCD 15561 (1956)
Wilburn Brothers, Decca 30787, DL5002 (1958)
Country Gentlemen, Stereo Spectrum SDLP-613, Rebel CD-7508 (1963)
Jim & Jesse, Old Dominion 498-07, Pinecastle PRC-9001 (1975)

The Last Letter (Rex Griffin)

We wouldn't do just old-time ballads and songs because we did have to keep up with numbers that were popular. In 1938 or early 1939 this was one of our most popular songs. As I recall, we were the first people that ever tried to sing it as a duet.

Rex Griffin's uncompromising 1937 suicide song became a hit when the Bolicks covered it in 1938. It has since become a country standard.

Rex Griffin, Decca 5383, Bear Family BCD 15911 (1937)
Blue Sky Boys, "My Last Letter," Bluebird B-7878, Montgomery Ward M-7568, Bear Family BCD 15951 (1938)
Sons of the Acadians, "La dernière lettre," Decca 17051 (1939)
Gene Autry, Conqueror 9800 (1940)
Pete Cassell, Majestic 6006, Mercury 6151, Old Homestead OH-4336 (1947)
Hank Snow, Thesaurus transcription 1671, Bear Family BCD 15488 (1951)
Willie Nelson, Liberty LST 7308, C2-8-28077-2 (1963)
Willie Nelson, RCA Victor LSP 3659, Bear Family BCD 15861 (1966)
Connie Smith, RCA Victor LSP 3889, Bear Family BCD 16814 (1967)
Merle Haggard, MCA 2267, Bear Family BCD 17250 (1976)

The Last Mile of the Way (Johnson Oatman Jr.-words, William Edie Marks-music, 1908)

FOR THE SON OF MAN SHALL COME IN THE GLORY OF HIS FATHER WITH HIS ANGELS AND THEN HE SHALL REWARD EVERY MAN ACCORDING TO HIS WORKS. —MATTHEW 16:27

Lester McFarland & Robert A. Gardner, Brunswick 276, Vocalion 5285 (1928)
Blue Sky Boys, Bluebird B-8597, Montgomery Ward M-8669, Bear Family BCD 15951 (1940)
Soul Stirrers, Specialty 921, SPCD-7052-25 (1955)

Last Night While Standing by My Window

See I Told the Stars About You

Let Me Be Your Salty Dog

The Morris Brothers altered Papa Charlie Jackson's original when they moved the line "Let me be your salty dog or I won't be your man at all" from a verse to the chorus. A "salty dog" reportedly is someone who slips out the back door while you're coming in the front.

Charlie Jackson, "Salty Dog Blues," Paramount 12236 (1924)
Morris Brothers, Bluebird B-7967, JSP 77118 (1938)
Morris Brothers, "Salty Dog Blues," Victor 20-1783 (1945), Vanguard VCD 121/22 (1963) (two versions)
Lester Flatt & Earl Scruggs, "Old Salty Dog Blues," Mercury 6396, Bear Family BCD 15472 (1950)
Blue Sky Boys, Rounder 0052 (1975)

Let the Lower Lights Be Burning (Philip P. Bliss, 1871)

This song can be found in old church hymnals. We heard it as far back as I can remember. We thought it was a pretty song and included it on our radio programs.

According to legend, a passenger boat on Lake Erie once crashed on the rocks while approaching a Cleveland harbor during a night storm. Though the lighthouse still functioned, two lights marking the channel to the dock had gone out. Philip Bliss heard the story from evangelist Dwight L. Moody, who moralized: "The Master will take care of the great lighthouse; let us keep the lower lights burning."

Harry Anthony & James F. Harrison, Edison 9272 (1906)
Jenkins Family, OKeh 45104 (1927)
Blue Sky Boys, WGST Program 38, October 23, 1946, Copper Creek CCCD-0145
Mac Wiseman, Dot DLP 25373, Bear Family BCD 15976 (1960)

Let's Not Sleep Again (Leslie York-Louis Buck, 1947)

This was sent to me by Steve Sholes.

York Brothers, "Let's Don't Sleep Again," King 669 (1947, in the Bolick collection)
Blue Sky Boys, RCA Victor 20-2755, Bear Family BCD 15951 (1947)

Lifeline *See* Throw Out the Lifeline

Life's Railway to Heaven (M. E. Abbey-words, Charles D. Tillman-music, 1890)

The first person I recall hearing sing this song was my father; it seemed to be one of his favorites. I'm sure he learned it while attending one of the singing schools; I don't think he missed any that were held at our church. I can't remember hearing him sing many songs other than those of a religious nature, but he told me that his mother used to sing some old ballads. However, I can never recall hearing my Grandmother Bolick sing any songs other than religious. My father did try to teach me the melody of "Lord Thomas" but I was never able to master it as he sang it, in what seemed a weird minor key. I first sang "Life's Railway to Heaven" as a solo. Earl and I sang it as a duet and, when Red Hicks joined us, we started to sing it as a trio. Although the song is commonly known now, one only heard it occasionally when we first started singing it. I have always liked it and think it is a pretty song.

The hymn is based on Will S. Hays's 1886 poem "The Faithful Engineer." Norm Cohen's railroad song collection, *The Long Steel Rail* (University of Illinois, 1981), documents popular train songs from 1828 onward, and observes that this one celebrates "the path of piety with the implicit warning that to stray from the route delineated by the steel rails of righteousness would lead elsewhere but heaven." In contrast, Nathaniel Hawthorne's short story "The Celestial Railroad" (1843) is skeptical of achieving salvation by substituting a comfortable modern train ride for the burdensome journey on foot described in John Bunyan's *The Pilgrim's Progress* (1678).

Ernest Thompson, Columbia 158-D (1924)
Blue Sky Boys, WGST Program 31, October 14, 1946
Blue Sky Boys, WGST Program 49, November 7, 1946, Copper Creek CCCD-0146
Bill Monroe, Decca DL 8769, Bear Family BCD 15423 (1958)
Seldom Scene, "Life Is Like a Mountain Railway," Sugar Hill SH-3709, CD-3926 (1979)

The Lightning Express (J. Fred Helf-E. P. Moran, 1898, as "Please Mister Conductor, Don't Put Me Off the Train")

A late 1890s vogue for tragic songs with railroad themes included "The East Bound Train" (a.k.a. "Going for a Pardon," 1896), two by Gussie L. Davis, "In the Baggage Coach Ahead" (1896), "He Is Coming to Us Dead" (1899), and this one. All became country standards by the 1920s. The list below excludes multiple versions by Vernon Dalhart made in 1925–26.

Byron G. Harlan, "Please Mister Conductor, Don't Put Me Off the Train," Edison 7219 (1899)

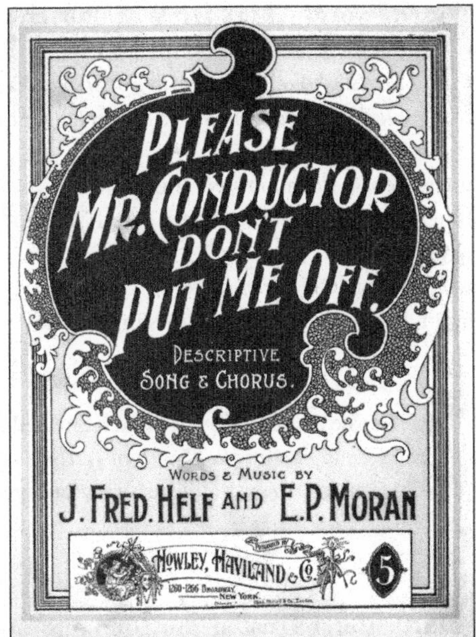

Courtesy of Lester S. Levy Collection of Sheet Music, Sheridan Libraries, Johns Hopkins University.

Ernest Thompson, Columbia 145-D (1924)
Lester McFarland and Robert A. Gardner, Brunswick 200, 326 (1927),
Bradley Kincaid, Melotone M12184, Vocalion 02683 (1931)
Blue Sky Boys, Bluebird B-8369, Montgomery Ward M-8414, Bear Family BCD 15951, BCD 17355 (1939)
Everly Brothers, Cadence CLP-3016, Ace CH75, Bear Family BCD 17355 (1958)

"The Lily of the Valley" (Charles W. Fry, 1881)

I AM THE ROSE OF SHARON AND THE LILY OF THE VALLEYS.
—SONG OF SOLOMON 2:1

This song is commonly known as "The Lily of the Valley."

The melody comes from Will S. Hays's "Little Old Log Cabin in the Lane" (1870).

Blue Sky Boys, "I've Found a Friend," Bluebird B-7933, Montgomery Ward M-7566, Bear Family BCD 15951 (1938)
Blue Sky Boys, "I Have Found a Friend," WGST Program 1, September 2, 1946, Copper Creek CCCD-0146
Willie Nelson, Arrival 719-4 (1992)

Little Bessie (R.-words (1852), arr. W. T. Porter, ca. 1875)

I learned this song from Lute Isenhour. There are five or six verses we weren't able to include on the recording. Eli didn't want our songs to run longer than 3 1/2 minutes.

Buell Kazee, Brunswick 215, Vocalion 5231 (1928)
Blue Sky Boys, Bluebird B-8017, Montgomery Ward M-7470, Bear Family BCD 15951 (1938)
Stanley Brothers, Columbia CK 86747 (1956)
Country Gentlemen, Folkways FA2410, Smithsonian Folkways CD 40022 (1961)

The original poem, "Little Bessie and the Way in Which She Fell Asleep," appeared in Samuel Irenaeus Prime's *Thoughts on the Death of Little Children* (New York: Anson D.F. Randolph, 1852, 89–91), an anthology of essays, prayers, and poems for grieving families.

Little Gal, I Trusted You Too Long (Josephine Friedlinger-Ben Shelhammer Jr.-Lew Mel)

This was sent to us by one of the many publishing companies that sent us songs, especially after World War II. Most wanted us to record their songs and offered part of the royalties. Usually we stayed clear of these offers. I don't remember how much fan mail we received for this song and I always considered it an average number.

Blue Sky Boys, WGST Program 7, September 10, 1946
Blue Sky Boys, WGST Program 47, November 5, 1946, Copper Creek CCCD-0145

Little Joe *See* The Death of Little Joe

Little Mother of the Hills (The Vagabonds-Herald, Dean and Curt, 1932)

The Vagabonds were a polished vocal trio that worked on the *Opry* in the early 1930s. Their best-known songs included "When It's Lamp Lighting Time in the Valley," "Ninety-Nine Years," and "Red River Valley."

The Vagabonds, Old Cabin (no number, 1933), Bluebird B-5197 (1933) (two versions)
Blue Sky Boys, RCA Victor 21-0108, Bear Family BCD 15951 (1949)
Ray & Ina Patterson, County 737 (1973)

The Little Paper Boy *See* Paper Boy

Lonely Tombs (B. F. White, 1847 / William Walker, 1866)

This is a song we sang early in our career. Our recording wasn't too good, as we hadn't sung it in years and had little time to rehearse it. It was written by William M. Golden, who wrote "A Beautiful Life," which we always sang as a trio. A notation beneath the title reads, "Composed after a walk through the city of the dead."

Origins of this hymn are unclear. It has been attributed to B. F. (Benjamin Franklin) White, whose "Lone Pilgrim" in *The Southern Harmony* (1847) has a similar first verse, and to William Walker in *The Christian Harmony* (1866). As Bill noted, it was later claimed by William M. Golden, who called it "Oh, Those Tombs."

Wade Mainer, Bluebird B-7424, Montgomery Ward M-7480, JSP 77124 (1937)
J.E. Mainer's Mountaineers, King 661, Gusto GT7-2206-2 (1946)
Stanley Brothers, Rebel CD-2003 (1947), King 698, Gusto GT7-2207-2 (1959) (two versions)
Blue Sky Boys, "Oh, Those Tombs," WCYB (Bristol, VA, 1949), Copper Creek CCCD-0125
Blue Sky Boys, "Oh, Those Tombs," Capitol T2483, ST2483, Arhoolie CD-9063 (1965)

Lonesome Road Blues

This is a song that I heard as far back as I can remember. I can't recall playing or singing it previous to Leslie [Keith's] *rendition.*

Also known as "I'm Going Down the Road Feeling Bad," this song and variants of it have been recorded hundreds of times. Henry Whitter's first version was instrumental; he sang on the second.

Henry Whitter, OKeh 40015 (1923)
Henry Whitter, "Goin' Down the Road Feeling Bad," OKeh 40169 (1924)
Blue Sky Boys, WCYB (Bristol, VA, 1949), Copper Creek CCCD-0126
Amber Sisters, Capitol 2289 (1952)
Bill Monroe, Decca DL 4080, Bear Family BCD 15529 (1960)

The Longest Train I Ever Saw / In the Pines

For a long time I confused this song with "In the Pines," that was supposedly written by Clayton McMichen. The tunes are similar and the chorus almost the same, but the verses are different. We generally sang this song as a trio but occasionally as a duet.

Bill's confusion is understandable since no two versions of this song are identical. Folk song scholars Norm Cohen and the late Judith McCulloh have written at length about its numerous variants.

Dock Walsh, "In the Pines," Columbia 15094-D, Old Hat CD-1006 (1926)
Tenneva Ramblers, "The Longest Train I Ever Saw," Victor 20861, Bear Family BCD 16094 (1927)
Clayton McMichen (as Bob Nichols), "Grave in the Pines, Columbia 15590-D (1930)
Clayton McMichen & His Georgia Wildcats, "In the Pines," Decca 5448 (1937)
Bill Monroe, "In the Pines," Bluebird B-8861, Bear Family BCD 16399 (1941)
Blue Sky Boys, "The Longest Train I Ever Saw," WGST Program 52, November 12, 1946, Copper Creek CCCD-0120
Lead Belly, "Black Girl (In the Pines)," Folkways FP4, Smithsonian Folkways CD 40044 (1947)
Bill Monroe, "In the Pines," Decca 28416, Bear Family BCD 15423 (1952)
Louvin Brothers, "In the Pines," Capitol T769, Bear Family BCD 15561 (1956)

Lord Be with Us—Amen (Karl Davis)

This recording features Leslie Keith singing lead while Earl sings bass and Bill sings tenor. Though the Blue Sky Boys featured vocal trios on broadcasts and personal appearances, this is the only time three voices are heard on a Blue Sky Boys Victor record.

Blue Sky Boys, RCA Victor 21-0318, Bear Family BCD 15951 (1950)

Lorena

We learned this from a Mac and Bob songbook published in the early thirties.

Country Music Sources attributes this slavery lament to one Louis Staab, with no date or indication of where it first appeared. Another song called "Lorena" was composed by Rev. H. D. L. Webster (words) and the unrelated J. P. Webster (music), and published in 1858. It became one of the best loved songs of troops fighting on both sides in the Civil War.

Mac & Bob's WLS Book of Songs (1931), 12

Smyth County Ramblers, "Way Down in Alabama," Victor V-40144, Old Hat CD-1001 (1928)

Carter Family, "No More the Moon Shines On Lorena," Victor 23523, Bear Family BCD 15865 (1930)

Renfro Valley Boys (John Lair, Karl Davis, Harty Taylor), "Loreena," Paramount 3321 (1931)

Delmore Brothers, "Lorena, the Slave," Bluebird B-5925, JSP 7727 (1935)

Blue Sky Boys, "On the Old Plantation," Bluebird B-8128, Bear Family BCD 15951 (1937)

Blue Sky Boys, WGST Program 38, October 23, 1946, Copper Creek CCCD-0145

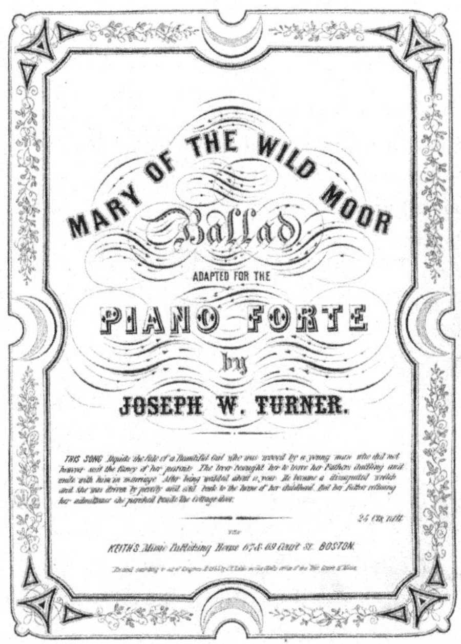

Courtesy of Lester S. Levy Collection of Sheet Music, Sheridan Libraries, Johns Hopkins University.

Mary of the Wild Moor (Laws P21)

We learned this song from a songbook sent to us by M.M. Cole. The author is listed as J. W. Turner. We recorded it on February 5, 1940, at the Kimball House in Atlanta, Georgia. I can't say this song was extremely popular, but we did receive quite a number of requests for it. Since World War II it has been recorded by other singers.

"Mary of the Wild Moor" was known in London, possibly as long ago as the 1820s, where it appeared on broadsides, song lyrics printed on paper sheets and sold by street vendors. An 1845 sheet music cover credits Joseph W. Turner with a piano arrangement, implying that the otherwise uncredited song was already considered traditional. It differs little from the Bolicks:

One night when the wind it blew cold
Blew bitter across the wild moor,
Young Mary she came with her child
Wand'ring home to her own father's door
Crying, "Father, oh pray let me in
Take pity on me, I implore
Or the child at my bosom will die
From the winds that blow 'cross the wild moor"
1845

'Twas on one cold wintry night
And the wind blew across the wild moor
As poor Mary came wandering home with her child
'Til she came to her own father's door
"Oh father, dear father," she cried
"Come down and open the door
Or the child in my arms it will perish and die
By the winds that blow across the wild moor"
BLUE SKY BOYS

Blue Sky Boys, Bluebird B-8446, Montgomery Ward M-8667, Bear Family BCD 15951 (1940)
Blue Sky Boys, WGST Program 25, October 4, 1946
Blue Sky Boys, WGST Program 37, October 22, 1946, Copper Creek CCCD-0146
Louvin Brothers, Capitol T769, Bear Family BCD 15561 (1956)
Mac Wiseman, Rural Rhythm RRMW 158, Bear Family BCD 16736 (1966)
Ray & Ina Patterson, County 737 (1973)
Dolly Parton, Columbia CK 66123, Music Mill 70050 (1994)
Johnny Cash, Columbia CK 69691 (2000)

Midnight on the Stormy Deep (Laws M1)

Steh ich in finsterer Mitternacht
So einsam auf der stillen Wacht,
So denk ich an mein fernes Lieb,
Ob mir auch treu und hold verblieb

Als ich zur Fahne fort gemüßt,
Hat sie so herzlich mich geküßt,
Mit Bändern meinen Hut geschmückt
Und weinend mich ans Herz gedrückt.

Sie liebt mich noch, sie ist mir gut,
Drum bin ich froh und wohlgemut.
Mein Herz schlägt warm in kalter Nacht,
Wenn es ans treue Lieb gedacht.

Jetzt bei der Lampe mildem Schein
Gehst du wohl in dein Kämmerlein,
Und schickst dein Dankgebet zum Herrn
Auch für den Liebsten in der Fern.

Doch wenn du traurig bist und weinst,
mich von Gefahr umrungen meinst,
Sei ruhig, bin in Gottes Hut,
Er liebt ein treu Soldatenblut.

Die Glocke schlägt, bald naht die Rund
und löst mich ab zu dieser Stund'.
Schlaf wohl im stillen Kämmerlein
und denk' in deinen Träumen mein.
—"Soldatenliebe," the original poem by Wilhelm Knauff, 1824

I'm pretty sure I learned this song from hearing Mac and Bob sing it over WLS.

Mac & Bob's WLS Book of Songs (1931), 42

An online article by Armin Hadamer and Susanne Koehler, "Warum Bill Monroe ein deutsches Volkslied sang: 'Midnight On The Stormy Deep' und sein Ursprung," traces "Midnight's" origins to the 1824 poem "Soldatenliebe" by Wilhelm Hauff (1802–1827), later known as "Die Schildwacht" or "Treue Liebe." After being set to music by Friedrich Silcher it was translated and published (minus a verse) by William Howitt in *The Student Life of Germany . . . Containing Nearly Forty of the Most Famous Student Songs* (Philadelphia, 1842).

It was reprinted in *War-Songs for Freemen, Dedicated to the Army of the United States* (1862), edited by Francis James Child, who later compiled *The English and Scottish Popular Ballads* (1882–1898). Paolo Dettwiler, editor-in-chief of the magazine *Bluegrass Europe,* observes that the anonymous author of "Midnight on the Stormy Deep" construed "deep" to mean "nautical," thus transferring Hauff's night guard to a naval post and changing the song considerably after the second verse (email, December 23, 2010).

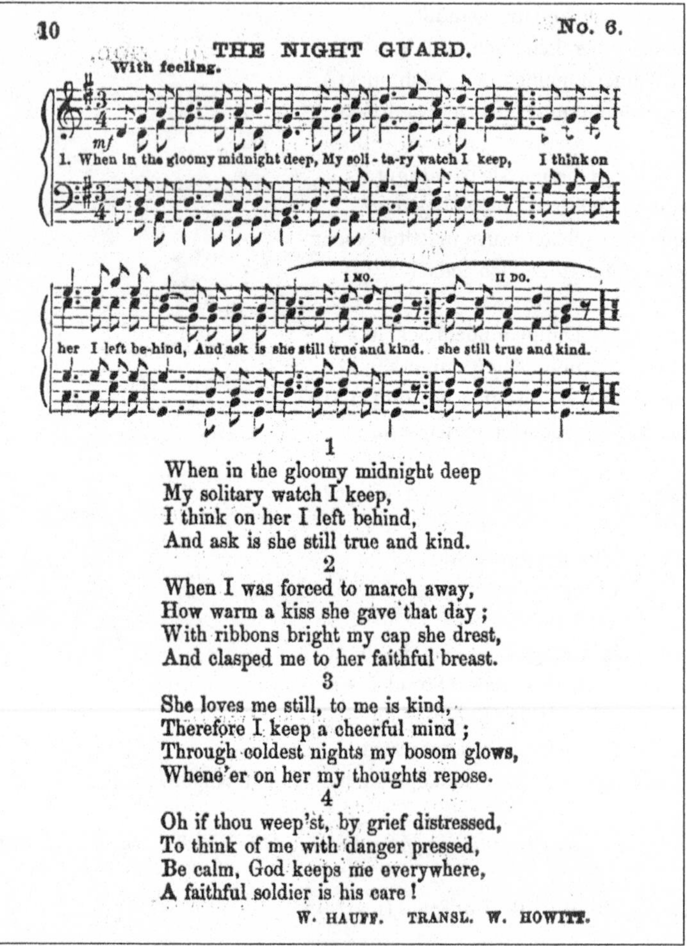
10 No. 6.

THE NIGHT GUARD.

With feeling.

mf

1. When in the gloomy midnight deep, My soli - ta-ry watch I keep, I think on

I MO. II DO.

her I left be-hind, And ask is she still true and kind. she still true and kind.

1

When in the gloomy midnight deep
My solitary watch I keep,
I think on her I left behind,
And ask is she still true and kind.

2

When I was forced to march away,
How warm a kiss she gave that day;
With ribbons bright my cap she drest,
And clasped me to her faithful breast.

3

She loves me still, to me is kind,
Therefore I keep a cheerful mind;
Through coldest nights my bosom glows,
Whene'er on her my thoughts repose.

4

Oh if thou weep'st, by grief distressed,
To think of me with danger pressed,
Be calm, God keeps me everywhere,
A faithful soldier is his care!

W. HAUFF. TRANSL. W. HOWITT.

"The Night Guard," William Howitt's 1842 translation of "Soldatenliebe" as it appeared in *War-Songs for Freemen* (1862).

McFarland and Gardner's 1931 text is nearly identical to the Blue Sky Boys version. "The Trail to Mexico" is a cowboy song based on "Midnight on the Stormy Deep." The Blue Sky Boys performed them both.

Carl Schlegel, "Steh' ich in finst'rer Mitternacht," Victor 69094 (1916)
Lester McFarland and Robert A. Gardner, Vocalion 5125 (1926)
Ernest Stoneman, Irma Frost & Eck Dunford, Country Music Foundation CMF-011, Bear Family BCD 16094 (1927)
Leroy Roberson, "Early Early in the Spring," Victor 23522 (1930)
Blue Sky Boys, "Midnight on the Stormy Sea," Bluebird B-6480, Montgomery Ward M-5033, Bear Family BCD 15951 (1936)

Blue Sky Boys, WGST Program 29, October 10, 1946
Blue Sky Boys, "It Was Midnight on the Stormy Deep," Rounder 11536 (1964)
Bill Monroe, Decca DL 74896, Bear Family BCD 15529 (1966)

Midnight Special

Lead Belly's versions of this song have circulated among folk singers since the 1930s. In country music the tune also fits "My Bucket's Got a Hole in It" and Faron Young's 1954 hit "If You Ain't Lovin." Carl Sandburg's 1927 collection *The American Songbag* includes two versions of "Midnight Special."

Dave Cutrell with McGinty's Oklahoma Cowboy Band, "Pistol Pete's Midnight Special," OKeh 45057 (1926)
Wilmer Watts & Frank Wilson, "Walk Right in Belmont," Paramount 3019, Old Hat CD-1007 (1927)
Sam Collins, "Midnight Special Blues," Gennett 6307 (1927)
Frenchy's String Band, "Texas and Pacific Blues," Columbia 14387-D, Yazoo 2024 (1928)
Lead Belly, Library of Congress 124A1, Elektra EKL 301/2, Rounder 1044 (1934)
Delmore Brothers, "Midnite Special," King 514, Ace CDCHD 1074 (1945)
Wilma Lee & Stoney Cooper, "Big Midnight Special," Hickory 1098, LPM-100, Bear Family BCD 16751 (1958)
Blue Sky Boys, Capitol T2483, ST2483, Arhoolie CD-9063 (1965)

Mommie, Will My Doggie Understand? (Jim Eanes)

Darnell Miller with the Swing Kings, Starday 422 (1959)
Dorsey Dixon, Bear Family BCD 16817 (1961)
Blue Sky Boys, Starday SLP-257, Gusto GT7-0549 (1963)
Jim Eanes, Leather (unissued, 1979)

Mother Went Her Holiness Way *See* The Holiness Mother

Mountain Dew (Scott Wiseman-Bascom Lamar Lunsford)

We used Scott Wiseman's version of this song. We often used a faster selection to change the format of our program. Most artists sing it as a solo; we tried to be different by singing the refrain as a trio. There are more verses but we seldom sang more than three.

The original Lunsford song described a lawyer defending a moonshiner in a courtroom trial. Scotty Wiseman dropped the courtroom narrative, modified the chorus, and wrote new comic verses about his brew's potency.

Bascom Lamar Lunsford, Brunswick 219, Smithsonian Folkways CD 40082 (1928)
Lulu Belle & Scotty, Vocalion 04690, Conqueror 9249 (1939)
Grandpa Jones, King 624, Gusto GT7-0880 (1947)
Blue Sky Boys, WCYB (Bristol, VA, 1949), Copper Creek CCCD-0125

The Murder of the Lawson Family (Walter Smith, 1930, Laws F35)

On Christmas Day 1929, Charlie Lawson murdered his wife and all but one of their seven children in their Lawsonville, North Carolina, home before shooting himself in the woods nearby. Evidence uncovered in the 1980s revealed an incestuous relationship between Charlie and his oldest daughter Marie, 17, who was pregnant at her death. The Carolina Buddies version of the song features its composer, Walter "Kid" Smith. Two histories have been inspired by the murders and the song:

M. Bruce Jones with Trudy J. Smith, *White Christmas, Bloody Christmas*. Trinity, NC: UpWords Publications, 1990.

Trudy J. Smith, *The Meaning of Our Tears: The Lawson Family Murders of Christmas Day 1929*. Asheboro, NC: DTS Group, 2006.

Carolina Buddies, Columbia 15537-D, Bear Family BCD 15521 (1930)
Cranford and Thompson, Champion 16261, Tompkins Square TSQ 2219 (1931)
Stanley Brothers, "The Story of the Lawson Family," Columbia CK 86747 (1956), King 772, Gusto GT7-2202-2 (1960), Copper Creek ST-CD-5003 (1961) (three versions)
Country Gentlemen, "The Story of Charlie Lawson," Folkways FA 2409, Smithsonian Folkways CD 40004 (1960)
Blue Sky Boys, "The Lawson Family Tragedy," Rounder 0052 (1975)

My God, Why Have You Forsaken Me? (Dorsey Dixon)

ABOUT THE NINTH HOUR JESUS CRIED WITH A LOUD VOICE, SAYING, "ELI, ELI, LAMA SABACHTHANI?" THAT IS TO SAY, "MY GOD, MY GOD, WHY HAST THOU FORSAKEN ME?" —MATTHEW 27:46

The Dixon Brothers recorded many original Dorsey Dixon songs in the 1930s. After the Dixons' record making stopped in 1938, Dorsey continued to write. Bill befriended Dorsey in the early 1960s and brought several of his songs to the 1963 Starday sessions.

Blue Sky Boys, Starday SLP-269, Gusto GT7-0549 (1963)

My Last Letter *See* The Last Letter

My Lord, What a Morning

It is a song that Earl and I heard from early childhood. Down through the years we added many verses to it, and I'm sure we know more than the ones presented here.

This is associated with Marian Anderson (1897–1993), who alternated old spirituals with German *Lieder* in concerts throughout her life. *My Lord, What a Morning* is the title of her 1956 autobiography.

Marian Anderson, Victor 19560, Eklipse EKR CD 26 (1924)
Pace Jubilee Singers, Victor 20225 (1926)
Blue Sky Boys, "When the Stars Begin to Fall," Bluebird B-7472, Montgomery Ward M-7471, Bear Family BCD 15951 (1938)
Blue Sky Boys, "When the Stars Begin to Fall," WGST Program 19, September 26, 1946, Copper Creek CCCD-0146
Marian Anderson, RCA Victor 10-1430, 09026-63306-2 (1947)
Harry Belafonte, RCA Victor LSP 2022 (1959)

My Main Trial Is Yet to Come (Pee Wee King-J. L. Frank)

Joseph Lee (J. L.) Frank (1900–1952) was a music agent and promoter who helped reshape the *Grand Ole Opry* in the 1930s by placing his son-in-law Pee Wee King's Golden West Cowboys on the show in 1937 and bringing Roy Acuff on board in 1938, though neither artist recorded this song. As Bill Bolick recounted (p. 86), Frank tried to recruit the Blue Sky Boys in 1947.

Cope Brothers, King 670 (1947)
Hank Williams, Mercury 34 536 084-2 (1949)
Blue Sky Boys, WCYB (Bristol, VA, 1949)
Jimmie Osborne, King 1231 (1953)
Stanley Brothers, King 698, Gusto GT7-2202-2 (1959)
Blue Sky Boys, Rounder 0052 (1975)

My Sweetheart Mountain Rose *See* Sweetheart Mountain Rose

The New Golden Rule (Karl Davis, 1949)

Blue Sky Boys, RCA Victor 21-0318, Bear Family BCD 15951 (1950)

Nine Pound Hammer

The first time I can really recall singing it was in 1942 when I was in the armed forces. A fellow from Del Rio, Tennessee, William Finchum, played the guitar and sang some. Occasionally we would try to sing it together. He knew several verses and I knew several more. Piecing them together, we seemed to make a pretty good version.

Al Hopkins & His Buckle Busters, Brunswick 177 (1927)
G.B. Grayson & Henry Whitter, Victor V-40105, County CD-3517 (1928)
Monroe Brothers, Bluebird B-6422, Montgomery Ward M-4747, Bear Family BCD 16399 (1936)
Merle Travis, Capitol 48000, 15124, 2176, T891, Bear Family BCD 15636, BCD 15637 (1946)
Blue Sky Boys, WCYB (Bristol, VA, 1949), Copper Creek CCCD-0126
Dick Curless, Event 4274, Bear Family BCD 15882 (1957)
Country Gentlemen, Starday 3510-2-2, Gusto GT7-3510-2-2 (1959)

No Disappointment in Heaven *See* There's No Disappointment in Heaven

No Home *See* No Place to Pillow My Head

No One to Welcome Me Home (Joe W. Earls, 1927)

You can find this song in early hymnbooks with shaped notes. The version Earl and I sang was pieced together from parts I had heard by different people.

Carver Boys, Paramount 3182 (1929)
Georgia Yellow Hammers, Victor 23542 (1929)
Blue Sky Boys, Bluebird B-6669, Montgomery Ward M-7158, Bear Family BCD 15951 (1936)

Delmore Brothers, "No One," Bluebird B-6998, Montgomery Ward M-7150 (1937)
Rambling Rangers, "No One," Vocalion 04949 (1938)
Hank Williams, Mercury 314 536 084-2 (1949), Time Life 80031-D (1951) (two versions)

No Place to Pillow My Head (Doc Hopkins, 1936)

This one was sent to us by M.M. Cole. The original title is "No Place to Pillow My Head." Eli changed it as he did many of our songs.

The Lester Flatt and Bill Monroe versions below each credit the song to themselves.

Karl & Harty, ARC 6-04-61, Conqueror 8626 (1936)
Blue Sky Boys, "No Home," Bluebird B-7311, Montgomery Ward M-7323, Bear Family BCD 15951 (1937)
(Charlie) Monroe's Boys, "No Home, No Place to Pillow My Head," Bluebird B-7922, Montgomery Ward M-7523, Bear Family BCD 16808 (1938)
Blue Sky Boys, WGST Program 16, September 23, 1946
Lester Flatt, RCA APL1-0131, Bear Family BCD 15975 (1973)
Bill Monroe, MCA 2251, Bear Family BCD 15606 (1976)

Oh, Marry in Time (Child 2)

The ballad scholar Francis James Child called this "The Elfin Knight." Like fairy tales, some ancient songs were inspired by riddles and impossible tasks. In England, it first appeared in print around 1670 and remains well known there. Bill learned it in 1942 from a Tennesseean named Brockett while both were serving with the Army in the South Pacific. More recent songs enumerate unlikely events that either strengthen or discourage true love. "Then I'll Stop Loving You" (Jim Reeves, the Browns), "The Twelfth of Never" (Johnny Mathis, the Browns), "Till the End of the World Rolls 'Round" (Flatt and Scruggs), "If Loving You Is Wrong" (Hank Thompson), and "Then I'll Stop Going for You" (Jim and Jesse) are meant to reassure. But "Maybe I'll Loan You a Dime" (Memphis Slim), "My Wife Has Gone to the Country" (Kelly Harrell), "Not Until Then" (Butterbeans and Susie), and "That's When I'll Come Back to You" (Louis and Lil Armstrong) are more like "Oh, Marry in Time," elaborate brush-offs with wishes that will be granted only when impossible things occur.

Blue Sky Boys, Capitol T2483, ST2483, Arhoolie CD 9063 (1965)
Simon & Garfunkel, "Scarborough Fair/Canticle," Columbia CS 9363 (1966)

Oh, Mary, Don't You Weep

There are five or six more verses that go with this song but [on broadcasts] *we didn't have time to sing that many.*

Fisk University Male Quartette, "Oh Mary, Mary, Don't You Weep, Don't You Mourn," Columbia A1895, Archeophone ARCH 5020 (1915)
Georgia Yellow Hammers, "Mary, Don't You Weep," Victor 20928 (1927)
Blue Sky Boys, "Oh, Sister Mary, Don't You Weep," WGST Program 51, November 11, 1946, Copper Creek CCCD-0120
Poplin Family, Melodeon MLP 7331 (1965)

Oh, Those Tombs *See* Lonely Tombs

An Old Account Was Settled (Frank Monford Graham, 1905)

See note to "Crying Holy Unto the Lord."

Perry Kim & Einar Nyland, "The Old Account Settled Long Ago," Victor 20868 (1926)
Norfolk Jubilee Quartette, "An Old Account Was Settled Long Ago," Paramount 12499, Broadway 5051 (1927)
Frank Welling & John McGhee, "The Old Account Was Settled Long Ago," Brunswick 258 (1928), Conqueror 7978 (1930) (two versions)
Blue Sky Boys, Bluebird B-6901, Montgomery Ward M-7161, Bear Family BCD 15951 (1936)
Johnny Cash, "The Old Account," Columbia CS 8125, Bear Family BCD 15562 (1959), Columbia CK 66017, C2K 75214 (1969) (two versions)
Wade & Julia Mainer, Old Homestead OHS-90016, OHCD-70068 (1973)
Jim & Jesse, "An Old Account Settled," Old Dominion 498-12, Pinecastle PRC-9001 (1979)

Old Camp Meeting Days (Adger McDavid Pace, 1934)

We never sang it prior to World War II. I have it in several different religious songbooks. We sang it as a trio.

Brown's Ferry Four, "Old Camp Meeting," King 750, 3506-2-2 (1946)
Blue Sky Boys, "Old Time Camp Meeting," WNAO audition disc, January 28. 1949

Blue Sky Boys, "Old Time Camp Meeting," WCYB (Bristol, VA, 1949), Copper Creek CCCD-0125
Carl Smith, Columbia CL 959, Bear Family BCD 15849 (1956)
Jim & Jesse, Epic BN 26107, Bear Family BCD 15716 (1964)
Doc Watson, "Old Camp Meeting Time," Vanguard VSD-79276, VSD4-155/58 (1968)
Mickey Gilley, Astro RH-81078 (1977)

Old Fashioned Meeting (Herbert W. Buffum, 1922)

I can recall Earl and I singing it as early as 1936 but can't associate it to any other artists. I believe Mr. Buffum is the author of "When I Take My Vacation in Heaven," a song that was popular in the thirties. We recorded it because we thought it was a good song that had never been previously recorded.

Blue Sky Boys, Bluebird B-7472, Bear Family BCD 15951 (1938)

Old Time Camp Meeting *See* Old Camp Meeting Days

On the Old Plantation *See* Lorena

On the Sunny Side of Life (Tillit S. Teddlie-words, J. Wesley Watts-music, 1918)

This was taken from an old First Church of God hymnal [Reformation Glory, 1923]. *It was one of the first songs Earl and I ever sang together. It was one of our most popular religious songs and we were still receiving requests for it when we quit entertaining.*

The Bolicks and Steve Sholes quarreled about songs to be recorded at their RCA session in Nashville on March 26, 1950. Sholes's working relationship with the music publisher Hill and Range involved pitching songs to RCA artists but, as Bill states elsewhere, he didn't always care for them. Six of the eight songs from the Bolicks' 1950 RCA session were licensed by Hill and Range. To placate them, Sholes invited them to record a new version of their first hit. It was their last song for the company they'd been associated with for fifteen years.

As we were packing our instruments to leave, I told Earl that in all probability we would never record for RCA again. Our contract was not renewed, partly because we were no longer entertaining when [it] *expired.*

Blue Sky Boys, "Sunny Side of Life," Bluebird B-6457, Montgomery Ward M-5029, Bear Family BCD 15951 (1936)
Blue Sky Boys, WGST Program 45, November 1, 1946, Copper Creek CCCD-0145
Ray & Ina Patterson, "Sunny Side of Life," Gold Star 1370 (1949)
Blue Sky Boys, "Sunny Side of Life," RCA Victor 21-0370, Bear Family BCD 15951 (1950)
Country Gentlemen, Folkways FA 2411, Smithsonian Folkways CD 40133 (1962), Rebel SLP 1497, CD-4002 (1970) (two versions)

One Cold Winter's Eve *See* The Dying Mother

Courtesy of Library of Congress, Music Division.

Only a Tramp (Dr. Addison D. Crabtre, 1877)

This sentimental classic moralized about indifference to poverty. It was recorded first by Uncle Pete and Louise, who followed the original closely. After Grady and Hazel Cole transformed it into a biblical allegory, Molly O'Day set their text to a modified melody and it became a career hit for her. The Blue Sky Boys learned the Coles' version from their record.

Uncle Pete & Louise, Conqueror 8342, Yazoo 2067 (1933)
Grady & Hazel Cole, "The Tramp on the Street," Bluebird B-8262, RCA 2100-2-R (1939, in the Bolick collection)

Cumberland Mountain Folks (with Molly O'Day), "The Tramp on the Street," Columbia 37559, 20187, Bear Family BCD 15565 (1946)
Wilma Lee Cooper, "Tramp on the Street," Rich-R'-Tone 424, Bear Family BCD 16751 (1947)
Bud Messner & the Skyline Boys, "Tramp On the Street," Banner B-566 (1947)
Hank Williams, "A Tramp on the Street," Mercury 314 517 862-2 (1949)
Joan Baez, "Tramp on the Street," Vanguard VSD 79700 (1961)
Blue Sky Boys, "The Tramp on the Street," Rounder 0052 (1975)

Only Let Me Walk with Thee (Johnson Oatman Jr.-words, James D. Vaughan-music, 1915)

Our father heard someone sing it, and thought it would be a good song for us. I managed to find the title in a James D. Vaughan songbook but the page had been removed.

Blue Sky Boys, Bluebird B-6669, Montgomery Ward M-7158, Bear Family BCD 15951 (1936)
Blue Sky Boys, WGST Program 11, September 16, 1946

Only One Step More

Origins of this hymn are obscure. The 1930s radio producer and songwriter John Lair made a statement that appears online and falls just short of an outright claim of authorship: "In my boyhood I knew many old mountain people who led a pretty hard life and, as they neared the end of it, looked forward to that hour when they would take that one last step from earth to heaven with the hope of better things to come that helped them over the hard places. I tried to write a song for them, in their own words expressing their philosophy of life and what lay ahead at the end of the long, long way. So far as I know this had never been published in any form except in hymnbook collections, some but now all of which were put out by Stamps-Baxter [*sic*]. None of their versions are exactly like the original which I was the first to get into print."

Blue Sky Boys, *Favorite Hymns and Folk Songs*, 10 (arrangement by J. R. Baxter Jr. from 1946)

Girls of the Golden West, Vocalion 04053, Conqueror 8997, Columbia 37758, 20335 (1938)
Prairie Ramblers, Vocalion 04796, Conqueror 9264, Columbia 37762, 20339 (1939)
Blue Sky Boys, Bluebird B-8552, Montgomery Ward M-8670, Bear Family BCD 15951 (1940)

Blue Sky Boys, WGST program transcription (unnumbered), December 18, 1947
Blue Sky Boys, WCYB (Bristol, VA, 1949)
Virginia Trio, "One Step More," Kentucky 517 (1951)
Hee Haw Gospel Quartet, *Hee Haw* 1981, Time Life 210792 (1981)

Paper Boy (Johnnie Wright-Jack Anglin-Eddie Hill)

Authorship claims for "Paper Boy" are in conflict. The Blue Sky Boys' 1949 record credits Johnnie Wright and Jack Anglin. Johnnie and Jack's 1947 disc cited Johnnie Wright, Jack Anglin, and Eddie Hill. Bill thought it was composed by Jim Anglin (Jack's brother), but Johnnie Wright told Eddie Stubbs that "the first people I ever heard sing that song was the Blue Sky Boys way back before I got into the business. We learned it from listening to them on one of their radio shows."

Johnnie & Jack, Apollo 154, Bear Family BCD 15553 (1947)
Blue Sky Boys, RCA Victor 21-0034, Bear Family BCD 15951 (1949)
Hank Williams, "Little Paper Boy," Mercury 314 536 081-2 (1949)
Jim & Jesse, "The Little Paper Boy," Epic BN 26074, Bear Family BCD 15716 (1963)

A Picture on the Wall (Bud Landress-words, Phil Reeve & Charles Ernest Moody-music, 1927)

Georgia Yellow Hammers, Victor 20943 (1927)
Carter Family, Victor 23636, Bluebird B-5185, Montgomery Ward M-4228, Bear Family BCD 15865 (1932)
Blue Sky Boys, Bluebird B-8646, Montgomery Ward M-8845, Bear Family BCD 15951 (1940)
Ray & Ina Patterson, County 737 (1973)
Maybelle Carter, Columbia KC-33084 (1974)

Pictures from Life's Other Side (Charles E. Baer, 1896)

The Smith's Sacred Singers record was a best seller in the 1920s.

Smith's Sacred Singers, Columbia 15090-D (1926).
Old Southern Sacred Singers, "'Tis a Picture From Life's Other Side," Brunswick 115 (1926, in the Bolick collection)

Sid Harkreader & Grady Moore, Paramount 3024, Broadway 8055 (as Harkins & Moran) (1927, in the Bolick collection)
Blue Sky Boys, Bluebird B-8646, Montgomery Ward M-8845, Bear Family BCD 15951 (1940)
Woody Guthrie, Folkways FA 2484, Smithsonian Folkways CD 40112 (1944)
Luke the Drifter (Hank Williams), MGM 11120, Mercury 314 536 081-2 (1951)
Seldom Scene, Rebel SLP-1561, CD-1561, CD-7516 (1976)

Poor Boy (Laws I-4)

Bill sang this with Lute Isenhour, mixing in elements from other songs. Both the Bolick version and Charlie Poole's "The Highwayman" are equal parts "Poor Boy" and "Maid Freed from the Gallows" (Child 95). Poole's "Hangman, Hangman" is exclusively the latter, with no traces of "Poor Boy."

Charlie Poole, "The Highwayman," Columbia 15160-D, County CD-3516 (1926)
B.F. Shelton, "Cold Penitentiary Blues," Victor V-40107, Bear Family BCD 16094 (1927)
Charlie Poole, "Hangman, Hangman, Slack the Rope," Columbia 15385-D (1928)
Charlie Jordan, "Dollar Bill Blues," Vocalion 1557, Yazoo 2028 (1930)
Lester McFarland & Robert A. Gardner, "Ninety-Nine Years" Parts 1 & 2, Brunswick 588 (1932)
Monroe Brothers, "I've Still Got Ninety-Nine," Bluebird B-7425, Montgomery Ward M-7448, Bear Family BCD 16399 (1938)
Woody Guthrie, Folkways FA 2484 (as "Gambling Man"), Smithsonian Folkways CD 40112 (1944)
Blue Sky Boys, Capitol T2483, ST2483, Arhoolie CD-9065 (1965)

Precious Memories (John Braselton Fillmore Wright, 1923)

This was sent to us by Stamps-Baxter. We started singing it in 1938 when "Red" Hicks joined us and we started singing trios. Through the years it was quite popular for us.

Blue Sky Boys, *Favorite Hymns and Folk Songs*, 9

Turkey Mountain Singers (Georgia Yellow Hammers), Bluebird B-5542 (1928)
Simmons Sacred Singers, OKeh 45299 (1928)

Wade Mainer, Bluebird B-8848, JSP 77124 (1941)
Blue Sky Boys, WGST Program 7, September 10, 1946
Blue Sky Boys, WGST Program 28, October 9, 1946, Copper Creek CCCD-0146
Blue Sky Boys, WGST program transcription (unnumbered), December 19, 1946
Blue Sky Boys, WGST program transcription (unnumbered), December 18, 1947
Jim Reeves, RCA Victor LSP-1950, Bear Family BCD 15656 (1958)
Bill Monroe, Decca DL 8769, Bear Family BCD 15423, BCD 16637 (1958), MCA MCAD-42286, Bear Family 16637 (1989) (two versions)
Mac Wiseman, Wise MAC-W108, 2001

Precious Moments (Don Fister)

Blue Sky Boys, Starday SLP-269, SLP-308, Gusto GT7-0549 (1963)
Carl Story, Starday SLP-348, Bear Family BCD 16839 (1965)

The Prisoner's Dream (Karl Davis-Harty Taylor-Patrick McAdory)

This was sent to us by M.M. Cole and was fairly popular with our radio audience. We were still receiving requests for it when we quit entertaining in 1951.

See Bill's comments for "The Answer to the Prisoner's Dream." Patrick McAdory was the pen name of Frank Johnson.

Karl & Harty, ARC 7-01-53 (1936)
Blue Sky Boys, Bluebird B-7411, Montgomery Ward M-7468, Bear Family BCD 15951 (1938)
Lulu Belle & Scotty, Vocalion 04841 (1939)
Bill Clifton, London HAU-8325, Bear Family BCD 16425 (1966)

The Promise of the Lord (Leon Payne)

Leon Payne (1917–1969) was a blind Texas singer/songwriter, best remembered for "I Love You Because," "They'll Never Take Her Love From Me," and "Lost Highway." He recorded for Starday in the 1950s and 60s.

Blue Sky Boys, Starday SLP-269, Gusto GT7-0549 (1963)

Quit That Tickling Me (Will S. Hays, 1872)

[The length of this song] *depended on how long we wanted to make it. In old live shows we always started off with an up-tempo number.*

Grandpa Jones, "Stop That Ticklin' Me," RCA Victor 20-4660, B.A.C.M. CD D 206 (1952)
Blue Sky Boys, Rounder 0236, 11536 (1964)

Radio Station S-A-V-E-D (Odell McLeod-Roy Acuff)

Mac Odell (Odell McLeod, 1916–2003) was this song's sole composer. Roy Acuff copyrighted it when he recorded it, under terms described by Roy's wife Mildred Acuff in a letter to Odell on October 10, 1943:

In regard to these songs I wrote you about, Roy said that he would use your name as writer on sheet music, records etc. but that he would want the copyright to the songs. He has never bought any songs that he has used the writer's name on, this way. He has always just bought them out right [*sic*], *therefore he would rather you make him a price on the songs and he will try to meet it.*

Odell's "Set Your Dial on Heaven" (1952) is a slightly modified version. Bill and Earl re-copyrighted it in 1963, using the original title.

Roy Acuff, Time-Life TLCW 09, Bear Family BCD 17300 (1944)
Mac Odell, "Set Your Dial on Heaven," King 1159, B.A.C.M. CD D 309 (1952)
Blue Sky Boys, Starday SLP-269, SLP-303, Gusto GT7-0549 (1963)
Pat Boone, DJM 22064 (1977)

Roll On, Buddy (Charles Bowman)

Lute Isenhour sang this and played it on a five-string banjo. We usually played it a bit faster than most of our selections. When Red Hicks joined us we sang the refrain as a trio but [we] *never sang it trio after Curly Parker joined us.*

Possibly they performed it with the fiddler Charlie Bowman himself when the three worked together in 1937.

Al Hopkins & His Buckle Busters, "Baby, Your Time Ain't Long," Brunswick 183, Vocalion 5182 (as the Hill Billies) (1927)

Charlie Bowman & His Brothers, Columbia 15357-D (1928)
Monroe Brothers, Bluebird B-6960, Montgomery Ward M-8455, Bear Family BCD 16399 (1937)
Blue Sky Boys, audition disc, November 20, 1939
Brother Oswald (Beecher Kirby) & Rachel Veach, Bear Family BCD 17300 (1942)
Blue Sky Boys, WCYB (Bristol, VA, 1949), Copper Creek CCCD-0125

Romans 6:23 (Karl Davis-Harty Taylor, 1947)

FOR THE WAGES OF SIN IS DEATH, BUT THE GIFT OF GOD IS ETERNAL LIFE IN JESUS CHRIST OUR LORD. —ROMANS 6:23

Karl and Harty link the biblical verse in Paul's letter to the plight of men lost on a raft at sea.

Blue Sky Boys, RCA Victor 20-2900, Bear Family BCD 15951 (1947)

Row Us Over the Tide (Edward C. Avis, 1888)

We were probably given help on this song from our father. It was composed by Homer F. Morris [*sic*]. *Footnotes read: "from an incident in a southern city during the great yellow fever epidemic."*

Bill's note refers to the 1878 yellow fever epidemic in Memphis. As he notes, it was later claimed by Homer F. Morris (1875–1955), who included it in *Trinity Songs of Faith, Hope and Love* (1910).

Bela Lam & His Greene County Singers, OKeh 45126 (1927)
Blue Sky Boys, Bluebird B-6567, Montgomery Ward M-7018, Bear Family BCD 15951 (1936)
Blue Sky Boys, Program 6, September 9, 1946, Copper Creek CCCD-0120
Carl Story, Starday SLP-219 (1962)

The Royal Telephone (Frederick M. Lehman, 1909 or 1919)

We learned this song early in our radio careers. The copyright reads 1909; not many people had telephones in those days. We sang this song quite regularly.

Some sources give the date of composition as 1919. Frederick Martin Lehman (1868–1953) also wrote "There's No Disappointment in Heaven." Stories, sermons, and songs about connecting with heaven (or hell) via railroads, automobiles, telephones, radios, and other novel inventions have been popular since the early days of the industrial revolution.

Rev. Sister Mary Nelson, "Telephone to Glory," Vocalion 1109 (1927)
Blind Roosevelt Graves & Brother, "Telephone to Glory," Paramount 12874, Crown 3326 (as Blind Willie Jackson & Brother) (1929)
Blue Sky Boys, Bluebird B-8369, Montgomery Ward M-8414, Bear Family BCD 15951 (1939)
Blue Sky Boys, WCYB (Bristol, VA, 1949), Copper Creek CCCD-0126

A Satisfied Mind (Joe "Red" Hayes-Jack Rhodes)

Starday Records' Don Pierce owned publishing rights to this 1954–55 hit and was undoubtedly pleased to have the Bolicks cover it.

Red Hayes, Starday 164 (1954)
Porter Wagoner, RCA Victor 20-6105, LPM-1358, Bear Family BCD 15499 (1954), RCA Victor LSP-2650 (1962) (two versions)
Jean Shepard, Capitol 3118, T1179, T1253, Bear Family BCD 15905 (1954)
Blue Sky Boys, Starday 677, SLP-257, Gusto GT7-0549 (1963)
Joan Baez, Vanguard 79200 (1965)

Searching for a Soldier's Grave (Roy Acuff)

Like "As Long As I Live," "Unloved and Unclaimed," and "This World Can't Stand Long," this is one of a group of songs Jim Anglin sold to Roy Acuff in 1943. See the note to "As Long As I Live."

Blue Sky Boys, *Favorite Hymns and Folk Songs*, 21 (The Soldier's Grave)

Bailes Brothers, Columbia 36932, 20016, Bear Family BCD 15973 (1945)
Wade Mainer, "Soldier's Grave," King 585, Gusto GT2-0957-2 (1946)
Hank Williams, Time Life 80031-D (1951)
Kitty Wells, Decca ED 2361, Bear Family BCD 15638 (1952)
Blue Sky Boys, Rounder 0052 (1975)

Shake Hands with Your Mother Today (Pete Roy-Bill Bolick)

Blue Sky Boys, RCA Victor 21-0108, Bear Family BCD 15951 (1949)

Shake My Mother's Hand for Me (Thomas A. Dorsey, 1934)

This is a song I heard one of many quartets sing. I looked it up in one of the Stamps-Baxter books and felt we could use it as a trio. It is also in several R. E. Winsett publications. The notes tell me that Stamps-Baxter copyrighted it in 1937. Almost all the mother songs we sang seemed to be well liked by our radio audience.

Thomas A. Dorsey (1899–1993) was a skilled songwriter and pianist who worked alongside Ma Rainey until 1928, when he began to make records as Georgia Tom. He wrote and sang a number of racy (for those days) songs, including three hit duets with Tampa Red, "Beedle Um Bum," "Selling That Stuff," and "It's Tight Like That." He turned to gospel songwriting full time in 1932. His "Precious Lord," "Peace in the Valley," and "If You See My Saviour" have become standards.

Thomas A. Dorsey, Vocalion (unissued, 1934)
Golden Eagle Gospel Singers, "Shake Mother's Hand for Me," Decca 7670 (1939)
Wade Mainer, Bluebird B-8848, JSP 77124 (1941)
Bill Monroe, Bluebird B-8953, Bear Family BCD 16399 (1941)
Blue Sky Boys, WGST Program 16, September 23, 1946
Blue Sky Boys, WGST Program 41, October 28, 1946, Copper Creek CCCD-0121
Johnnie & Jack, RCA Victor 20-4878, Bear Family BCD 15553 (1952)
Kitty Wells, Decca 74679 (1965)

Shall I Miss It? (Barney E. Warren)

We learned this song from a First Church of God hymnal, in the church we attended as children. Barney E. Warren was affiliated with the Church of God and wrote a great number of religious songs including "Beautiful" and "The Blood of Jesus." Several were among our most requested religious songs.

See note to "Beautiful."

Blue Sky Boys, WGST Program 46, November 4, 1946, Copper Creek CCCD-0146

She Has Forgotten
(Karl Davis-Harty Taylor, 1936)

Blue Sky Boys, "There Was a Time," Bluebird B-8110, Montgomery Ward M-7567, Bear Family BCD 15951 (1939)
Blue Sky Boys, WGST Program 3, September 4, 1946
Bailes Brothers, King 1130, Bear Family BCD 17132 (1946)
Bailey Brothers, "Have You Forgotten," Canary 002 (1950), WWVA Jamboree EP-1155 (1953) (related song, two versions)
Don Reno & Red Smiley, King 45-5296, LP-701, Gusto GT7-0959-2 (1959)
Ray & Ina Patterson, County 737 (1973)

She'll Be There
(Fisher Hendley-Edgar Lee Boswell)

This is better known as "What a Friend We Have in Mother." It was inspired by "What a Friend We Have in Jesus" [Joseph Scriven-words, 1855, Charles Converse-music, 1868].

Dixie Reelers, "What a Friend We Have in Mother," Bluebird B-6461, Montgomery Ward M-5030 (1936)
Fisher Hendley & His Aristocratic Pigs, Vocalion 04658 (1938)
Blue Sky Boys, Bluebird B-8356, Montgomery Ward M-8413, Bear Family BCD 15951 (1939)
Louvin Brothers, "What a Friend We Have in Mother," Rounder CD 1030 (1952)

She's My Curly Headed Baby

The Callahan Brothers from Madison County, North Carolina, worked at WWNC in Asheville in 1933–34. Their first records in 1934 included this career hit.

Callahan Brothers, Melotone M12898, Conqueror 8275 (1934)
Callahan Brothers, "She's My Curly Headed Baby No. 2," ARC 35-10-28, Conqueror 8584 (1935)
Louvin Brothers, "My Curly Headed Baby," Capitol 4255, T1547, Bear Family BCD 15561 (1958)
Blue Sky Boys, "Curly Headed Baby," Rounder 0052 (1975)

She's Somebody's Darling Once More (Bobby Gregory, 1938)

Bobby Gregory (1900–1971) is best remembered for "Sunny Side of the Mountain," written with Harry McAuliffe, aka Big Slim, the Lone Cowboy.

Shelton Brothers, Decca 5630 (1938)
Blue Sky Boys, Bluebird B-8446, Montgomery Ward M-8667, Bear Family BCD 15951 (1940)
Blue Sky Boys, WCYB (Bristol, VA, 1949)

Short Life of Trouble

Lute Isenhour and I sang this before Earl and I started singing together. Lute's wife said we sang it better than anyone she had ever heard. Of course, she could have been a bit prejudiced. Earl and I picked up new verses here and there, and this is the version we finally used. We never heard our recording of it until 1963 when RCA reissued it on a Camden album. The 1949 version is better than our initial effort for Bluebird.

The Burnett and Rutherford record sold well and the song was recorded over a dozen times in the 1920s and 1930s. By the time the Blue Sky Boys' Bluebird record was published late in 1941, they were serving in the US army. By the time they were discharged in 1945, almost all their records had been deleted from the catalog.

Dick Burnett & Leonard Rutherford, Columbia 15133-D (1926, in the Bolick collection)
G.B. Grayson & Henry Whitter, Victor V-40105, County CD-3517 (1928)
Wade Mainer & Zeke Morris, "Short Life and It's Trouble," Bluebird B-6936, Montgomery Ward M-7128 (as Mainer's Mountaineers), JSP 77118 (1937)
Blue Sky Boys, Bluebird B-8829, Montgomery Ward M-8849, Bear Family BCD 15951 (1940)
Blue Sky Boys, WCYB (Bristol, VA, 1949), Copper Creek CCCD-0126
Ralph Stanley, Rebel CD-1735, 1996

Silver Threads Among the Gold (Eben E. Rexford-words, Hart Pease Danks-music, 1873)

This song was well known when I was a boy and I heard it often in the thirties.

Richard Jose, Victor 2556 (1903), 2556 (1904), 31342 (1904) (three versions)
John McCormack, Victor 64260 (1912), 1173 (1925) (two versions)

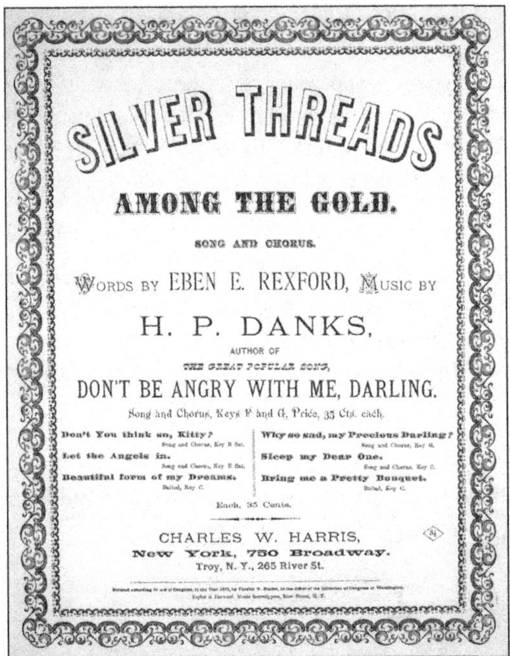

Courtesy of Lester S. Levy Collection of Sheet Music, Sheridan Libraries, Johns Hopkins University.

Blue Sky Boys, WGST Program 44, October 31, 1946, Copper Creek CCCD-0146
Don Reno, Dot DLP 3617, Bear Family BCD 15728 (1964)
Slim Whitman, Imperial LP-12277 (1964)

Since the Angels Took My Mother Far Away (George Filenius-Beth Rhodes-Hal Kent)

This was released on Montgomery Ward soon after it was made but didn't appear on Bluebird until 1944. It prompted the Blue Sky Boys' first record review, from an anonymous, condescending writer in *Billboard* on November 4, 1944:

The harmony singing of Bill and Earl Bolick, as the Blue Sky Boys, is outdoorish with a vengeance. Boys are strictly from the hay-stacks, and for selling the tear-jerking tunes, there's enough cry in their vocal twangs to dampen any disk.

Blue Sky Boys, Montgomery Ward M-8847, Bluebird 33-0516, Bear Family BCD 15951 (1940)
Blue Sky Boys, WCYB (Bristol, VA, 1949)

The Sinking of the Titanic

This is one of many songs appearing over the years that commemorated the ship's fatal collision with an iceberg on April 14, 1912, on its maiden voyage from Southampton, England to New York. To some, the tragedy was a warning from God about hubris, materialism, and viewing technological progress as superior to the divine will.

Cofer Brothers, "The Great Ship Went Down," OKeh 45137 (1927)
Dixon Brothers, "Down With the Old Canoe," Bluebird B-7449, Montgomery Ward M-7489, Bear Family BCD 16817 (1938)
Blue Sky Boys, "The Sinking of the Titanic," WNAO program transcription (1949)

Sing a Song for the Blind *See* Song of the Blind

Skip to My Lou

Wikipedia describes "Skip to My Lou" as a "partner-stealing dance from the 1840s." It's also been a children's play-party favorite from then until now.

Uncle Eck Dunford, "Skip to My Lou, My Darling," Victor 20938, Yazoo 2051, Bear Family BCD 16094 (1927)
Georgia Organ Grinders, "Skip to My Lou, My Darling," Columbia 15415-D (1929)
Blue Sky Boys, audition disc for KWKH (Shreveport, LA, 1941)

Sold Down the River (Vaughn Horton, 1947)

The phrase originated with slave trafficking before the Civil War, and became a metaphor for betrayal and deception.

Blue Sky Boys, RCA Victor 20-2380, Bear Family BCD 15951 (1947)
Bill Monroe, Decca DL 74080, Bear Family BCD 15529 (1960)
Bob Paisley & the Southern Grass, Rounder 0142 (1980)
Michael Cleveland & Flamekeeper, Rounder 11661 0596-2 (2008)

Somebody Makes Me Think of You
See Somebody's Tall and Handsome

Somebody's Boy Is Homeless Tonight (R. S. Hanna, 1894)

Carter Family, "The Wandering Boy," Victor 20877, Bear Family BCD 15865 (1927)
Carter Family, "Bring Back My Boy," Decca 5649, Bear Family BCD 15865 (1938)
Blue Sky Boys, "Bring Back My Wandering Boy," Bluebird B-8128, Bear Family BCD 15951 (1938)
Stanley Brothers, "The Wandering Boy," Columbia 20953, Bear Family BCD 15564 (1952)
Rodney Crowell, "Wandering Boy," Sugar Hill CD-1065 (2000)

Somebody's Tall and Handsome (J.R.M., 1884)

Eli Oberstein changed this title to "Somebody Makes Me Think of You." It's a song I learned as a child.

The original lyric is fairly insipid:

Somebody's tall and handsome, somebody's fair to see
Somebody's sweet and loving, somebody smiles on me
Somebody's heart is faithful, somebody's heart is true
Somebody waits for somebody, somebody knows — do you?

The Blue Sky Boys' parody tempers sentiment with cynicism:

Somebody called for Mama, Mama went out to see
Mama came back a-crying, saying, "Daughter, you'd best stay with me" . . .
Somebody called for Papa, Papa went out to see
Papa came back a-laughing, was glad to get rid of me

Carolina Tar Heels, Victor V-40138, Yazoo 2052 (1929)
Blue Sky Boys, "Somebody Makes Me Think of You," Bluebird B-6714, Montgomery Ward M-7159, Bear Family BCD 15951 (1936)
Three Tobacco Tags, "Tall and Handsome Comedy," Bluebird B-6853, Montgomery Ward M-7164 (1937)
Morris Brothers, "Somebody Loves You, Darling," Victor 20-1783 (1945)

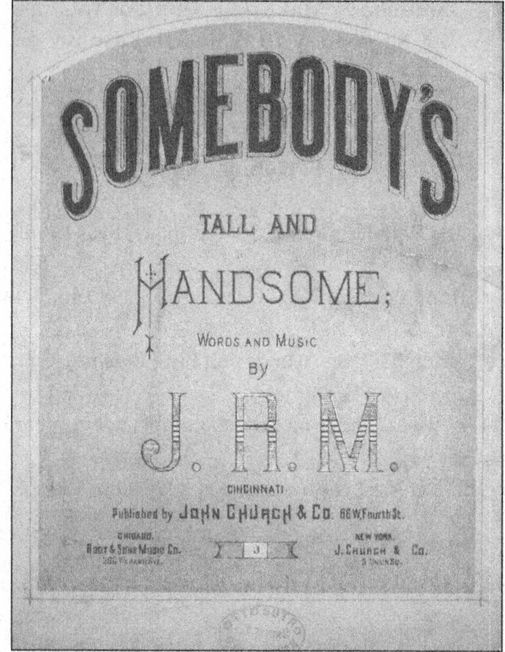

Courtesy of Lester S. Levy Collection of Sheet Music, Sheridan Libraries, Johns Hopkins University.

Jim & Jesse, "Somebody Loves You, Darling," Epic BN 26031, Bear Family BCD 15716 (1962)

Marty Stuart & Curly Seckler, "Somebody Loves You, Darlin," CMH 8000, 1992

Someone's Last Day (M. H. McKee, 1924)

We learned this from our father, who probably learned it at one of the singing schools he attended.

Blue Sky Boys, Bluebird B-8356, Montgomery Ward M-8413, Bear Family BCD 15951 (1939)

Blue Sky Boys, WGST Program 34, October 17, 1946, Copper Creek CCCD-0120

Carl Sauceman, Mercury 6173, Rounder 1019 (1948)

Carter Sisters & Mother Maybelle, "This Is Someone's Last Day," RCA Victor 21-0057, B.A.C.M. CD D 176 (1949)

Stanley Brothers, Wango LP-103 (as John's Gospel Quartet), County 753 (1963)

Song of the Blind (Doc Hopkins)

This song was sent to us by M.M. Cole and was written by Doc Hopkins. Doc doesn't seem to be very well remembered by many artists or people but to me he was, at one time, one of the best singers of ballads and folk songs in the country. I especially liked his guitar playing and soft voice. When Doc was in his prime, he was about the best guitar player and singer there was. As he got older, he lost his voice and I don't think he was too good. When he was young I'd listen to him on the Suppertime Frolic *on WJJD in Chicago. I felt very fortunate to meet him when we were at the UCLA Folk Festival in 1965.*

"Song of the Blind" is a moving tribute from one artist to another. Doctor Howard "Doc" Hopkins (1900–1988) told Stephen Wade that this song was written about Dick Burnett (1883–1977), who first published (and possibly wrote) "I Am a Man of Constant Sorrow" in 1913. They met in Rockcastle County, Kentucky, where Doc first heard "Song of the Orphan Boy." Though he learned from other blind musicians, Doc Hopkins claimed it was Blind Burnett who affected him most.

See "Song of the Orphan Boy," pg. 212.

Karl & Harty, ARC (unissued, 1936)
Blue Sky Boys, "Sing a Song for the Blind," Bluebird B-8143, Montgomery Ward M-7324, Bear Family BCD 15951 (1937)
Blue Sky Boys, WGST Program 5, September 6, 1946, Copper Creek CCCD-0146
Mac Martin & Ed Brozi, "God Have Pity on the Blind," Patuxent CD-207 (1970)

Speak to Me, Little Darling (Leslie York, 1943)

It was composed by the York Brothers, who were members of the Grand Ole Opry. *Steve Sholes sent us this song and requested that we do it on our first recording session after World War II. He stated that he was asking this favor for a good friend of his, Murray Nash. Had we known that we would only record four songs, it is doubtful that we would have learned this one.*

The broadcast and RCA versions of this song were made in Atlanta on the same day, in the order shown.

York Brothers, Decca 5933 (1941)
Blue Sky Boys, WGST Program 21, September 30, 1946
Blue Sky Boys, RCA Victor 20-2022, Bear Family BCD 15951 (1946)
Blue Sky Boys, WGST program transcription (unnumbered), December 19, 1946

Song of The Orphan Boy

O, I once was a man who worked hard in the land,
For support I worked hard every day,
I worked in the oil green on a seven star machine,
But now, dear friends, I cannot see my way.

Cho.- Oh, dear friends today, if you could not see your way
Oh, how lonely and sad you would be,
Don't think it any wrong to buy one of my sons,
Won't you buy from a blind man likeme.

When I went out in the field I did not know how to drill,
I went to work in Nineteen Hundred and One,
Nothing then troubled me, it was then I could see,
But now my working days are all done.

Oh, I once had a home, happy home sweet home,
But my father died when I was four years old;
Just eighteen years ago mother left this world below,
She has gone to walk the pearly streets of gold.

Oh, it was one dark night, there was not any moonlight,
I was going through the railroad camp,
I was going home when I met my fatal doom,
I was shot and robbed by a railroad tramp.

I went away upon the train, my eyes I tried to gain;
Oh, my body how it pained and throbbed,
It was the eighth month in the year when the trouble did appear,
On Wednesday night when I was shot and robbed

Oh, when I was found, my face lying on the ground,
They picked me up and laid me on a cot;
Then the robber took his flight, I was carried home that night
From the place where I had been shot.

In God's own holy Word He has promised a reward,
When from sorrow and afflictions set free;
The deaf and dumb shall hear and talk, the blind shall see, the lame shall walk,
Oh, what a glorious time that will be.

In that happy land at last when our troubles all have past,
When our sorrows and afflictions are o'er,
In that blessed home there no death can ever come
We shall never be blind any more.

Now dear friend my song is done, are you father, or a son?
In the Bible do you believe?
If you think it is right to help a man that has no sight,
You can help a poor blind man to live.

Blind Dick Burnett songbook, 1913.

Blue Sky Boys, WGST program transcription (unnumbered), December 18, 1947

Blue Sky Boys, WGST Program 136, March 10, 1947, Copper Creek CCCD-0121

Shorty Morris, Mercury 6159 (1948, in the Bolick collection)

Story of the Knoxville Girl *See* The Knoxville Girl

Sunny Side of Life *See* On the Sunny Side of Life

Sweet Allallee (Charles E. Stewart-words, James W. Porter-music, 1852 (as "Ella Ree") / Septimus Winner, 1865)

This song I associate with Mac and Bob. Although we didn't own a phonograph until after I left home, we were one of the first families in our vicinity to own a radio. We generally listened to the [National] *Barn Dance in Chicago on Saturday nights. My father ordered one of Mac and Bob's songbooks because he liked many of the songs they sang. He told me he remembered hearing some of these songs when he was a boy and recalled hearing his mother sing some of them. I'm quite certain that "Sweet Allallee" was one of the songs in this book. Dad purchased about all the books that were offered at singing schools but seldom bought any that were advertised over the radio.*

This was a sentimental favorite of Christy's Minstrels, promoting the lost happiness of life in slavery on the "old plantation," a comfortable myth that persisted long after the Civil War. Septimus Winner (1827–1902) claimed and republished it in 1865 as "Carry Me Back to Tennessee." He wrote lyrics to "Listen to the Mocking Bird" (1855) and "Whispering Hope" (1868). Both were credited to the pseudonymous "Alice Hawthorne" and both were recorded by the Blue Sky Boys.

Lester McFarland & Robert A. Gardner, Vocalion 5199 (1927, in the Bolick collection)
Blue Sky Boys, Bluebird B-6854, Montgomery Ward M-7162, Bear Family BCD 15951 (1936)
Blue Sky Boys, WGST Program 23, October 2, 1946
Country Gentlemen, "Darling Alalee," Starday 487, SLP-136, 3510-2-2, Folkways FA 2409, Smithsonian Folkways CD 40004 (1960)
Maybelle Carter, "Sweet Allie Lee," Columbia KG 32436 (1973)

Sweet Evelina (M.-words, T.-music, 1860)

In searching for information regarding this song, I ran across a pamphlet entitled 200 Favorite Old Songs. *There was no music to any of the songs, only words. "Sweet Evalina" was one of them. The words are identical to the way Earl and I sang it but the chorus wasn't included. I'm certain that our version was taken from this book. There was no information about any songs in the pamphlet.*

Phil Reeve & (Charles) Ernest Moody, Victor 21188 (1927)
Sons of the Pioneers, "Dear Evelina," Standard Transcription B-1694-A, Bear Family BCD 15710 (1934)
Shelton Brothers, Decca 5261 (1935)
Blue Sky Boys, "Sweet Evalina," Bluebird B-7348, Montgomery Ward M-7323, Bear Family BCD 15951 (1936)

The Sweetest Gift (A Mother's Smile) (J. B. Coats)

We learned this song in 1946 or 1947. James and Martha Carson were the first entertainers I ever heard sing it when they were on WSB's Cross Roads Follies. I looked it up in one of the Stamps-Baxter songbooks, thinking it would be a good song for Earl and myself. This is another song in which the harmony singer takes the lead in the chorus [see "When the Ransomed Get Home"]. *It proved to be successful for us but, as I have stated previously, almost any mother song was popular with our radio audiences.*

James & Martha (Carson), White Church 1120 (1946, in the Bolick collection)
Blue Sky Boys, WNAO audition disc, January 28. 1949
Blue Sky Boys, RCA Victor 21-0034, Bear Family BCD 15951 (1949)
Blue Sky Boys, WCYB (Bristol, VA, 1949), Copper Creek CCCD-0125
Bailey Brothers, Rich-R'-Tone 446 (1949)
Snuffy Jenkins, Folk Lyric LP 123, Arhoolie CD 9027 (1962)
Seldom Scene, "Sweetest Gift," Rebel SLP 1520 (1972)
Gibson Brothers, "The Sweetest Gift," Rounder 11661 35986 02 (2014)

Sweetest Mother (Gertrude Stoddard Dennstedt-Will M. Ramsey, 1939)

I found this in several religious songbooks. Earl and I started singing it not too long after we started in radio.

Humbard Family, Vocalion 05562 (1940)
Blue Sky Boys, WCYB (Bristol, VA, 1949), Copper Creek CCCD-0126

Sweetheart Mountain Rose (Bill Bolick-Earl Bolick)

This was actually written by Ralph ("Zeke") Hamrick, who also wrote "Why Not Confess" (see note). Curly Parker learned it while performing with the Holden Brothers (Fairley and Jack) in the late 1930s, before he joined the Blue Sky Boys in 1940 and taught it to them.

Blue Sky Boys, "My Sweetheart Mountain Rose," County 752 (1963)
Blue Sky Boys, Starday SLP-257, Gusto GT7-0549 (1963)
Blue Sky Boys, Rounder 11536 (1964)
Hamrick Brothers, Marbone (1975)

Take Me Back to Renfro Valley (John Lair)

This was sent to us by M.M. Cole. We seldom sang it although I think it has a pretty melody.

This account by John Lair appears online:

> At the time I wrote this song, I was employed as a musical director of radio station WLS in Chicago. I was also writing and producing my own show with talent I had taken to Chicago from an area surrounding my old home on Renfro Creek near Mount Vernon, Kentucky. I went home on vacation and was so depressed by the changes I found that, upon my return, I put it all into this song. The more I heard it sung, the more homesick I got, and the more determined I became to go back and make it more like it had been in my boyhood. With a boy I had put on radio, Red Foley, his brother Cotton Foley, Whitey Ford and five hundred dollars borrowed money, I went and got to work. Renfro Valley became the first community in the nation to originate and broadcast a radio program put on by the actual residents of that community. Success was instantaneous, overwhelming—and surprising—and we owed it mostly to this song. Beginning in 1942, it was the theme song of our network program for more than twelve years on CBS.

Linda Parker, Conqueror 8164 (1933)
Chuck Wagon Gang, ARC 7-03-70, Conqueror 9784, Bear Family BCD 17348 (1936)
Blue Sky Boys, WGST Program 32, October 15, 1946, Copper Creek CCCD-0120
Bailey Brothers, "Take Me Back to Happy Valley," Old Homestead OCHS-138 (1957), Rounder 0030, CD-11510 (1974) (two versions)

Take Me Back to Tennessee

To the best of my knowledge, Fiddling Arthur Smith was the first person I ever heard sing this. I think Leslie does a good job playing and singing it; I hear a shade of Arthur in his fiddling on this. [Leslie] *played much rougher than Curly, but he did try to tone his playing down and he was gifted in many ways. He played many old selections that I had never heard.*

Arthur Smith's record was the model for Leslie Keith, a singing fiddler who joined the Blue Sky Boys at WCYB in 1949 after working there with the Stanley Brothers. The tune is "Careless Love" with new lyrics.

Arthur Smith, Bluebird B-6514, Montgomery Ward M-4869 County CD-3526 (1936)
Blue Sky Boys, WCYB (Bristol, VA, 1949), Copper Creek CCCD-0126

Take Up Thy Cross (Rev. Alfred H. Ackley, 1922)

HE SAID TO THEM ALL, "WHOEVER WANTS TO BE MY DISCIPLE MUST DENY THEMSELVES AND TAKE UP THEIR CROSS DAILY AND FOLLOW ME." —LUKE 9:23

This is another song my father helped us with, taken from one of the hymnbooks he purchased.

Charles Richardson & O.S. Gabehart, OKeh 45403 (1929)
Blue Sky Boys, Bluebird B-6567, Bear Family BCD 15951 (1936)
Mac & Bob (Lester McFarland & Robert A. Gardner), Vocalion 05488 (1940)
Blue Sky Boys, WGST Program 20, September 27, 1946

Tears on Her Bridal Bouquet (Arthur Q. Smith, 1949)

Arthur Q. Smith (James Arthur Pritchett, 1909–1963) was a prolific alcoholic songwriter who, for modest sums, frequently sold songs that became hits for others. They included "I Wouldn't Change You If I Could," "Wedding Bells," "Missing in Action," and "I Overlooked an Orchid."

Blue Sky Boys, RCA Victor 21-0317, Bear Family BCD 15951 (1950)
Orval Prophet, Decca 28338, Bear Family BCD 16376 (1952)
Stonewall Jackson, Columbia 4-41114, Bear Family BCD 16421 (1957)

That Beautiful Home (H. W. Elliott-words, Emmett S. Dean-music, 1895)

Murphy Sacred Quartet, OKeh 45172 (1927)
Carter Family, "Beautiful Home," Conqueror 9568, Bear Family BCD 15985 (1940)
Blue Sky Boys, Program 5, September 6, 1946, Copper Creek CCCD-0120
Hank Williams, Time-Life 25526 (1951)

There Was a Time *See* She Has Forgotten

There'll Be No Broken Hearts for Me (Bill Bolick-Earl Bolick)

This was one of a pair of original songs that only appeared on a 1970s reissue; the other was "Where Our Darling Sleeps Tonight." Bill's authorship claims are ambiguous but his assessment of Steve Sholes's motives isn't:

I think both numbers were written by me; I know I definitely put the music to them. Whether I wrote the songs [i.e., lyrics] *I'm not quite sure. Steve and I had so much trouble on this last session that he refused to issue this and "Where Our Darling Sleeps Tonight," I think because they were the only numbers we had anything to do with writing. I felt it was kind of a personal thing.*

Blue Sky Boys, Bluebird AXM2-5525, Bear Family BCD 15951 (1950)

There'll Come a Time (Charles K. Harris, 1895)

I learned this song from Lute Isenhour, from Alexander County near Taylorsville, NC. He was one of the finest banjo players I have ever heard. I can't recall singing this with Lute but I did learn it from him.

Charlie Poole's record of this song was a best seller. For a note on Charles K. Harris, see "After the Ball."

Steve Porter, Berliner 1729, Columbia 4544 (two versions, both 1897)
Charlie Poole, Columbia 15116-D, County CD-3508 (1926)
Karl & Harty, ARC (unissued, 1935)
Blue Sky Boys, Bluebird B-6538, Montgomery Ward M-7016, Bear Family BCD 15951 (1936)
Wade Mainer, King 603, Gusto GT2-0957-2 (1946)

There's Been a Change (Calvin Van Pelt-Bill Bolick-Earl Bolick, 1947)

Blue Sky Boys, RCA Victor 20-2570, Bear Family BCD 15951 (1947)

There's No Disappointment in Heaven (Frederick M. Lehman, 1914)

This was one of our father's favorite songs. I can't recall hearing it sung as a duet prior to our recording. In later years I obtained a recording by Mac and Bob, who recorded it much earlier.

The McFarland and Gardner record was one of the best-selling country discs of the 1920s. Frederick Martin Lehman (1868–1953) also wrote "The Royal Telephone."

Perry Kim & Einar Nyland, "No Disappointment in Heaven," Rainbow 1066 (ca. 1922), Victor (unissued, 1926) (two versions)
Homer Rodeheaver-Doris Asher, "No Disappointment in Heaven," Victor 20529 (1925)
Lester McFarland & Robert A. Gardner, Brunswick 111, Vocalion 5123 (1926)
Bob Wills, "No Disappointment in Heaven," Columbia P 15853, Bear Family BCD 15933 (1936)
Blue Sky Boys, "No Disappointment in Heaven," Bluebird B-7113, Montgomery Ward M-7325, Bear Family BCD 15951 (1937)
Dock Boggs, "No Disappointment in Heaven," Folkways FA2392, Smithsonian Folkways CD 40108 (1964)

There's No Other Love for Me (Karl Davis-Harty Taylor, 1936)

The gypsy and deep water death themes suggest mid-nineteenth-century origins for this song.

Blue Sky Boys, Bluebird B-8339, Montgomery Ward M-8412, Bear Family BCD 15951 (1939)
Blue Sky Boys, WGST Program 18, September 25, 1946

They're All Going Home But One (Karl Davis-Harty Taylor-Patrick McAdory, 1936)

This was sent to us by M.M. Cole. Patrick McAdory was listed as co-writer; I learned later that it was not the author's true name. He wrote a number of songs including some that became popular.

About "Patrick McAdory" (Frank Johnson), see the note to "Answer to 'The Prisoner's Dream.'" The 1936 copyright entry lists all three composers as shown.

Karl & Harty, "They Are All Going Home But One," ARC 7-01-69, Conqueror 8721 (1936)
Blue Sky Boys, "They're All Home But One," Bluebird B-7173, Bear Family BCD 15951 (1937)
Anglin Twins, "They Are All Going Home But One," Vocalion 02963 (1937)
Blue Sky Boys, WGST Program 2, September 3, 1946
Blue Sky Boys, WCYB (Bristol, VA, 1949)
Mac Wiseman, Music Mill MME-70038, Bear Family BCD 15976 (1964)

This Evening Light (Daniel Sidney Warner-H. R. Jeffrey, 1885)

IT WILL BE A UNIQUE DAY, KNOWN ONLY TO THE LORD, WITHOUT DISTINCTION BETWEEN DAY AND NIGHT. WHEN EVENING COMES, THERE WILL BE LIGHT. — ZECHARIAH 14:7

Mr. Warner was the founder of the Church of God that we attended in our boyhood days. We took it from a hymnal [Reformation Glory, 1923] *used by the church. We knew this song as far back as we can remember.*

D. S. Warner also wrote "I Know My Name Is There," recorded by Ernest V. Stoneman's Dixie Mountaineers in 1927.

Blue Sky Boys, Bluebird B-8597, Montgomery Ward M-8669, Bear Family BCD 15951 (1940)
Blue Sky Boys, WGST Program 25, October 4, 1946
Blue Sky Boys, WCYB (Bristol, VA, 1949), Copper Creek CCCD-0126

This Is Like Heaven to Me (J. E. French, 1903)

Carter Family, Victor 23845, Montgomery Ward M-7358, Bear Family BCD 15865 (1933)
Blue Sky Boys, Bluebird B-7973, Montgomery Ward M-7566, Bear Family BCD 15951 (1938)

This Train

Although this song is somewhat religious, we thought of it more as a novelty number. We simply tried to piece enough of it together to be able to sing it.

"This Train Is Bound for Glory" has been widely recorded; it inspired the title for Woody Guthrie's autobiography *Bound for Glory* (1943). Willie Dixon's humorous parody "My Babe" was recorded by himself, Little Walter, and others after 1955.

Woods' Famous Blind Jubilee Singers, "This Train Is Bound for Glory," Paramount 12315 (1925)
Sebren & Wilson (Vaughan Happy Two), "Dis Train," Vaughan 1675 (1929)
Sister Rosetta Tharpe, Decca 2558, Fremeaux FA 017 (1939)
Lulu Belle & Scotty, Vocalion 04910 (1939, in the Bolick collection)
Elder Roma Wilson, Arhoolie CD-429 (1948)
Blue Sky Boys, WCYB (Bristol, VA, 1949), Copper Creek CCCD-0125
Hank Thompson, Capitol T618, Bear Family BCD 15904 (1954)
Little Walter, "My Babe," Checker 811, MCA CHD-9384 (1955)
Elder Roma Wilson, "This Train Is a Clean Train," Arhoolie CD-429 (1994)

This World Can't Stand Long (Roy Acuff)

As with "As Long As I Live," "Unloved and Unclaimed," and "Searching for a Soldier's Grave," Jim Anglin sold this song to Roy Acuff, who then claimed authorship. See note to "As Long As I Live."

Roy Acuff, Columbia 20454, CK-48956, Bear Family BCD 17300 (1947)
Wilma Lee & Stoney Cooper, Rich-R'-Tone 424, Bear Family BCD 16751 (1947)
King's Sacred Quartet, King 674, Bear Family BCD 15553 (1947)
Blue Sky Boys, WCYB (Bristol, VA, 1949)

Throw Out the Life Line (Rev. Edwin S. Ufford, 1888, arr. George C. Stebbins, 1890)

Reportedly this hymn was inspired by a life-saving drill Rev. Ufford observed at Port Allerton, near his Boston home.

Mr. and Mrs. J. Douglas Swagerty, OKeh 40274 (1924)
Alcoa Quartette, Columbia 15022-D (1925)
William MacEwen, Columbia 2385-D, 1930
Blue Sky Boys, "Life Line," Bluebird B-7984, Montgomery Ward M-7471, Bear Family BCD 15951 (1938)
Ella Fitzgerald, Capitol ST2685, CDP-7-95151-2 (1967)

The Trail to Mexico (Laws B13)

We obtained this song from a book sent to us by M.M. Cole that I haven't been able to find. I have [it in] *another book sent to us by Stamps-Baxter,* Centennial Songs of Texas, 1836 to 1936. *The song is listed as traditional with arrangement copyrighted by V. O. Stamps.*

This is a recasting of "Midnight on the Stormy Deep" (c.f.), with the lonely seafarer transformed into a Texas trail rider.

Carl T. Sprague, "Following the Cow Trail," Victor 20067 (1925)
Jules Allen, "The Cow Trail to Mexico," Victor 23757, B.A.C.M. CD D 250 (1929)
Blue Sky Boys, WGST Program 36, October 21, 1946, Copper Creek CCCD-0120

Tramp on the Street *See* Only a Tramp

Turn Your Radio On (Albert E. Brumley, 1938)

Albert E. Brumley wrote a number of pretty religious songs. "Turn Your Radio On" was dedicated to the Stamps Quartet and copyrighted by Stamps-Baxter in 1938.

Blue Sky Boys, *Favorite Hymns and Folk Songs*, 14

See note to "I'll Meet You in the Morning."

Lulu Belle & Scotty, Vocalion 04910 (1939, in the Bolick collection)
Blue Sky Boys, Bluebird B-8843, Montgomery Ward M-8846, Bear Family BCD 15951 (1940)
Blue Sky Boys, WGST Program 24, October 3, 1946, Copper Creek CCCD-0121
King's Sacred Quartet, King 674, Bear Family BCD 15553 (1947)
Blue Sky Boys, WGST program transcription (unnumbered), December 18, 1947
Ray Stevens, Barnaby Z-30809 (1971)
Blackwood Brothers, ARAA LPG-106 (1973)

Two Little Rosebuds (Dorsey Dixon, 1932)

Lute Isenhour and I may have sung this together; I'm certain Earl and I sang it not long after we started in radio. Dorsey Dixon, who composed "Wreck on the Highway, wrote many songs including comical ones: "The Intoxicated Rat," "Sales Tax on the Women," etc. I got to know Dorsey during the sixties when I was living in Greensboro, North Carolina. My wife Doris and I visited him several times in Rockingham. He was a likeable fellow and we enjoyed his company.

This was one of Dixon's best-known songs. It mourns the drowning of two young girls in East Rockingham's Pee Dee mill pond during the summer of 1932.

Dixon Brothers, Bluebird B-6441, Montgomery Ward M-7015, Bear Family BCD 16817 (1936)
Wade Mainer & Zeke Morris, "Little Rosebuds," Bluebird B-6993, JSP 77118 (1937)
Curley King & His Tennessee Hilltoppers, Rich-R'-Tone 433 (1947)
Karl & Harty, Capitol Transcription G 62 (ca. 1947)
Blue Sky Boys, WCYB (Bristol, VA, 1949), Copper Creek CCCD-0126

J.E. Mainer, Arhoolie CD 456 (1963)
Red Ellis & the Huron Valley Boys, Starday SLP-273, SLP-308 (1963)
Mac Martin & Ed Brozi, Patuxent CD-207 (1970)

The Unfinished Rug (Karl Davis)

Blue Sky Boys, RCA Victor 21-0317, Bear Family BCD 15951 (1950)

Unloved and Unclaimed (Roy Acuff)

This was sent to us by Acuff-Rose. We recorded it for Rounder Records in May of 1975. I think it sounds much better on the WCYB transcriptions. We weren't actively engaged in entertaining when we did the Rounder album and didn't have the time to rehearse the song. [The WCYB] *effort was done when possibly we were at our best.*

Like "As Long As I Live," "This World Can't Stand Long," and "Searching For a Soldier's Grave," this is a song Jim Anglin sold to Roy Acuff, who then claimed authorship. See the note to "As Long As I Live."

Roy Acuff, Columbia 38189, 20425, Bear Family BCD 17300 (1947)
Blue Sky Boys, WGST program transcription (unnumbered), December 19, 1946
Blue Sky Boys, WCYB (Bristol, VA, 1949), Copper Creek CCCD-0126
Blue Sky Boys, Rounder 0052 (1975)

The Unquiet Grave (Child 78)

The Bolicks learned this from Ray and Ina Patterson in 1948. Printed texts survive from the early nineteenth century but the song is older. Songs sung by the dead, dying, and doomed aren't unknown in country music ("Green, Green Grass of Home," "Long Black Veil") but conversations between impatient corpses and mourning survivors don't show up often. The English composer Ralph Vaughan Williams published an arrangement of this one in 1912, subtitled "How Cold the Wind Doth Blow," and a Wikipedia article lists a number of folk and folk rock versions.

"The Unquiet Grave" recommends that bereavement following death of a loved one should last no more than a year. The Bolicks' version omits a verse that warns against necrophilia:

You crave one kiss of my clay-cold lips but my breath smells earthy strong
If you have one kiss from my lily-white lips your time will not be long

Andrew Rowan Summers, Folkways FP 64 (1950)
Joan Baez, Vanguard VSD 79160 (1964)
Blue Sky Boys, Capitol T2483, ST2483, Arhoolie CD 9063 (1965)

Wandering Boy *See* Somebody's Boy Is Homeless Tonight

Watching You (James Melvin Henson, 1915)

We knew this hymn for many years. Instead of a duet, we thought it sounded better as a trio.

Whitey & Hogan, Decca 5810 (1939)
Blue Sky Boys, "There's an Eye Watching You," WGST Program 25, October 4, 1946
Blue Sky Boys, WGST Program 44, October 31, 1946, Copper Creek CCCD-0121

We Buried Her Beneath the Willow (Cumberland Ridge Runners, 1936)

This is on sheet music from M.M. Cole. It was written by the Cumberland Ridge Runners in honor of Linda Parker, a member of their group.

The copyright authors of record are "the Cumberland Ridge Runners, pseud. of Karl Davis, Doc Hopkins & Harty Taylor," performers on Chicago's WLS National Barn Dance in the 1930s, as was Linda Parker (née Genevieve Elizabeth Muenich [1912–1935]), a popular singer who died from peritonitis following a ruptured appendix while on tour with the Cumberland Ridge Runners.

Karl & Harty, ARC 6-04-61 (1936)
Blue Sky Boys, "We Buried Her," Bluebird B-8017, Bear Family BCD 15951 (1937)
Blue Sky Boys, WGST Program 1, September 2, 1946
Blue Sky Boys, WCYB (Bristol, VA, 1949)
Kitty Wells, Decca 78858, Bear Family BCD 15638 (1958)
Mac Martin & the Dixie Travelers, Copper Creek CCCD-0235 (2004)

Courtesy of Lester S. Levy Collection of Sheet Music, Sheridan Libraries, Johns Hopkins University.

We Parted by the Riverside (Will S. Hays, 1866)

I generally associate this song with the original Carter Family.

William Shakespeare Hays (1837–1907) was a versatile Louisville, Kentucky, songwriter who bequeathed several evergreens to country music, starting with this one:

We Parted by the Riverside (1866)
You've Been a Friend to Me (1867)
I'll Remember You Love in My Prayers (1869)
The Little Old Log Cabin in the Lane (1870)
The Old Man's Drunk Again (1872)
Molly Darling (1872)
Quit Dat Tickling Me (1872)
Take This Letter to My Mother (1873)
Jimmie Brown (The Paper Boy) (1875)

Ernest Stoneman, Edison 52312, County CD-3510 (1928)
Stoneman Family, Victor V-40030, Bear Family BCD 16094 (1928)
Carter Family, "Tell Me That You Love Me," Victor 23656, Montgomery Ward M-4250, Bear Family BCD 15865 (1932)
Blue Sky Boys, Bluebird B-8482, Montgomery Ward M-8668, Bear Family BCD 15951 (1940)
Blue Sky Boys, WCYB (Bristol, VA, 1949), Copper Creek CCCD-0125

Wednesday Night Waltz (Spencer Williams-words, anonymous melody)

The Leake County Revelers' popular record inspired numerous covers, including some with lyrics supplied by the versatile New Orleans songwriter Spencer Williams (1889–1965), who later added lyrics to "Basin Street Blues."

Leake County Revelers, Columbia 15189-D, 37600, 20199, County CD-3514 (1927)
Frank Luther & Carson Robison, Brunswick 297 (1928)
Wiley Walker & Gene Sullivan, OKeh 05711 (1940)
Cope Brothers, King 806 (1947)
Blue Sky Boys, Starday SLP-257, Gusto GT7-0549 (1963)

Were You There?

This is one of the spirituals popularized by the Fisk University Jubilee Singers, who toured the country to raise funds for the school after the Civil War.

Fisk University Jubilee Singers, Columbia A3919, Archeophone ARCH 5020 (1920), Folkways FA2372 (1955) (two versions)
Marian Anderson, HMV DA 1670 (1936), RCA Victor 10-1431, LM-2032 (1947) (two versions)
Wade Mainer, Bluebird B-8273, JSP 77124 (1939)
Bill Monroe, Bluebird B-8953, Bear Family BCD 16399 (1941), Decca 74896, Bear Family BCD 15529 (1963) (two versions)
Blue Sky Boys, WGST Program 139, March 13, 1947, Copper Creek CCCD-0120

What Does the Deep Sea Say? (Bob Miller-Charlotte Kay, 1929)

Mac and Bob were the first people I remember singing this song. Whenever I hear it, I usually think of them.

Bob Miller (1895–1955) was a professional composer who specialized in country themes. His successes included "Eleven Cent Cotton and Forty Cent Meat" (1928), "Twenty-One Years" (1930), and "There's a Star Spangled Banner Waving Somewhere" (1942).

Vernon Dalhart, Harmony 960-H (as Mack Allen), Diva 2960-G, Velvet Tone 1960-V (1929)
Lester McFarland & Robert A. Gardner, Brunswick 483 (1930)
Bob Miller (as Bob Ferguson), Columbia 15727-D (1931)
Bob Miller Trio, Victor 23737, Bluebird B-5034 (1932)
Monroe Brothers, "Where Is My Sailor Boy," Bluebird B-6762, Montgomery Ward M-7140, Bear Family BCD 16399 (1936)
Blue Sky Boys, WCYB (Bristol, VA, 1949), Copper Creek CCCD-0125
Bill Monroe & Doc Watson, "Where Is My Sailor Boy," Smithsonian Folkways CD 40064 (1963)
Blue Sky Boys, Rounder 0052 (1975)
Tim O'Brien, Sugar Hill CD-3954 (2001)

What Have You Done? *See* Darling, Think of What You've Done

What Would You Give in Exchange for Your Soul? (F. J. Berry-words, James H. Carr-music, 1912)

When we first went to WGST in 1936, we usually rehearsed in the storage room of the Crazy Water Crystal Company's office located in the Arcade Building. Mr. J. W. Fincher spent as much time in Georgia as he did in the Carolinas, even though the [company's] *headquarters were in Charlotte. During one of his visits to Atlanta, he asked if we knew "What Would You Give in Exchange for Your Soul?" We informed him that we didn't. He said this song had been popular for the Monroe Brothers and he would like for us to learn it. He brought us the book and taught us the melody. For us, the song wasn't the attraction we thought it would be but we were glad to learn it.*

Wade Mainer and Zeke Morris made the first recording of this song in Charlotte on February 14, 1936. The Monroe Brothers recorded it there three days later and persuaded Eli Oberstein to suppress the Mainer version. Theirs became a career hit, prompting cover versions and reply songs (including three more by the Monroes) over the next couple of years. The Mainer-Morris version was quietly released on Montgomery Ward in 1937 and Bluebird in 1939, attracting little attention. (See Rosenberg and Wolfe, *The Music of Bill Monroe* [University of Illinois, 2007], 6–7, for a detailed discussion.)

Wade Mainer & Zeke Morris, Montgomery Ward M-7134 (as Mainer's Mountaineers), Bluebird B-8073, JSP 77118 (1936)
Monroe Brothers, Bluebird B-6309, Montgomery Ward M-4745, Bear Family BCD 16399 (1936)
Blue Sky Boys, WGST Program 2, September 3, 1946
Blue Sky Boys, WGST Program 30, October 11, 1946, Copper Creek CCCD-0120
Webb Pierce, Decca 74384 (1962)
Louvin Brothers, Capitol ST2331, Bear Family BCD 15561 (1963)
Bill Monroe & Doc Watson, Smithsonian Folkways CD 40064 (1963)

When Heaven Comes Down (Johnnie Bailes-Al Robinson)

All the lost sinners with mansions so fine
Will give up their millions, their whiskey and wine . . .
God in his glory will level the ground
On the great day of judgment when Heaven comes down

Populist resentments like these are echoed in other pessimistic songs of the period, like "No Vacancy," "This World Can't Stand Long," and "Building on the Sand," reflecting discontent in the face of postwar inflation, a severe housing shortage affecting returning veterans, the emerging Cold War, and other issues.

Blue Sky Boys, RCA Victor 21-0156, Bear Family BCD 15951 (1949)

When I Reach That City on the Hill (Johnson Oatman Jr.-R. E. Winsett)

YE ARE THE LIGHT OF THE WORLD. A CITY THAT IS SET ON A HILL CANNOT BE HID. —MATTHEW 5:14

J.E. Mainer's Mountaineers, "City on the Hill," Bluebird B-6160, Montgomery Ward M-4711, JSP 77118 (1935)
Blue Sky Boys, WGST Program 17, September 24, 1946, Copper Creek CCCD-0120

James & Martha Carson, Capitol 954 (1950)
Porter Wagoner, RCA Victor LSP-3488 (1965)
Wade & Julia Mainer, "City on the Hill," Old Homestead OHTR-4000, OHCD-4013, OHCD-70068 (1976)

When I Take My Vacation in Heaven (Herbert W. Buffum, 1925)

Ruth Donaldson & Helen Jepsen, Gennett 6192, Challenge 341 (1927), Superior 2735 (1931) (two versions)
Mother McCollum, Vocalion 1532 (1930)
Ernest Tubb, Decca 14506, Bear Family BCD 15498 (1949)
Rose Maddox, Capitol ST1439, Bear Family BCD 15743 (1960)
Johnny Cash, Columbia CS 8522, Bear Family BCD 15562 (1961)
Blue Sky Boys, Rounder 0052 (1975)

When My Blue Moon Turns to Gold Again (Wiley Walker-Gene Sullivan, 1940)

We learned this song by hearing the recording by Wiley Walker and Gene Sullivan, the duo who composed it. As I remember, the lyrics we used are those sent by the publishers.

Wiley Walker & Gene Sullivan, OKeh 06374, Columbia 37665, 20264 (1941)
Blue Sky Boys, WGST Program 27, October 8, 1946, Copper Creek CCCD-0145
Elvis Presley, RCA Victor LPM 1382 (1956)
Bill Monroe, Decca 32075, 74896, Bear Family BCD 15529 (1966)
Merle Haggard, MCA 2267 (1977)

When the Ransomed Get Home (Samuel William Beazley, ca. 1905)

We learned this from our father. I don't think anyone ever noticed, but in the chorus the harmony singer takes the lead on parts of the song:

Bill:When the ransomed get home
    Earl:When the ransomed get home
Bill:What a joy it will be
    Earl:What a joy it will be
Earl: To be gathered up there
    Bill: To be gathered up there
Earl: Blessed Savior with Thee

Bill: Blessed Savior with Thee
Bill:Where no partings e'er come
Earl:Where no partings e'er come
Bill:And we never more roam
Earl:And we never more roam
Earl: In the beautiful land
Bill: In the beautiful land
Earl:When the ransomed get home
Bill:When the ransomed get home

The verses are sung in regular two-part harmony with the harmony following the lead. This is the way it was written and the way our father taught it to us.

Blue Sky Boys, Bluebird B-6764, Montgomery Ward M-7160, Bear Family BCD 15951 (1936)

When the Roses Bloom Again
See I'll Be with You When the Roses Bloom Again

When the Roses Bloom in Dixieland
(George "Honey Boy" Evans, 1913)

Honey Boy Evans (1870–1915) was a Welsh-born entertainer and composer whose other songs included "Come Take a Trip in My Airship" (1904), "In the Good Old Summer Time" (1912), and numerous 1890s relics in the coon song genre.

Carter Family, Victor V-40229, Bluebird B-5716, Montgomery Ward M-4544, Bear Family BCD 15865 (1929)
Blue Sky Boys, Bluebird B-8294, Montgomery Ward M-8410, Bear Family BCD 15951 (1939)

When the Stars Begin to Fall *See* My Lord, What a Morning

When the Valley Moon Was Low

Bill Bolick told Charles Wolfe that this song came to the Blue Sky Boys via Hugh Anglyn of Griffin, Georgia, when they were on WGST in the 1930s. Anglyn is also credited with "Angel Mother" from 1947.

Blue Sky Boys, Bluebird B-8152, Bear Family BCD 15951 (1938)

Where Our Darling Sleeps Tonight (William A. Bolick-Earl Bolick)

On a 2007 broadcast of "Back to the Blue Ridge" (WVTF-FM, Roanoke), host Kinney Rorrer credited this song to Virginia Richardson, who knew the Bolicks, but see the note to "There'll Be No Broken Hearts for Me."

Blue Sky Boys, Bluebird AXM2-5525, Bear Family BCD 15951 (1950)

Where Shall I Be? (Charles P. Jones, 1899)

Charles Price Jones (1865–1949), from Kingston, Georgia, was a prolific composer and Baptist pastor active in the Holiness movement starting in the 1890s. This spiritual appears in *The Negro and His Songs,* by Howard W. Odum and Guy B. Johnson (University of North Carolina, 1925), 134–35. Jones's "I Would Not Be Denied" is also still well known.

See note to "Crying Holy Unto the Lord."

Norfolk Jubilee Quartet, Paramount 12234, (1924, re-recorded 1927)
Blind Lemon Jefferson (as Deacon L. J. Bates), Paramount 12585, JSP 7706 (1927)
Carter Family, Victor 23523, Bluebird B-6055, Montgomery Ward M-4229, Bear Family BCD 15865 (1930)
Coleman Brothers, Decca 48041 (1944)
Blue Sky Boys, WGST Program 19, September 26, 1946
Gospel Harmonettes, Specialty 846, LP-2107, CD7205 (1952)
Hylo Brown, Starday SEP-215, SLP-204 (1962)

Where the Soul Never Dies (William M. Golden, 1914)

In all probability we learned this song from our father, who could read shaped notes. He attended a lot of singing schools sponsored at the church. Usually teachers used one or two songbooks they sold to their pupils and my father always purchased them. He would sing bits of these songs around the house and if there were any I liked I would get him to help me [learn them].

This popular hymn was first titled "To Canaan's Land I'm on My Way." It was coupled with "Sunny Side of Life" on the Bolicks' first release in 1936, and remained a best-selling record for years.

Rev. M.L. Thrasher & His Gospel Singers, Columbia 15271-D (1928)

Blue Sky Boys, Bluebird B-6457, Montgomery Ward M-5029, Bear Family BCD 15951 (1936)
Blue Sky Boys, "Where the Soul of Man Never Dies," WGST Program 34, October 17, 1946, Copper Creek CCCD-0121
Hank & Audrey Williams, "Where the Soul of Man Never Dies," Health and Happiness Show no. 1, Mercury 314 517 862-2 (1949)
Jim & Jesse, Epic BN 26107, Bear Family BCD 15716 (1964)
Kitty Wells, Decca 74679 (1965)
Oak Ridge Boys, Columbia 3-10320, KC-33502, KC-33935 (1976)
Ricky Skaggs, Sugar Hill SH-3711 (1980)

Where We'll Never Grow Old (James C. Moore, 1914)

This can be found in many old religious songbooks. James C. Moore dedicated it to his father and mother. We knew it before we ever got into radio.

The Smith's Sacred Singers record was coupled with "Pictures from Life's Other Side." It became a best seller that made both hymns perennial favorites.

Smith's Sacred Singers, Columbia 15090-D (1926)
Lester McFarland & Robert A. Gardner, Brunswick 115, Vocalion 5119 (as Smoky Mountain Sacred Singers) (1926)
Alfred G. Karnes, Victor 20840, Bear Family BCD 16094 (1927)
Carter Family, Victor 23656, Bluebird B-5058, Bear Family BCD 15865 (1932)
Blue Sky Boys, WGST Program 23, October 2, 1946, Copper Creek CCCD-0121
Jim Reeves, RCA Victor LSP-2552, Bear Family BCD 15656 (1962)

Whispering Hope (Alice Hawthorne [Septimus Winner], 1868)

WHICH HOPE WE HAVE AS AN ANCHOR OF THE SOUL, BOTH SURE AND STEADFAST, AND WHICH ENTERETH INTO THAT WITHIN THE VEIL. —HEBREWS 6:19

This is a selection we heard as far back as we can remember. Earl and I sang it from our first time in show business until we quit. When we did it for Victor, we changed the song to suit our own peculiar style. When we decided to put it on again for Starday, we thought we would do it the way it was written.

Septimus Winner (1827–1902) claimed "Sweet Allalee" and "Listen to the Mocking Bird," crediting the pseudonymous "Alice Hawthorne" on the latter.

Alma Gluck, Victor 87107 (1914)
Lester McFarland & Robert A. Gardner, Vocalion 5192 (1927)
Sons of the Pioneers, Standard Transcription B-3391-A, Bear Family BCD 16104 (1936)
Blue Sky Boys, Bluebird B-8401, Montgomery Ward M-8666, Bear Family BCD 15951 (1940)
Blue Sky Boys, WCYB (Bristol, VA, 1949), Copper Creek CCCD-0126
Hank Snow, Thesaurus transcription 1649, Bear Family BCD 15488 (1951)
Mac Wiseman, Dot DLP 3135, Bear Family BCD 15976 (1959)
Blue Sky Boys, Starday SLP-269, Gusto GT7-0549-2 (1963)

White Flower for You *See* I'll Wear a White Flower for You

Who Wouldn't Be Lonely? (Leon Chappelear-Jimmie Davis)

In 1933 the Lone Star Cowboys vocal trio consisted of the Shelton Brothers and Leon Chappelear. Their "Just Because" and "Deep Elm Blues" were also recorded that year and overshadowed this lovely song.

Lone Star Cowboys, Bluebird B-5283 (1933)
Shelton Brothers, Decca 5100 (1935)
Blue Sky Boys, Bluebird B-7661, Montgomery Ward M-7469, Bear Family BCD 15951 (1938)
Ray & Ina Patterson, County 715 (1969)

Who's Gonna Shoe Your Pretty Little Feet? (Child 76)

I have heard this sung so many different ways. I can recall us singing it similar to the Monroes' "Little Red Shoes," and also a version without the little yodel. Our final version was a combination of the two.

The two title verses hark back to the eighteenth century or earlier and figure prominently in Charlie Poole's "Don't Let Your Deal Go Down Blues" (1925). McCartt and Patterson's popular "Green Valley Waltz" attached the words to a waltz tune that included the second strain Bill played on the mandolin, along with the "little yodel." "Where did you get those high top shoes?" can be heard in "John Henry" and other folk songs.

Charlie Poole, "Don't Let Your Deal Go Down Blues," Columbia 15038-D, County CD-3503 (1925, words only)

McCartt Brothers & Patterson, "Green Valley Waltz," Columbia 15454-D, County CD-3511 (1928)
Renfro Valley Boys, Paramount 3321, Broadway 8334 (1931)
Monroe Brothers, "Little Red Shoes," Bluebird B-6645, Montgomery Ward M-4748, Bear Family BCD 16399, BCD 17355 (1936)
Woody Guthrie, Asch A432, Smithsonian Folkways CD 40112 (1944)
Patti Page, "Who's Gonna Shoe My Pretty Little Feet," Mercury MG-25101, Bear Family BCD 17355 (1951), Columbia CL 2353, CS 9153 (1965) (two versions)
Everly Brothers, Cadence CLP-3016, Ace CH75, Bear Family BCD 17355 (1958)
Blue Sky Boys, Capitol T2483, ST2483, Arhoolie CD-9063 (1965)

Why Not Confess (Ralph Hamrick)

Ralph Hamrick was a songwriter and working musician on West Virginia radio in the 1930s. When he and Curly Parker worked with the Holden Brothers (Fairley and Jack), Parker learned the song and reportedly taught it to the Blue Sky Boys when he joined them on WPTF (Raleigh) in October 1940, in time for them to record it on October 7. It was issued first on Montgomery Ward. When the Bluebird version was belatedly published in 1944, it sold well and probably influenced RCA's decision to re-sign the Bolicks in 1946. The Bolicks recorded Hamrick's "Sweetheart Mountain Rose" in 1963.

"Why Not Confess," with "Since the Angels Took My Mother Far Away," was the only Blue Sky Boys disc issued between 1941 and 1946. It was also their first to be reviewed in *Billboard.*

Blue Sky Boys, Montgomery Ward M-8846, Bluebird 33-0516, Bear Family BCD 15951 (1940)
Maddox Brothers & Rose, Decca 28551 (early 1950s)
Johnnie & Jack, Bear Family BCD 15553 (1956)
Louvin Brothers, Capitol T910, Bear Family BCD 15561 (1957)
Brother Oswald, Starday SLP-192, Gusto GT7-0632-2 (1962)
Blue Sky Boys, Starday 677, SLP-257, Gusto GT7-0549-2 (1963)
Jim & Jesse, Epic BN 26074, Bear Family BCD 15716 (1963)

Why Should It End This Way?

This was sent to us by one of our radio audience, written in freehand and without the name of the sender. I reworked the song several times before we sang it. We had heard it previous to the time it was sent to us but the lyrics were quite different.

Tobacco Tags, Bluebird B-6790 (1936, in the Bolick collection)
Melody Boys, Montgomery Ward M-7691 (1938)
Blue Sky Boys, WGST Program 139, March 13, 1947, Copper Creek CCCD-0120

Why Should You Be Troubled and Sad? (Dorsey Dixon)

Dorsey Dixon (1897–1968) of Rockingham, North Carolina, appeared with his brother Howard as the Dixon Brothers on the *Crazy Barn Dance* in the mid-'30s and on records from 1936 to 1938. See the note to "Two Little Rosebuds."

Blue Sky Boys, Starday SLP-269, Gusto GT7-0549 (1963)

Wild and Reckless Hobo (Laws H2)

Bill claimed that Lute Isenhour "was the first I ever heard sing 'A Wild and Reckless Hobo' and several old-time numbers like that." It shares one verse with Jimmie Rodgers's "Waiting for a Train" and another with "Danville Girl." Blind Dick Burnett from Monticello, Kentucky, printed it around 1913 in a songbook that also included "I Am a Man of Constant Sorrow" and "Going Around the World." The George Reneau record draws from Burnett's text and Bill Bolick acknowledged that the Blue Sky Boys version was "basically the same as the Burnett and Rutherford recording."

George Reneau ("Blind Musician of the Smoky Mountains"), Vocalion 14999, 5059 (1925)
(Dick) Burnett & (Leonard) Rutherford, "Rambling Reckless Hobo," Columbia 15240-D, Yazoo 2200 (1927, in the Bolick collection)
Blue Sky Boys, Capitol T2483, ST2483, Arhoolie CD-9063 (1965)

Will My Mother Know Me There? (Johnson Oatman Jr.-words, William M. Golden-music, 1906)

L.V. Jones and His Virginia Singing Class, OKeh 45187, Yazoo 2021 (1927)
Carter Family, Montgomery Ward M-7155, Bear Family BCD 15865 (1933)
Blue Sky Boys, WGST Program 22, October 1, 1946, Copper Creek CCCD-0120

The Reckless Hobo

A rambling, reckless Hobo Left his happy home,
Started on a western trip By himself alone,
He said, upon this western trip I guess I'll have some fun;
Standing at a station house. This is the song he sung:
Standing on a platform Smoking a cheap cigar,
Waiting for a freight train To catch an empty car
Thinking of those good old times, Wishing they'd come again;
I'm a thousand miles away from home, Bumming a railroad tra

Kind Miss, kind Miss, Won't you give me a bite to eat,
A little piece of cold corn bread A little piece of meat?
She threw her arms around me Say I'll love you as a friend,
But if I give to you this time
You'll be bumming around again.
Kind Miss, kind Miss, Don't talk to me so rough;
You think I am a hobo Because I look so tough.
She took me in her kitchen, She treated me nice and kind,
She put me in the notion Of bumming all the time.

When I left her kitchen I went strolling down in town,
I heard a double-header blow, I thought it was western bound
I walked out to the railroad, Out to the railroad shop,
I heard the agent tell a man The freight train would not stop
My heart began to rove around And I began to sing
If that freight train goes through this town
I'll catch it on the wing
I pulled my cap down over my eyes And walked out to the track
And caught the stirrup of empty car And never did look back.

I got off in Danville, Got stuck on a Danville girl,
You bet your life she's out of sight
She wears the Danville curl.
She wears her hair on the back of her head
Like high toned people do,
But if a west-bound train pulls out tonight
I'll bid that girl adieu.
Now I am in your city, boys, Trying to do what is right;
Don't think because I am a railroad boy
That I am not all right.

My pocketbook is empty, My heart is filled with pain;
Ten thousand miles away from home.
Bumming a railroad train.

Blind Dick Burnett songbook, 1913.

Will the Angels Play Their Harps for Me?
(Walter Hirsch-Monte Wilhite, 1928)

Garland Bolick heard the Happiness Boys (Billy Jones and Ernest Hare) sing this on a 1920s NBC broadcast and bought the sheet music. No known recordings of it by Bill and Earl survive.

Frank Luther, Banner S-6225, OKeh 45275 (as Jimmie Black) (two versions, both 1928)
Carson Robison Trio, Cameo 8380 (1928)

Blue Sky Boys, Bluebird (master broken, 1940)
Hylo Brown, Capitol T1168, Bear Family BCD 15572 (1958), Copper Creek CCCD-0135 (1959), Rural Rhythm RRHB-183 (1967) (three versions)

Will the Circle Be Unbroken?
(Ada R. Habershon-words, Charles H. Gabriel-music, 1907)

Modern versions of this song derive from the Carter Family's "Can the Circle Be Unbroken" (1935), that substitutes verses about a mother's death and funeral for the original hymn. The record sold well and the Carter lyrics, later re-titled "Will the Circle Be Unbroken," all but eclipsed the original, especially after being chosen as the title song for a best-selling Nitty Gritty Dirt Band album in 1972. Versions below are from the 1907 original.

Silver Leaf Quartette of Norfolk, OKeh 8777, Vocalion 04395 (1930)
Monroe Brothers, Bluebird B-6820, Montgomery Ward M-7142, Bear Family BCD 16399 (1936)
Eddy Arnold, RCA Victor LPM 1224, Bear Family BCD 15726 (1956)
Rose Maddox, Capitol T1437, ST1437, Bear Family BCD 15743 (1960)
Blue Sky Boys, Capitol T2483, ST2483, Arhoolie CD-9063 (1965)
Pentangle, Transatlantic TRASM29, TRS106 (1973)

Will You Meet Me Over Yonder?
(R. E. Winsett, 1923)

This was taken from a Stamps-Baxter book and we probably heard quartets around Atlanta sing it. There seemed to be an abundance of quartets in Georgia. With my small knowledge of music and having first heard others sing it, we didn't have too much trouble learning songs of this type.

Robert Emmett Winsett (1876–1952) wrote popular hymns and ran publishing houses in Arkansas and Tennessee that produced hymnbooks for many years.

Chuck Wagon Gang, Vocalion 04342, Conqueror 8837, Bear Family BCD 17348 (1936)
Blue Sky Boys, WGST Program 18, September 25, 1946, Copper Creek CCCD-0120
Osborne Brothers, Decca 75079, Bear Family BCD 15748 (1968)
Doyle Lawson & Quicksilver, Crossroads 1075 (ca. 2004)

Will You Miss Me When I'm Gone?
(Rev. George Beebe-H. E. McAfee, ca. 1900)

This song was among our most requested trios, taken from a book by Stamps-Baxter. It has five verses, but we usually sang only three and the chorus. We never tried to sing this as a duet.

Blue Sky Boys, *Favorite Hymns and Folk Songs*, 16

Carter Family, Victor 21638, Bear Family BCD 15865 (1928)
Blue Sky Boys, audition disc, November 20, 1939
Blue Sky Boys, WGST Program 2, September 3, 1946
Blue Sky Boys, WGST Program 36, October 21, 1946
Blue Sky Boys, WCYB (Bristol, VA, 1949), Copper Creek CCCD-0126
Stanley Brothers, Wango LP-104, LP-105 (as John's Gospel Quartet), County 739, 754, Rebel CD-1110 (1963)

Within the Circle *See* I'm Going Home This Evening

Won't It Be Wonderful There?
(James Rowe-words, Homer F. Morris-music, 1930)

This is a song we knew before we started singing over the air. Our first complete version was probably sent by Stamps-Baxter.

Knippers Brothers & Parker, Champion 16829, 45128 (1934)
Blue Sky Boys, Program 33, October 16, 1946, Copper Creek CCCD-0146
George Jones, Musicor MS-3061, MS-3203, Bear Family BCD 16928 (1966)
Ricky Skaggs Family, Rounder 0151 (1978–79)

Worried Man Blues

We didn't learn it from the Carter Family, for I heard it before I ever heard their record, and sang it with Lute Isenhour.

Carter Family, Victor V-40317, 27497, Bear Family BCD 15865 (1930)
Carter Family, ARC 7-05-55, Conqueror 8816, Bear Family BCD 15865 (1935)
Woody Guthrie, Smithsonian Folkways CD 40101 (1944)
Blue Sky Boys, WCYB (Bristol, VA, 1949)
Jerry Reed, "A Worried Man," RCA 74-0211, LSP-4204 (1969)

Worried Mind (Ted Daffan-Jimmie Davis)

In the late 1930s, the Bar-X Cowboys' steel guitarist Ted Daffan wrote a few songs. One became a hit when OKeh recorded it with several of the Cowboys and issued it under Daffan's name. His "Born to Lose" and "I'm a Fool to Care" were also major hits.

Ted Daffan's Texans, OKeh 05668, Conqueror 9563, 9699, Columbia 37013, 20039 (1940)
Blue Sky Boys, audition disc, 1941
Roy Acuff, OKeh 06229, Conqueror 9889, Columbia 37020, 20046, Bear Family BCD 17300 (1941)
Wayne King & His Orchestra, Victor 27373 (1941)
Bob Wills, "New Worried Mind," OKeh 06101, Bear Family BCD 15933 (1941), Kaleidoscope F-29, K-29 (1946) (two versions)
Blue Sky Boys, Gusto GT7-0549 (1963)

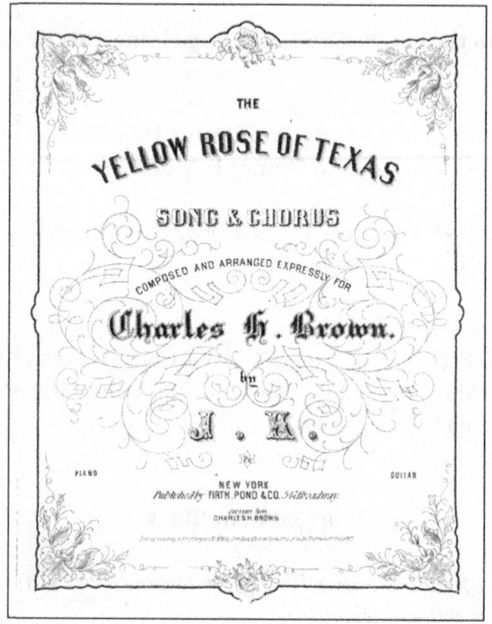

Courtesy of Lester S. Levy Collection of Sheet Music, Sheridan Libraries, Johns Hopkins University.

Yellow Rose of Texas (J.K., 1858)

I first heard this song in the early thirties. I can remember [hearing it by] *Mac and Bob, Gene Autry, and Karl and Harty. I haven't heard this sung to the tune that we used in many years; the melody is now altogether different. Boyd Hilton, who lived in the Blackburn community not far from Hickory, knew the song and I'm quite certain I learned the words from him. His family attended the same church as we did and we came to be good friends. This song has three different tunes that I am aware of. One came from Boyd Hilton, one came from artists on WLS out of Chicago, and the other is used most widely by people who sing it today. Boyd and I liked the way WLS artists sang it. He and I sang it that way as did Earl and I.*

Ben Jarrell, Gennett 6143 (1927)
Renfro Valley Boys (Karl & Harty), Paramount 3316 (1932)
Gene Autry & Jimmy Long, Perfect 12912, Conqueror 8096 (1933, in the Bolick collection)
Blue Sky Boys, WGST Program 12, September 17, 1946
Blue Sky Boys, WGST Program 40, October 25, 1946, Copper Creek CCCD-0145
Mitch Miller with Orchestra & Chorus, Columbia 40540 (1955)

You Can Be a Millionaire with Me (Grady and Hazel Cole)

Hazel and Grady Cole wrote a number of pretty songs. They sent me a handwritten copy of [this one] *in the late thirties or early forties. Their most popular song was "Tramp on the Street."*

Also see "Tramp on the Street."

Grady & Hazel Cole, Bluebird B-8262 (1939, in the Bolick collection)
Pappy "Gube" Beaver, Capitol 284, Cattle CCD-332 (1944)
Blue Sky Boys, WCYB (Bristol, VA, 1949), Copper Creek CCCD-0125
Blue Sky Boys, "You Could Be a Millionaire," Rounder 0052 (1975)
J.D. Crowe, Rounder 11661-0512-2 (ca. 2006)

You Give Me Your Love and I'll Give You Mine (L. A. Davis-words, M. J. Fitzpatrick-music, 1902)

This is a song I associate with Mac and Bob. I'm sure it was from their early songbook that we learned this song.

Mac & Bob's WLS Book of Songs (1931), 52

J.W. Myers, Zon-O-Phone 858, Phonozoic 004 (1902)
Lester McFarland, Brunswick 109, Vocalion 5129 (1926)

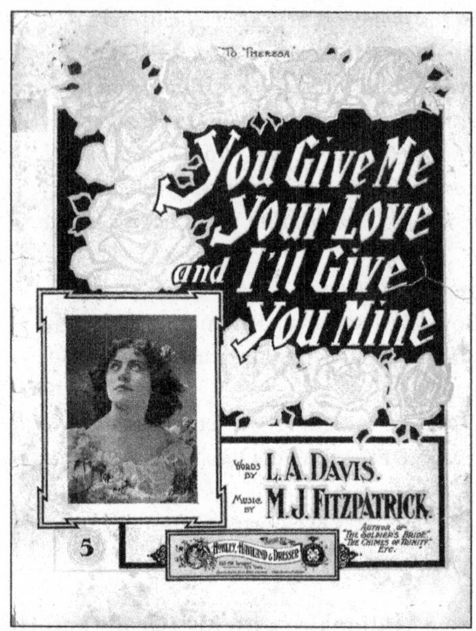

Courtesy of Lester S. Levy Collection of Sheet Music, Sheridan Libraries, Johns Hopkins University.

Blue Sky Boys, Bluebird B-6714, Montgomery Ward M-7159, Bear Family BCD 15951 (1936)
Carter Family, "Give Me Your Love and I'll Give You Mine," Decca 5318, Bear Family BCD 15865 (1936)
Claude King, "Give Me Your Love and I'll Give You Mine," Columbia CS 8610 (1962)
Morris Brothers, Vanguard VCD 121/22 (1963)
Maybelle Carter, "Give Me Your Love and I'll Give You Mine," Columbia CS 9275 (1965)
Don Reno and Bill Harrell, King 6155, 1033, Gusto GT7-2121-2 (1967)

You've Branded Your Name on My Heart (Bill and Earl Bolick)

Blue Sky Boys, WNAO audition disc, January 28. 1949
Blue Sky Boys, RCA Victor 21-0075, Bear Family BCD 15951 (1949)
Blue Sky Boys, WCYB (Bristol, VA, 1949)
Ray & Ina Patterson and The Pacos Valley Boys, Cozy 346 (ca. 1950)
Blue Sky Boys, "Your Brand Will Remain on My Heart," Starday SLP-257, Gusto GT7-0549 (1963)

FIDDLE AND DANCE TUNES

The Bolicks' troubles with Homer Sherrill from 1935–37 did nothing to make them like hillbilly fiddling. Bill liked Curly Parker's backups and fills, but he found fiddle tunes most useful for running out the clock on broadcasts, when they could be as short or as long as necessary. Those cited here were featured on the Blue Sky Boys' 1946–49 broadcasts that survive on transcriptions. Bill's comments are taken from Copper Creek CD notes, prepared by Gary Reid. There are many more recorded versions of these tunes, and just a few samples appear here.

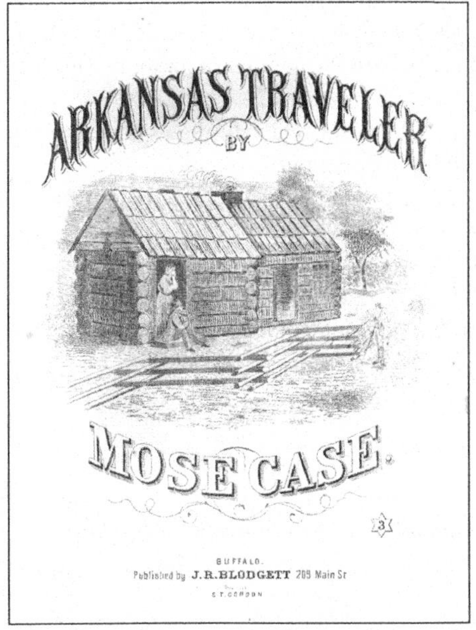

Courtesy of Lester S. Levy Collection of Sheet Music, Sheridan Libraries, Johns Hopkins University.

Arkansas Traveler

Most fiddlers consider this number a classic. Curly's rendition of it is somewhat different, as he picks some of the melody with his fingers instead of using the bow.

Don Richardson, Columbia A2140 (1916), OKeh 1255 (1919) (two versions)
Henry C. Gilliland & A.C. (Eck) Robertson, Victor 18956, County CD-3515 (1922)
Blue Sky Boys, WGST Program 30, October 11, 1946, Copper Creek CCCD-0121
Blue Sky Boys, WCYB (Bristol, VA, 1949)
Tommy Jackson, Dot 1085 (1951)

Black Mountain Blues

This fiddle tune was without doubt the most popular fiddle number Curly Parker played. He learned this tune from Leslie Keith, who composed it. Curly played "Black Mountain Blues" much better than Leslie, who worked with us at a later date. In order to play it, the fiddle had to be tuned in A. The way Curly twanged the strings gave it a much better, lonesome sound. He received more requests for this than all the other fiddle tunes he played combined. I have heard a number of variations of this but no one could come up to Curly and Leslie.

Leslie Keith (1906–1977) learned the fiddle tune he called "Black Mountain Blues" in the 1920s from a Birmingham, Alabama–area fiddler named Jim Montgomery and from the fiddling of Charlie Stripling, famous for playing it as "The Lost Child."

Stripling Brothers, "The Lost Child," Vocalion 5321, County 401 (1928)
Blue Sky Boys, audition disc, 1941
Blue Sky Boys, WGST Program 34, October 17, 1946, Copper Creek CCCD-0121
Curly Fox, "Black Mountain Rag," King 710 (1947)
Leslie Keith, Rich-R'-Tone 428 (ca. 1948, unissued)
Tommy Jackson, "Black Mountain Rag," Mercury 6310, 72026 (1950), Dot DEP-1036 (1954) (two versions)

Buffalo Gal

This song is also commonly known as "Alabama Gal." Uncle Josh sometimes sang a line or two but it was generally used by us as a fill-in at the end of our programs.

Gid Tanner & Riley Puckett, "Alabama Gal," Columbia 119-D (1924)
Riley Puckett, "Alabama Gal," Columbia 15185-D (1927)
Blue Sky Boys, WGST Program 22, October 1, 1946, Copper Creek CCCD-0146
Blue Sky Boys, WCYB (Bristol, VA, 1949)
Tommy Jackson, Dot 1247 (1954)

Cacklin' Hen

This is a traditional instrumental used by most fiddlers, although I'm not sure how many play it today. I think most fiddlers today have entered into what they consider a higher plane of music. Sometimes Uncle Josh joined in with "All my chickens gone, all my chickens gone."

Fiddlin' John Carson, "The Old Hen Cackled and the Rooster's Going to Crow," OKeh 4890 (1923)
Blue Sky Boys, WGST Program 38, October 23, 1946, Copper Creek CCCD-0145
Blue Sky Boys, WCYB (Bristol, VA, 1949)

Chicken Reel

This is another fiddle tune we used as a fill-in at the end of the radio program. I'm sure that every old-time fiddler is familiar with it.

E.F. "Poss" Acree, OKeh 40197 (1924)
Varsity Eight, Cameo 8141 (1928)
Blue Sky Boys, WGST Program 43, October 30, 1946, Copper Creek CCCD-0146
Tommy Jackson, Mercury 70974 (1950)
Roy Acuff, "Sixteen Chickens and a Tambourine," Capitol 2548, T2278, Bear Family BCD 15562 (1953)

Cumberland Gap

This is a breakdown fiddle tune I have known for many years. Uncle Josh usually sang a few lines when we used it.

Gid Tanner & Riley Puckett, Columbia 210-D (1924)
Blue Sky Boys, Program 24, October 3, 1946, Copper Creek CCCD-0146
Blue Sky Boys, WCYB (Bristol, VA, 1949)

Danced All Night with a Bottle in My Hand

We used this number at the end of our programs. The only words I ever heard with it are:

Danced all night with a bottle in my hand,
A bottle in my hand, a bottle in my hand,
Danced all night with a bottle in my hand,
Just before dawn gave the fiddler a dram

Gid Tanner & His Skillet Lickers, Columbia 15108-D (1926)
Clayton McMichen's Georgia Wildcats, "Give the Fiddler a Dram," Varsity 5011, Joe Davis 3510 (1932)
Blue Sky Boys, WGST Program 44, October 31, 1946, Copper Creek CCCD-0145

Devil's Dream

Charles D'Almaine, Victor 4985, 16042 (1906)
Blue Sky Boys, WGST Program 6, September 9, 1946, Copper Creek CCCD-0145
Tommy Jackson, Mercury 6261 (1950)

East Tennessee Blues

We didn't know this number until Curly Parker joined us in 1940. I played very few breakdowns on the mandolin. We felt our listeners liked the songs we sang better than the instrumentals. With the exception of several selections, we didn't receive too many requests for fiddle tunes, although I think Curly was one of the best fiddlers.

This fiddle tune acquired lyrics and became "She's Killing Me" on a 1931 Nichols Brothers record made in Charlotte. It was covered by the Callahan Brothers, Bob Wills, and others in the 1930s.

Al Hopkins & the Buckle Busters, Brunswick 103, Vocalion 5016 (as The Hill Billies) (1926)
Nichols Brothers, "She's Killing Me," Victor 23582 (1931)
Callahan Brothers, "She's Killing Me," Banner 33004, Conqueror 8334 (1934)
Bob Wills, "She's Killing Me," Vocalion 03424, Columbia 37622, 20221, Bear Family BCD 1593 (1936)
Blue Sky Boys, WCYB (Bristol, VA, 1949), Copper Creek CCCD-0126
Tommy Jackson, Dot 1232 (1954)
Fred Price & Clint Howard, Folkways FA 2355, Smithsonian Folkways CD 40029/30 (1960)

Eighth of January

This was played by Curly [Parker]*'s younger brother Ruel. Both were very good fiddlers.*

"Eighth of January" commemorates General Andrew Jackson's 1815 victory over British troops at the end of the War of 1812; it was once known as "Jackson's Victory." Jimmie Driftwood's lyrics turned the old tune into "The Battle of New Orleans" and started a vogue for country songs with historical themes.

Blue Sky Boys, WGST Program 32, October 15, 1946, Copper Creek CCCD-0120
Tommy Jackson, Dot 1218 (1954)
Jimmie Driftwood, "The Battle of New Orleans," RCA Victor LPM 1635, Bear Family BCD 15465 (1957)
Johnny Horton, "The Battle of New Orleans," Columbia 4-41339, C2K 64761 (1959)

Fire on the Mountain

This is another instrumental that we used at the end of most of our programs. The length depended on the time we had left. Many times Uncle Josh sang a few lines. I have no idea as to when or where this song originated or who composed the few lyrics.

Clayton McMichen & Riley Puckett, Columbia 15185-D (1927)
Blue Sky Boys, WGST Program 4, September 5, 1946
Blue Sky Boys, WGST Program 139, March 13, 1947, Copper Creek CCCD-0145
Curly Fox, "Come Here, Son," King 710 (1947)
Blue Sky Boys, WCYB (Bristol, VA, 1949)
Ed Haley, Rounder CD 1134 (1940s)
Tommy Jackson, Mercury 6313 (1950)

Fisher's Hornpipe

Blue Sky Boys, audition disc, November 20, 1939

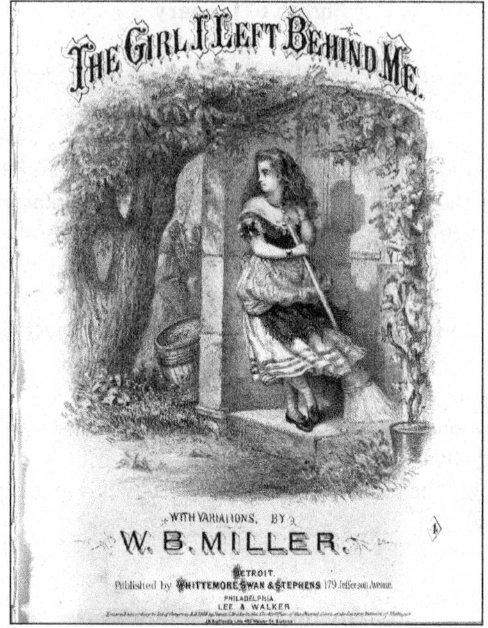

Courtesy of Lester S. Levy Collection of Sheet Music, Sheridan Libraries, Johns Hopkins University.

The Girl I Left Behind Me (Samuel Lover, 1797–1868)

We regarded this song as strictly a fiddle tune although there are words to it. I have heard a number of variant verses but never gave much thought to singing them.

Jasper Bisbee, Edison 51381 (1924)
Blue Sky Boys, WCYB (Bristol, VA, 1949), Copper Creek CCCD-0125
Tommy Jackson, "The Gal I Left Behind," Dot 1252 (1954)

Golden Slippers (James A. Bland, 1879)

Curly Parker and his brother Ruel played a large number of instrumentals in this manner and could work up some beautiful duets.

The Bolicks' vocal version survives from a WCYB broadcast in 1949.

Blue Sky Boys, WGST Program 28, October 9, 1946, Copper Creek CCCD-0121
Tommy Jackson, Dot 1218 (1954)

Hop Light Ladies *See* Miss McLeod's Reel

Ida Red

Riley Puckett, Columbia 15102-D (1926)
Clayton McMichen's Georgia Wildcats, "Ider Red," Crown 3397, Varsity 5011 (1932)
Bob Wills, Vocalion 05079, Conqueror 9404, Bear Family BCD 15933 (1938)
Blue Sky Boys, audition disc, November 20, 1939
Blue Sky Boys, WGST Program 32, October 15, 1946, Copper Creek CCCD-0120

Katy Hill

We didn't use this fiddle tune until Curly Parker joined us. He plays it as well or better than most fiddlers. I seldom played any breakdowns on the mandolin. When I did, it was usually a hornpipe, schottische, or polka.

Allen Sisson, Edison 51690 (1925)
Bill Monroe, Bluebird B-8693, Montgomery Ward M-8863, Bear Family BCD 16399 (1940)
Blue Sky Boys, WGST Program 1, September 2, 1946, Copper Creek CCCD-0120
Blue Sky Boys, WGST Program 21, September 30, 1946
Tommy Jackson, Dot 1186 (1953)

Leather Britches

Leake County Revelers, Columbia 15149-D, County LP 532 (1927)
Michael Coleman, "Lord McDonald's Reel," Columbia 33237-F, 33507-F, Gael-Linn CED 161 (1927)
Blue Sky Boys, WGST Program 7, September 10, 1946, Copper Creek CCCD-0146
Tommy Jackson, Dot 1137 (1952)

Courtesy of Lester S. Levy Collection of Sheet Music, Sheridan Libraries, Johns Hopkins University.

Listen to the Mocking Bird (Alice Hawthorne [Septimus Winner]-words, Richard Milburn-music, 1855)

Many people have never heard the words to this song. I can remember singing it when I was a boy. If my memory serves me correctly, it was in one of my school songbooks. Earl and I never tried to sing it, although I remember most of the words. It seemed to be a favorite of most fiddlers, and the lyrics faded away. It was quite popular with our radio audience. Curly Parker received more fan mail for this than [anything else] *he played with the exception of "Black Mountain Blues."*

The lyricist Septimus Winner (1827-1902) wrote numerous songs under pseudonyms. Richard Milburn was an African American barber in Philadelphia who whistled this tune to his own guitar accompaniment. He is credited only on the first 1855 editions; his name was soon dropped and is absent from this 1856 sheet music cover.

Blue Sky Boys, WGST Program 25, October 4, 1946
Blue Sky Boys, WCYB (Bristol, VA, 1949), Copper Creek CCCD-0125

Lost Train Blues

Arthur Smith had considerable influence on other fiddlers in the 1930s and '40s; his all but forgotten "Lost Train Blues" was a predecessor of "Orange Blossom Special." Youtube video excerpts from 1940s Jimmy Wakely films show Smith playing both tunes.

Arthur Smith, Bluebird B-5858 (1935)
J.E. Mainer's Mountaineers, "New Lost Train Blues," Bluebird B-6424, Montgomery Ward M-7003, JSP 77118 (1936)
Blue Sky Boys, WGST Program 42, October 29, 1946, Copper Creek CCCD-0124
Blue Sky Boys, WCYB (Bristol, VA, 1949)

Miss McLeod's Reel

I have heard some words to ["Hop Light, Ladies"] *but never tried to sing it. We always considered it a fiddle tune and used it that way.*

American versions of this old Scots-Irish tune are sometimes called "Hop Light Ladies" or "Did You Ever See the Devil, Uncle Joe."

James C. McAuliffe, "Miss McCloud's Reel," Edison 7230 (1899), 8184 (1902) (two versions)
Don Richardson, Columbia A2575 (1916)
Fiddlin' John Carson, "Hop Light Lady," OKeh 45011 (1925)
Gid Tanner & His Skillet Lickers, Columbia 15730-D, County CD-3509 (1931)
Blue Sky Boys, "Hop Light Ladies," WCYB (Bristol, VA, 1949), Copper Creek CCCD-0126

Mississippi Sawyer

This southern version of "Downfall of Paris" harks back to an eighteenth-century French *contredanse*, "Le carillon national," that became the melody for "Ah! ça ira!," a provocative anthem of the French Revolution in 1790. The phrase originated with Benjamin Franklin, America's minister to France from 1778 to 1785, who enthusiastically predicted victory for the American Revolution, saying, "Ah! ça ira!" (It'll be fine!). Under that heading, there were respectable and vernacular versions of the song:

Malgré les mutins tout réussira.

In spite of the mutineers everything shall succeed.

Nos ennemis confus en restent là
Et nous allons chanter Alléluia!
Ah!! ça ira, ça ira, ça ira

Our enemies, confounded, stay petrified
And we shall sing Hallelujah!
Ah! It'll be fine, it'll be fine, it'll be fine!

Ah! ça ira, ça ira, ça ira
Les aristocrates on les pendra!
Et quand on les aura tous pendus
On leur fichera la pelle au cul

Ah! It'll be fine, it'll be fine, it'll be fine
The aristocrats, we'll hang them!
And when we've hung them all
We'll stick a shovel up their arse

Don Richardson, Columbia A2018 (1916)
Murphy Brothers Harp Band, "The Downfall of Paris," Columbia 15646-D (1930)
Blue Sky Boys, WCYB (Bristol, VA, 1949)
Tommy Jackson, Dot 1086 (1951)

Old Joe Clark

Two versions feature fiddlers Curly Parker (WGST) and Leslie Keith (WCYB) respectively. On the latter, Bill leads on the verses and tenor in the chorus, while Earl sings bass and Leslie takes the lead. Bill Bolick preferred Curly's unassertive melodic style to the rougher hoedown sound of Leslie Keith, who had played and recorded with the Stanley Brothers in 1947–48 before joining the Blue Sky Boys in 1949–51.

Fiddlin' John Carson, "Fare You Well, Old Joe Clark," OKeh 40038 (1923)
Fiddlin' John Carson, "Old Joe Clark," OKeh 45198 (1927)
Blue Sky Boys, WGST Program 50, November 8, 1946, Copper Creek CCCD-0120
Blue Sky Boys, WCYB (Bristol, VA, 1949), Copper Creek CCCD-0126
Tommy Jackson, Mercury 6280 (1950), Dot 1252 (1954) (two versions)

Ragtime Annie

A.C. (Eck) Robertson, Victor 19149, County CD-3515 (1922)
Blue Sky Boys, Program 34, October 17, 1946, Copper Creek CCCD-0146
Tommy Jackson, Dot 1137 (1952)

Rubber Dolly/Back Up and Push

Curly played this number a bit differently from the way I learned it. Lute Isenhour, with whom I worked when I first started in radio, sang three or four verses. One was: "Somebody told her I loved a soldier, now she won't buy me that rubber dolly."

Georgia Organ Grinders, "Back Up and Push," Columbia 15394-D (1929)
Ella Fitzgerald, "My Wubba Dolly," Decca 2816 (1939, parody)
Bill Monroe, "Back Up and Push," Bluebird B-8988, Bear Family BCD 16399 (1941)
Blue Sky Boys, WCYB (Bristol, VA, 1949), Copper Creek CCCD-0125
Tommy Jackson, "Back Up and Push," Mercury 6313 (1950)
Tommy Jackson, "My Wubba Dolly," Dot 1234 (1954)

Sally Goodin'

Before I learned to play an instrument of any kind, I can recall hearing my mother sing a few words to it.

A.C. (Eck) Robertson, Victor 18956, County CD-3515 (1922)
Blue Sky Boys, WGST Program 11, September 16, 1946
Blue Sky Boys, WGST Program 37, October 22, 1946, Copper Creek CCCD-0146
Blue Sky Boys, WCYB (Bristol, VA, 1949)
Tommy Jackson, Mercury 6246, 72026 (1950), Dot 1232 (1954) (two versions)

Skip to My Lou

Blue Sky Boys, audition disc, 1941

Soldier's Joy

"Soldier's Joy" appeared in print in the eighteenth century. It's one of the oldest documented fiddle tunes still current in the English-speaking world and is known in Scandinavia under various names.

Samantha Bumgarner & Eva Davis, "I Am My Mama's Darling Child," Columbia 191-D (1924)

Gid Tanner & His Skillet Lickers, Columbia 15538-D, County CD-3509 (1930)
Gid Tanner & His Skillet Lickers, Bluebird B-5658, Montgomery Ward M-4907, RCA Victor 20-2168, 8416-2 (1934)
Blue Sky Boys, WGST Program 27, October 8, 1946, Copper Creek CCCD-0145
Tommy Jackson, Dot 1085 (1951)
Lindbäck Family (Finland), Rounder 82161-1160-2 (1952)

Sourwood Mountain

This is known to most old-time fiddlers. Occasionally Uncle Josh would sing a verse or more. We usually played it at the end of a program.

Uncle Am Stuart, Vocalion 14840, 5036 (1924)
Blue Sky Boys, WGST Program 19, September 26, 1946
Blue Sky Boys, WGST Program 47, November 5, 1946, Copper Creek CCCD-0121
Blue Sky Boys, WCYB (Bristol, VA, 1949), Copper Creek CCCD-0125

Tugboat

(Dick) Burnett & (Leonard) Rutherford, "Ladies on the Steamboat," Columbia 15209-D, Yazoo 2200 (1927)
Kessinger Brothers, Brunswick 315 (1929)
Dad Massey, "Tugboat and Pineywoods," ARC 7-03-53, Rounder 82161 1160-2 (1936)
Blue Sky Boys, WGST Program 16, September 23, 1946
Benny Thomasson, County 724, CD-2737 (1970)

Turkey in the Straw (as "Zip Coon": J. B. Farrell, 1834/G. W. Dixon, 1834)

Before I ever learned to play any type instrument, I learned the words to it in some magazine or book. I remember copying at least three or four verses and having it in my possession for a number of years. I haven't been able to locate it in any of my memorabilia.

Billy Golden, Berliner 726 (1896), Edison 4011 (1890s) (two versions)
Don Richardson, "Old Zip Coon," Columbia A2140 (1916)

Don Richardson, "Turkey In the Straw," Columbia A3452 (1921)
Henry C. Gilliland & A.C. ("Eck") Robertson, Victor 19149, County CD-3515 (1922)
Blue Sky Boys, WGST Program 48, November 6, 1946, Copper Creek CCCD-0145
Tommy Jackson, Mercury 6261 (1950)

Whistlin' Rufus (W. Murdock Lind-words, Frederick Allen "Kerry" Mills-music, 1899)

I can recall hearing it years ago on the WLS Barn Dance, sung by the Arkansas Woodchopper. I can remember him singing "Little Ah Sid," "The Old Swimming Hole," and "Just Plain Folks."

Arkie, the Arkansas Woodchopper (Luther Ossenbrink, 1906–1981), performed on the WLS National Barn Dance in Chicago from 1930 through 1959.

Len Spencer, Berliner 04 (1899)
Vess L. Ossman (banjo), Berliner 092 (1899)
Ernest Thompson, Columbia 15006-D, Harmony 5109-H (as Jed Tompkins) (1924)
Blue Sky Boys, WGST Program 26, October 7, 1946, Copper Creek CCCD-0121
Tommy Jackson, Dot 1139 (1952)

SOURCES FOR BLUE SKY BOYS SONGS

Ballads and Songs in Laws and Child Collections

Barbara Allen (Child 84)
The Butcher's Boy (Laws P24)
Down on the Banks of the Ohio (Laws F5)
Fair Eyed Ellen (Laws F1a)
I Never Will Marry (Laws K17)
Katie Dear (Laws M4)
The Knoxville Girl (Laws P35)
Maid Freed from the Gallows (Child 95)
Mary of the Wild Moor (Laws P24)
Midnight on the Stormy Deep (Laws M1)
The Murder of the Lawson Family (Walter Smith 1930, Laws F35)

Oh, Marry in Time (Child 2)
Trail to Mexico (Laws B13)
The Unquiet Grave (Child 78)
Who's Gonna Shoe Your Pretty Little Feet? (Child 76)

From Hymn Books

The ABC Song
Amazing Grace
Beautiful
A Beautiful Life
The B-I-B-L-E
The Blood of Jesus
Boat of Life
Come to the Saviour
The Cross on the Hill
Crying Holy Unto the Lord
Death Is Only a Dream
Didn't They Crucify My Lord?
Drifting Too Far from the Shore
Drop Your Net
Dust on the Bible
The Dying Boy's Prayer
The Dying Mother
Farther Along
Gathering Buds
God Is Still on the Throne
Heaven Holds All to Me
The Hills of Home
How Beautiful Heaven Must Be
Hymns My Mother Sang
I Believe It for My Mother Told Me So
I Need the Prayers (Of Those I Love)
If I Could Hear My Mother Pray Again
If We Never Meet Again
I'll Be Listening
I'll Be No Stranger There
I'll Meet You in the Morning
I'll Take My Saviour by the Hand
I'll Wear a White Flower for You
I'm Going to Write to Heaven
I'm S-A-V-E-D

Just a Little Talk with Jesus
Just One Way to the Pearly Gate
Kneel at the Cross
The Last Mile of the Way
Let the Lower Lights Be Burning
Lifeline
Life's Railway to Heaven
The Lily of the Valley
Lonely Tombs
Lord Be with Us—Amen
My God, Why Have You Forsaken Me?
My Main Trial Is Yet to Come
The New Golden Rule
No Disappointment in Heaven
No One to Welcome Me Home
Oh, Sister Mary, Don't You Weep
An Old Account Was Settled
Old Camp Meeting Days
Old Fashioned Meeting
Only Let Me Walk with Thee
Only One Step More
A Picture on the Wall
Pictures from Life's Other Side
Precious Memories
Precious Moments
The Promise of the Lord
Radio Station S-A-V-E-D
Romans 6:23
Row Us Over the Tide
The Royal Telephone
A Satisfied Mind
Searching for a Soldier's Grave
Shake Hands with Your Mother Today
Shake My Mother's Hand for Me
Shall I Miss It
She'll Be There (What a Friend We Have in Mother)
Silent Night
Someone's Last Day
Sunny Side of Life
Sweetest Mother
Take Up Thy Cross
That Beautiful Home
This Evening Light

This Is Like Heaven to Me
This World Can't Stand Long
Throw Out the Lifeline
Turn Your Radio On
Watching You
Were You There?
What Would You Give in Exchange for Your Soul?
When Heaven Comes Down
When I Take My Vacation in Heaven
When the Ransomed Get Home
Where Shall I Be?
Where the Soul Never Dies
Where We'll Never Grow Old
Whispering Hope
Will My Mother Know Me There?
Will the Circle Be Unbroken?
Will You Meet Me Over Yonder?
Will You Miss Me When I'm Gone?
Won't It Be Wonderful There?
You Can Be a Millionaire with Me

Jim Anglin (credited to Roy Acuff)

As Long As I Live
Searching for a Soldier's Grave
This World Can't Stand Long
Unloved and Unclaimed

Bill Bolick (with co-writers)

Angel Mother (Hugh Anglyn)
Behind These Prison Walls of Love (Hazel Hope Jarrard)
Don't Take the Light (From My Dark Cell) (Calvin Van Pelt)
Shake Hands with Your Mother Today (Pete Roy)

Bill and Earl Bolick (with co-writers)

Come to the Saviour (Thomas D. Lynn)
God Is Still on the Throne
I Cannot Take You Back Now

I Love Her More, Now Mother's Old
Sweetheart Mountain Rose (Ralph Hamrick)
There'll Be No Broken Hearts for Me
There's Been a Change (Calvin Van Pelt)
Where Our Darling Sleeps Tonight
You've Branded Your Name on My Heart

Garland Bolick (hymns sung at home)

Amazing Grace
The Blood of Jesus
Death Is Only a Dream
The Dying Boy's Prayer
The Hills of Home
Life's Railway to Heaven
There's No Disappointment in Heaven
An Old Account Was Settled
Only Let Me Walk with Thee
Row Us Over the Tide
Someone's Last Day
Take Up Thy Cross
When the Ransomed Get Home
Where the Soul Never Dies

Albert E. Brumley

Her Mansion Is Higher Than Mine

Herbert W. Buffum

Old Fashioned Meeting
When I Take My Vacation in Heaven

M.M. Cole (publisher)

Asleep in the Briny Deep
Goodbye Maggie
Hymns My Mother Sang
Mary of the Wild Moor

No Place to Pillow My Head
Song of the Blind
Take Me Back to Renfro Valley
They're All Going Home But One
Trail to Mexico (also Stamps-Baxter)

Jimmie Davis (with co-writers)

Don't Say Goodbye If You Love Me (Bonnie Dodd)
Who Wouldn't Be Lonely (Leon Chappelear)
Worried Mind (Ted Daffan)

Karl Davis

Lord Be with Us—Amen
The New Golden Rule
The Unfinished Rug

Karl Davis–Harty Taylor

The B-I-B-L-E
The Chapel in the Hills
Darling, Think of What You've Done
God Sent My Little Girl
The Holiness Mother
The House Where We Were Wed (with Will Carleton)
I'm Just Here to Get My Baby Out of Jail
Kentucky
Romans 6:23
She Has Forgotten
There's No Other Love for Me
We Buried Her Beneath the Willow

Karl Davis–Harty Taylor–Patrick McAdory

Answer to 'The Prisoner's Dream'
I'm Going Home This Evening
The Prisoner's Dream
They're All Going Home But One

Dorsey Dixon

I'll Wear a White Flower for You
My God, Why Have You Forsaken Me?
Two Little Rosebuds
Why Should You Be Troubled and Sad?

William M. Golden

A Beautiful Life
Lonely Tombs
Where the Soul Never Dies
Will My Mother Know Me There?

Doc Hopkins

Asleep in the Briny Deep
No Place to Pillow My Head
Song of the Blind

Lute Isenhour

Can't You Hear That Night Bird Crying?
Darling, Think of What You've Done
Didn't They Crucify My Lord?
In My Little Home in Tennessee
Katie Dear
(The) Knoxville Girl
Little Bessie
Roll On, Buddy
Rubber Dolly
Short Life of Trouble
There'll Come a Time
Two Little Rosebuds

Frederick M. Lehman

The Royal Telephone
There's No Disappointment in Heaven

Lester McFarland and Robert A. Gardner (records and songbooks)

Are You Tired of Me, My Darling?
The East Bound Train
I Believe It for My Mother Told Me So
I Told the Stars About You
I Wish I Had Died in My Cradle
I'll Be with You When the Roses Bloom Again
(The) Knoxville Girl
The Last Mile of the Way
Midnight on the Stormy Deep
(There's) No Disappointment in Heaven
On the Old Plantation
Sweet Allallee
Take Up Thy Cross
What Does the Deep Sea Say?
Where We'll Never Grow Old
Whispering Hope
You Give Me Your Love and I'll Give You Mine

Johnson Oatman, Jr. (lyrics)

The Last Mile of the Way
Only Let Me Walk with Thee
When I Reach That City on the Hill
Will My Mother Know Me There?

Ray & Ina Patterson

ABC Song
The Dying Mother
Unquiet Grave
You've Branded Your Name on My Heart

Reformation Glory (hymnal, 1923)

Beautiful
The Blood of Jesus
Heaven Holds All to Me
Shall I Miss It?
On the Sunny Side of Life
This Evening Light

James Rowe and James D. Vaughan

Gathering Buds (James Rowe-words, James D. Vaughan-music, 1921)
Give Me My Roses Now (James Rowe-words, R. H. Cornelius-music, 1925)
The Hills of Home (James Rowe-words, James D. Vaughan-music, 1914)
I Dreamed I Searched Heaven for You (Mary Ethel Weiss-James D. Vaughan, 1931)
I Need the Prayers (Of Those I Love) (J. E. Rankin, ca.1878/James D. Vaughan, 1908)
If I Could Hear My Mother Pray Again (James Rowe-words, James D. Vaughan-music, 1922)
Just One Way to the Pearly Gate (James Rowe-words, James D. Vaughan-music, 1920)
Only Let Me Walk with Thee (Johnson Oatman Jr.-words, James D. Vaughan-music, 1915)
Won't It Be Wonderful There? (James Rowe-words, Homer F. Morris-music, 1930)

Stamps-Baxter Music Company (publisher)

Farther Along
I'll Be Listening
I'll Be No Stranger There
Just a Little Talk with Jesus
Only One Step More
Precious Memories
Shake My Mother's Hand for Me
The Sweetest Gift (A Mother's Smile)
Trail to Mexico (also published by M.M. Cole)
Turn Your Radio On
What Would You Give in Exchange for Your Soul?
Will You Meet Me Over Yonder?
Will You Miss Me When I'm Gone?
Won't It Be Wonderful There?

Barney Elliott Warren

Are You Building on the Rock?
Beautiful
The Blood of Jesus
Farther Along (arranger)
Shall I Miss It?

APPENDIX 2

Blue Sky Boys Discography

This account documents all known studio recordings by the Blue Sky Boys and includes all available information about each session. All Bluebird and RCA Victor titles from 1936 through 1950 first appeared as ten-inch 78 rpm discs, with some re-published on 45 rpm discs after 1948.

All surviving published records from 1936 through 1950 appear in the comprehensive Bear Family box set *The Blue Sky Boys: The Sunny Side of Life* (Bear Family BCD 15951) and on JSP 7782, *The Blue Sky Boys.* To conserve space and avoid repetition, neither boxed set is cited in individual entries.

The discography includes broadcast and audition transcriptions that were part of Bill Bolick's personal collection. As noted below, excerpts from them have been published.

These labels are cited, some with abbreviations:

Bear Family (CD)
Bb [Bluebird] (78, 33)
Blue Tone (CD)
Cam [RCA Camden] (33)
Capitol (33)
Copper Creek (CD)
County (33, CD)
Dust-to-Digital (CD)
Gusto (CD)
JEMF [John Edwards Memorial Foundation] (33)
LC [Library of Congress] (33)
London (Japan) (33)
MW [Montgomery Ward] (78)
Old Timey (33)
RCA [RCA Victor] (all formats)
Rimrock (33)
RZ [Regal Zonophone] (78)
    G series: Australia
    MR series: England
Rounder (33, CD)
Starday (33)
Twin (India) (78)

BLUEBIRD AND RCA VICTOR STUDIO SESSIONS, 1936–46

All titles from 1936 through 1940 feature Bill and Earl Bolick, almost always in duets with, respectively, their mandolin and guitar. A fiddle and string bass were added to postwar sessions. Matrix numbers (at left) apply to 78 rpm releases only. When RCA introduced 45 rpm discs in 1949, separately coded matrix numbers were assigned to 78 and 45 rpm metal parts. Virtually all original labels include the sub-credit "Bill and Earl Bolick."

BS 102640-1	I'm Just Here to Get My Baby Out of Jail	Bb B-6621, MW M-7017, Bb AXM2-5525 (33), Blue Tone BSR-CD-1001/2 (CD)
BS 102641-1	Sunny Side of Life	Bb B-6457, MW M-5029, Cam CAL-797 (33), Rounder 1006 (33), RCA (Japan) RA-5331 (33), RCA 8417-2R (CD), Blue Tone BSR-CD-1001/2 (CD)
BS 102642-1	There'll Come a Time	Bb B-6538, MW M-7016, Blue Tone BSR-CD-1001/2 (CD)
BS 102643-1	Where the Soul Never Dies	Bb B-6457, MW M-5029, Blue Tone BSR-CD-1001/2 (CD)
	Where the Soul of Man Never Dies	RCA 2100-2R (CD)
BS 102644-1	Midnight On the Stormy Sea	Bb B-6480, MW M-5033, Bb AXM2-5525 (33), Blue Tone BSR-CD-1001/2 (CD)
BS 102645-1	Take Up Thy Cross	Bb B-6567, MW M-7018, Bb AXM2-5525 (33), Blue Tone BSR-CD-1001/2 (CD)
BS 102646-1	Row Us Over the Tide	Bb B-6567, MW M-7018, Blue Tone BSR-CD-1001/2 (CD)
BS 102647-1	Down On the Banks of the Ohio	Bb B-6480, MW M-5033, Cam CAL-797 (33), AL2-0726 (33), Rounder 1006 (33), RCA (Japan) RA-5220 (33), RA-5331 (33), Blue Tone BSR-CD-1001/2 (CD)
BS 102648-1	I'm Troubled, I'm Troubled	Bb B-6538, MW M-7016, Blue Tone BSR-CD-1001/2 (CD)
BS 102649-1	The Dying Boy's Prayer	Bb B-6621, MW M-7017, Blue Tone BSR-CD-1001/2 (CD)

Southern Radio Corporation, 208 S. Tryon Street, Charlotte, Tuesday, 16 June 1936, 1-3 PM. Eli Oberstein, producer.

BS 02569-1	No One to Welcome Me Home	Bb B-6669, MW M-7158, Blue Tone BSR-CD-1001/2 (CD)
BS 02570-2	Short Life of Trouble	unissued (file note: "cannot find wax")
BS 02571-1	Didn't They Crucify My Lord	Bb B-6764, MW M-7160, Blue Tone BSR-CD-1001/2 (CD)
BS 02572-1	Only Let Me Walk with Thee	Bb B-6669, MW M-7158, Blue Tone BSR-CD-1001/2 (CD)
BS 02573-1	Can't You Hear That Night Bird Crying	Bb B-6854, MW M-7162, Blue Tone BSR-CD-1001/2 (CD)
BS 02574-1	An Old Account Was Settled	Bb B-6901, MW M-7161, Blue Tone BSR-CD-1001/2 (CD)
BS 02575-1	Sweet Allallee	Bb B-6854, MW M-7162, Twin FT 8337, Rounder 1006 (33), RCA (Japan) RA-5331 (33), Blue Tone BSR-CD-1001/2 (CD)
BS 02576-1	You Give Me Your Love	Bb B-6714, MW M-7159, RZ G23374, Bb AXM2-5525 (33), Blue Tone BSR-CD-1001/2 (CD)
BS 02577-1	I Believe It	Bb B-6808, MW M-7085, Blue Tone BSR-CD-1001/2 (CD)
BS 02578-1	When the Ransomed Get Home	Bb B-6764, MW M-7160, Blue Tone BSR-CD-1001/2 (CD)
BS 02579-1	Fair Eyed Ellen	Bb B-6808, MW M-7161, Blue Tone BSR-CD-1001/2 (CD)
BS 02580-1	Somebody Makes Me Think of You	Bb B-6714, MW M-7159, Rounder 1006 (33), RCA (Japan) RA-5331 (33), Blue Tone BSR-CD-1001/2 (CD)

Southern Radio Corporation, 208 S. Tryon Street, Charlotte, Tuesday, 13 October 1936, 2–4:35 PM. Eli Oberstein, producer.

BS 011800-1	Sweet Evalina	Bb B-7348, MW M-7323, Blue Tone BSR-CD-1003/4 (CD)
BS 011801-1	No Home	Bb B-7311, MW M-7323, Blue Tone BSR-CD-1003/4 (CD)

BS 011802-1	What Have You Done?	Bb B-7173, MW M-7324, Blue Tone BSR-CD-1003/4 (CD)
BS 011803-1	Sing a Song for the Blind	Bb B-8143, MW M-7324, Blue Tone BSR-CD-1003/4 (CD)
BS 011804-1	Within the Circle	Bb B-7113, MW M-7325, Blue Tone BSR-CD-1003/4 (CD)
BS 011805-1	They're All Home But One	Bb B-7173, Blue Tone BSR-CD-1003/4 (CD)
BS 011806-1	Hymns My Mother Sang	Bb B-7311, MW M-7326, Bb AXM2-5525 (33), Blue Tone BSR-CD-1003/4 (CD)
BS 011807-1	Have No Desire to Roam	Bb B-7348, MW M-7326, Bb AXM2-5525 (33), Blue Tone BSR-CD-1003/4 (CD)
BS 011808-1	No Disappointment in Heaven	Bb B-7113, MW M-7325, Blue Tone BSR-CD-1003/4(CD)
BS 011809-1	Story of the Knoxville Girl	Bb B-7755, MW M-7327, Cam CAL-797 (33), ADL2-0726 (33), RCA (Japan) RA-5220 (33), Blue Tone BSR-CD-1003/4 (CD)
BS 011810-1	On the Old Plantation	Bb B-8128, Old Timey 102 (33), Blue Tone BSR-CD-1003/4 (CD)
BS 011811-1	In My Little Home in Tennessee	Bb B-8143, MW M-7327, Blue Tone BSR-CD-1003/4 (CD)

Rooms 1050, 1052, 1054, Hotel Charlotte, Charlotte, NC, Monday, 2 August 1937, 9:30–11:30 AM. Eli Oberstein, producer. RCA Camden ADL2-0726 is in artificial stereo.

BS 018671-1	Beautiful, Beautiful Brown Eyes	Bb B-7755, MW M-7470, Cam ADL2-0726 (33), Bb AXM2-5525 (33), RCA (Japan) RA-5276 (33), Blue Tone BSR-CD-1003/4 (CD)
BS 018672-1	The Prisoner's Dream	Bb B-7411, MW M-7468, Bb AXM2-5525 (33), Blue Tone BSR-CD-1003/4 (CD)
BS 018673-1	The Answer to "The Prisoner's Dream"	Bb B-7411, MW M-7469, Blue Tone BSR-CD-1003/4 (CD)
BS 018674-1	When the Stars Begin to Fall	Bb B-7472, MW M-7471, Blue Tone BSR-CD-1003/4 (CD)

BS 018675-1	We Buried Her	Bb B-8017, RZ MR 3021, Blue Tone BSR-CD-1003/4 (CD)
BS 018676-1	Heaven Holds All for Me	Bb B-7803, MW M-7472, Blue Tone BSR-CD-1003/4 (CD)
BS 018677-1	Little Bessie	Bb B-8017, MW M-7470, RZ MR 3021, Cam ADL2-0726 (33), ACL1-0535 (33), RCA LPV-569 (33), Bb AXM2-5525 (33), Blue Tone BSR-CD-1003/4 (CD)
BS 018678-1	I Need the Prayers	Bb B-7803, MW M-7472, Bb AXM2-5525 (33), Blue Tone BSR-CD-1003/4 (CD)
BS 018679-2	Old Fashioned Meeting	Bb B-7472, Blue Tone BSR-CD-1003/4 (CD)
BS 018680-1	Katie Dear	Bb B-7661, MW M-7468, Cam CAL-797 (33), ADL2-0726 (33), Rounder 1006 (33), RCA (Japan) RA-5220 (33), RCA 8417-2R (CD), Blue Tone BSR-CD-1003/4 (CD)
BS 018681-1	Who Wouldn't Be Lonely	Bb B-7661, MW M-7469, Blue Tone BSR-CD-1003/4 (CD)
BS 018682-1	Life Line	Bb B-7984, MW M-7471, Blue Tone BSR-CD-1003/4 (CD)

Hotel Charlotte, Rooms 1050, 1052, 1054, Charlotte, NC, Tuesday, 25 January 1938, 11:30 AM–1:30 PM. Eli Oberstein, producer, Raymond Sooy and Fred Lynch, engineers.

Regal Zonophone MR 3021 as ALABAMA BARNSTORMERS. RCA Camden ADL2-0726 is in artificial stereo.

BS 027739-1	When the Valley Moon Was Low	Bb B-8152
BS 027740-1	My Last Letter	Bb B-7878, MW M-7568, Bb AXM2-5525 (33), Cam ADL2-0726 (33)
BS 027741-1	Mother Went Her Holiness Way	Bb B-7984
BS 027742-1	Hang Out the Front Door Key	Bb B-8110, MW M-7567
BS 027743-1	This Is Like Heaven to Me	Bb B-7933, MW M-7566
BS 027744-1	I've Found a Friend	Bb B-7933, MW M-7566

BS 027745-1	Asleep in the Briny Deep	MW M-7568, Cam CAL-797 (33), Rounder 1006 (33), RCA (Japan) RA-5331 (33)
BS 027746-1	Last Night While Standing by My Window	Bb B-7878
BS 027747-1	There Was a Time	Bb B-8110, MW M-7567
BS 027748-1	Bring Back My Wandering Boy	Bb B-8128

Rooms 121, 123, Andrew Jackson Hotel, 223 E. Main Street, Rock Hill, SC, Tuesday, 27 September 1938, 1–3 PM. Frank Walker and Dan Hornsby, producers.

BS 041222-1	When the Roses Bloom in Dixieland	Bb B-8294, MW M-8410, Bb AXM2-5525 (33)
BS 041223-1	Are You from Dixie?	Bb B-8294, MW M-8410, Cam CAL-797(33), ADL2-0726 (33), Rounder 1006 (33), RCA (Japan) RA-5220 (33), RCA 8417-2R (CD)
BS 041224-1	Give Me My Roses Now	Bb B-8308, MW M-8411
BS 041225-1	The House Where We Were Wed	Bb B-8308, MW M-8411
BS 041226-1	There's No Other Love for Me	Bb B-8339, MW M-8412
BS 041227-1	God Sent My Little Girl	Bb B-8339, MW M-8412
BS 041228-1	Someone's Last Day	Bb B-8356, MW M-8413
BS 041229-1	She'll Be There	Bb B-8356, MW M-8413
BS 041230-1	The Lightning Express	Bb B-8369, MW M-8414, Cam CAL-797 (33), Rounder 1006 (33), RCA (Japan) RA-5331 (33)
BS 041231-1	The Royal Telephone	Bb B-8369, MW M-8414
BS 041232-1	The Convict and the Rose	Bb B-8522, MW M-8415, Twin FT 8998, Cam ADL2-0726 (33), RCA (Japan) RA-5276 (33)
BS 041233-1	Father, Dear Father, Come Home	Bb B-8522, MW M-8415, Twin FT 8998

Rooms 104, 106, Kimball House, 30 S. Pryor Street, Atlanta, GA, Monday, 21 August 1939, 3:45–6 PM. Frank Walker and Dan Hornsby, producers.

Introduction by John Fulton and theme
Will You Miss Me When I'm Gone?
Uncle Josh comedy
I Told the Stars About You
Fisher's Hornpipe
I Need the Prayers
Ida Red
Roll On Buddy
Outro and theme

Richard "Red" Hicks (vocal, guitar) added. Acoustical Equipment Company, Atlanta, GA, Monday, 20 November 1939. This is a privately made audition disc.

BS 047500-1	Will the Angels Play Their Harps for Me	Master broken
BS 047501-1	We Parted by the Riverside	Bb B-8482, MW M-8668
BS 047502-1	Only One Step More	Bb B-8552, MW M-8670, Bb AXM2-5525 (33), RCA 2100-2R (CD)
BS 047503-1	The East Bound Train	Bb B-8552, MW M-8670
BS 047504-1	Since the Angels Took My Mother Far Away	Bb unissued
BS 047505-1	The Last Mile of the Way	Bb B-8597, MW M-8669, Cam ADL2-0726 (33)
BS 047506-1	She's Somebody's Darling Once More	Bb B-8446, MW M-8667
BS 047507-1	I'm S-A-V-E-D	Bb B-8401, MW M-8666, Rounder 1006 (33)
BS 047508-1	Whispering Hope	Bb B-8401, MW M-8666
BS 047509-1	The Butcher's Boy	Bb B-8482, MW M-8668, Bb AXM2-5525 (33), Cam CAL-797 (33), ADL2-0726 (33), RCA (Japan) RA-5276 (33)
BS 047510-1	This Evening Light	Bb B-8597, MW M-8669
BS 047511-1	Mary of the Wild Moor	Bb B-8446, MW M-8667, Cam CAL-797 (33), ADL2-0726 (33), RCA (Japan) RA-5220 (33)

Rooms 104, 106, Kimball House, 30 S. Pryor Street, Atlanta, GA, Monday, 5 February 1940, 9–11:15 AM. Frank Walker and Dan Hornsby, producers.

BS 054508-1	Why Not Confess	MW M-8846, Bb 33-0516, AXM2-5525 (33)
BS 054509-1	Turn Your Radio On	Bb B-8843, MW M-8846, Rounder 1006 (33), RCA (Japan) RA-5331 (33)
BS 054510-1	Since the Angels Took My Mother Far Away	MW M-8847, Bb 33-0516, AXM2-5525 (33)
BS 054511-1	In the Hills of Roane County	Bb B-8693, MW M-8848, Cam CAL-797 (33), ADL2-0726 (33), Rounder 1006 (33), RCA (Japan) RA-5331 (33)
BS 054512-1	Kneel at the Cross	Bb B-8843, MW M-8847, Bb AXM2-5525 (33), RCA (Japan) RA-5331 (33)
BS 054513-1	Brown Eyes	Bb B-8693, MW M-8848, Cam ADL2-0726 (33), RCA (Japan) RA-5331 (33)
BS 054514-1	Short Life of Trouble	Bb B-8829, MW M-8849, Cam CAL-797 (33), ADL2-0726 (33), RCA (Japan) RA-5220 (33)
BS 054515-1	A Picture on the Wall	Bb B-8646, MW M-8845, RCA (Japan) RA-5331 (33)
BS 054516-1	Pictures from Life's Other Side	Bb B-8646, MW M-8845, Cam ADL2-0726 (33), Rounder 1006 (33), RCA (Japan) RA-5331 (33)
BS 054517-1	Don't Say Goodbye If You Love Me	Bb B-8829, MW M-8849, Rounder 1006 (33), RCA (Japan) RA-5331 (33)

Rooms 104, 106, Kimball House, 30 S. Pryor Street, Atlanta, GA, Monday, 7 October 1940, 9–11:30 AM. Frank Walker and Dan Hornsby, producers. Bluebird 33-0516 was released in 1944.

Theme
Black Mountain Blues
In the Hills of Roane County
A Beautiful Life
Worried Mind
Skip to My Lou

Earl Bolick: lead voice in duets, guitar; Bill Bolick: lead voice (tenor voice in duets), mandolin; Curly (Samuel Messer) Parker: fiddle, vocal. WPTF, Raleigh, NC, early 1941. This is a privately made audition disc.

D6-VB-2964-1	Speak to Me, Little Darling (Leslie York)	RCA 20-2022, 48-0036 (45)
D6-VB-2965-1	Have You Seen My Daddy Here (Fowler-Hull-Lammers)	RCA 20-2151
D6-VB-2966-1	I Love Her More, Now Mother's Old (Bill and Earl Bolick)	RCA 20-2151
D6-VB-2967-2	Dust on the Bible (Johnny and Walter Bailes)	RCA 20-2022, 48-0036 (45), Cam ADL2-0726 (33), Bb AXM2-5525 (33), Rounder 1006 (33), RCA (Japan) RA-5331 (33)

Earl Bolick: lead voice in duets, guitar; Bill Bolick: lead voice (tenor voice in duets), mandolin; Curly Parker: fiddle; Charles Grean: bass. Piedmont Hotel, 100–118 Peachtree Street, Atlanta, Monday, 30 September 1946. Stephen H. Sholes, producer.

WGST RADIO TRANSCRIPTIONS, ATLANTA, 1946–47

After we had been at WGST for approximately six months, John Fulton, the station manager, called me into his office. He told me he had worked out a good deal for us with the Willys-Overland Company of Toledo, Ohio, Jack Briscoe, Inc. of Atlanta, and the Willys jeep dealers of Georgia. They wanted to sponsor us over three 5,000-watt Georgia radio stations: WGST in Atlanta, WMAZ in Macon, and a station in Savannah. I can't recall the letters of the Savannah station. To do this, we would have to record five fifteen-minute programs in one afternoon. A master disc would be made and two more transcriptions dubbed from the master. The dubs would be sent to the other radio stations which I have mentioned. The transcriptions were to be played over these three stations at 6:30 in the morning each morning, Monday *through Friday. Time would be allotted to plug for personal appearances. If we could send a list of our appearances to the stations, they would be advertised at the end of each program. In addition to this, we would receive a $15.00 raise in salary. The only drawback to this project was that WGST could not do the recordings. Due to some type of contract with the musicians union we would have to be paid union scale. Rather than lose the project entirely, they worked out something with Acoustic Equipment Company of Atlanta. A WGST announcer and an engineer would be furnished by the station. The programs, though actually performed in the studios of WGST, would be run by telephone wire to Acoustic Equipment Company and they would do the actual recording. I feel the transcriptions would have been much better had WGST been allowed to record them.*

Imagine, if you can, doing five fifteen-minute programs in one afternoon. On four or five occasions we did as many as ten programs in one day. It was very tiresome saying the same thing, listening to the same commercials, trying to work out something with Uncle Josh, singing songs you didn't have time to rehearse and hadn't sung in some time. These programs were only to be played one time. If you made a mistake and it was only heard one time, it isn't noticed much. However, when you played it time and time again, it stuck out like a sore thumb. Luckily we didn't make too many mistakes. To the best of my knowledge, Acoustic Equipment made as many, or more, than we did. A number of times we were almost finished with a program when they would call and tell us they were having technical problems and we would do the same program again. Tape recorders hadn't come into their own as yet and these programs were recorded [in real time] *on sixteen-inch discs. A fifteen-minute program was recorded on each side. Our programs for Willys Overland lasted for seven to eight months.*

On most of our sponsored programs, we used the following format: we started an opening theme. The announcer would then read a commercial for the sponsor. After the commercial, he would introduce me as the emcee. The first song was usually a religious one and it was generally sung by the trio. Following that, Earl and I would generally sing. The announcer would read another commercial. After that we would play our theme song. This was usually faded out while the local announcer gave the name and location of the Willys Jeep dealers in the surrounding territory covered by their station. One reason for using our theme at this time was that the time allotted worked out perfectly with this particular number. We tried other songs but they didn't work out as well as our theme. Most of the other songs were either too short or too long. After this information was given during our theme, we were brought back again. Earl and I would sing another song, usually a religious selection. A visit with Uncle Josh was done before this song or immediately after. Curly Parker usually ended the program with a fiddle tune. Most fiddle tunes could be shortened or lengthened depending on how much time we had remaining. This was followed by another commercial. Our closing theme and sign-off completed the show.

[When] *WMAZ in Macon, Georgia, sent a number of these discs addressed to me instead of WGST, I thought at first I would not let WGST know but my conscience wouldn't allow me to do it. I went to John Fulton and told him that if the station wanted them back I'd return them. If not, I would like to have them. He told me to keep them, that WGST had all the transcriptions we had made. Had I known what the future would be, I'd have asked for all the transcriptions. At the time I had no idea what I would do with them. They couldn't be played on a regular turntable. I did think of asking WGST to sell me a used one, or getting one of the engineers to make one for me. After we left WGST I don't know what was done with the transcriptions. I do know that for several months after we left, they had a daily program by us, using the songs lifted from them.*

The announcers on these transcriptions were Jack Colby, John McLean, Francis Hardin, and Percy Hearle. They were very nice fellows and we got along with them exceptionally well. Some didn't like having to put in that much extra time, but after a few programs they seemed to enjoy it, especially the chats with Uncle Josh.

Each of the following transcribed broadcasts was made on one side of a sixteen-inch acetate disc. Recording dates are unknown, but programs are numbered and broadcast dates indicated. Participants are Earl Bolick: lead voice (bass in trios), guitar; Bill Bolick: tenor vocal, mandolin; Curly Parker: fiddle, lead voice in trios; (1) Ruel Parker (fiddle) replaces his brother Curly; (2) they play twin fiddles. Published titles are on compact discs unless otherwise indicated.

Program 1, Monday, 2 September 1946:

An Empty Mansion	
We Buried Her Beneath the Willow	
I Have Found a Friend	Copper Creek CCCD-0146
Katy Hill	Copper Creek CCCD-0120
Comedy	Copper Creek CCCD-0145

Program 2, Tuesday, 3 September 1946:

Will You Miss Me

They're All Going Home But One

What Would You Give in Exchange for Your Soul?

The Arkansas Traveler

Program 3, Wednesday, 4 September 1946:

Shake My Mother's Hand for Me	Copper Creek CCCD-0121	(Partial introduction from Program 140)
The Holiness Mother	Copper Creek CCCD-0120	
She Has Forgotten		
Soldier's Joy	Copper Creek CCCD-0145	
Request for cards and letters	Copper Creek CCCD-0145	
Request for show dates	Copper Creek CCCD-0145	
Closing theme	Copper Creek CCCD-0145	

Program 4, Thursday, 5 September 1946:

Just a Little Talk with Jesus	
Song of the Blind	Copper Creek CCCD-0146
I'm Going Home This Evening	
Fire on the Mountain	
Comedy	Copper Creek CCCD-0120

Program 5, Friday, 6 September 1946 (only three titles listed):

Opening theme and introduction	Copper Creek CCCD-0145
Farther Along	Copper Creek CCCD-0145
Darling, Think of What You've Done	Copper Creek CCCD-0146
That Beautiful Home	Copper Creek CCCD-0120
Advertisement	Copper Creek CCCD-0120
Comedy	Copper Creek CCCD-0120

Program 6, Monday, 9 September 1946:

As Long As I Live	

Row Us over the Tide	Starday SLP-205 (33), Pine Mountain PMR-205 (33), London SLC (M) 353/4 (33), Gusto GT7-0695-2 (CD), GT7-0816-2 (CD), Copper Creek CCCD-0120	
Goodbye Maggie	Copper Creek CCCD-0121	
Devil's Dream	Copper Creek CCCD-0145	

Program 7, Tuesday, 10 September 1946:

Precious Memories		
Little Gal, I Trusted You Too Long	Copper Creek CCCD-0145	
Dust on the Bible	Starday SLP-205 (33), Pine Mountain PMR-205 (33), London SLC(M) 353/4 (33), Gusto GT7-0695-2 (CD) (CD)	(These issues may be from Program 36)
Leather Britches	Copper Creek CCCD-0146	

Program 11, Monday, 16 September 1946:

Nothing But the Blood of Jesus		
Bring Back My Blue Eyed Boy to Me		
Only Let Me Walk with Thee		
Sally Goodin'		

Program 12, Tuesday, 17 September 1946:

Oh, Sister Mary, Don't You Weep	Copper Creek CCCD-0121	
Yellow Rose of Texas		
Just One Way to the Gate	Copper Creek CCCD-0145	
Turkey in the Straw	Copper Creek CCCD-0145	

Program 16, Monday, 23 September 1946:

Shake My Mother's Hand for Me	
No Place to Pillow My Head	
I Have Found the Way	Starday SLP-205 (33), Pine Mountain PMR-205 (33), London SLC(M) 353/4 (33), Gusto GT7-0695-2 (CD), GT7-0816-2 (CD), Copper Creek CCCD-0145
Tugboat	

Program 17, Tuesday, 24 September 1946:

When I Reach That City on the Hill	Copper Creek CCCD-0120
Answer to the Prisoner's Dream	
This Train	Copper Creek CCCD-0125
Danced All Night with a Bottle in My Hand	Copper Creek CCCD-0145

Program 18, Wednesday, 25 September 1946:

Will You Meet Me Over Yonder?	Copper Creek CCCD-0120
There's No Other Love for Me	
Where the Soul Never Dies	Copper Creek CCCD-0121
Ida Red	Copper Creek CCCD-0120

Program 19, Thursday, 26 September 1946:

Where Shall I Be?	
The House Where We Were Wed	Copper Creek CCCD-0146
When the Stars Begin to Fall	Copper Creek CCCD-0146
Sourwood Mountain	
Comedy	Copper Creek CCCD-0145

Program 20, Friday, 27 September 1946:

Getting Ready to Leave This World	
I'm Just Here to Get My Baby out of Jail	
Take Up Thy Cross	
Ragtime Annie	Copper Creek CCCD-0146
Advertisement	Copper Creek CCCD-0146
Comedy	Copper Creek CCCD-0145

Program 21, Monday, 30 September 1946:

Great Grand Dad	Library of Congress LBC-10 (33)
Speak to Me, Little Darling	
That Beautiful Home	Copper Creek CCCD-0120
Katy Hill	
Advertisement	Copper Creek CCCD-0145

Program 22, Tuesday, 1 October 1946:

Will My Mother Know Me There?	Copper Creek CCCD-0120
The Last Letter	Starday SLP-205 (33), Pine Mountain PMR-205 (33), London SLC(M) 353/4 (33), Gusto GT7-0695-2 (CD)
If I Could Hear My Mother Pray Again	
Buffalo Gal	Copper Creek CCCD-0146
Comedy	Copper Creek CCCD-0145

Program 23, Wednesday, 2 October 1946:

Where We'll Never Grow Old	Copper Creek CCCD-0121
Sweet Allalee	

I Dreamed I Searched Heaven for You	
Fire on the Mountain	Copper Creek CCCD-0145

Program 24, Thursday, 3 October 1946:

A Beautiful Life	Copper Creek CCCD-0146
Turn Your Radio On	Starday SLP-205, Pine Mountain PMR-205, London SLC(M) 353/4 (all 33), Gusto GT7-0695-2 (CD), Copper Creek CCCD-0121
The East Bound Train	
Cumberland Gap	Copper Creek CCCD-0146

Program 25, Friday, 7 October 1946:

There's an Eye Watching You	
Mary of the Wild Moor	
This Evening Light	
Listen to the Mocking Bird	

Program 26, Monday, 7 October 1946:

The Blood of Jesus	
When the Roses Bloom Again	Copper Creek CCCD-0145
I'll Be Listening	Copper Creek CCCD-0121
Whistlin' Rufus	Copper Creek CCCD-0121

Program 27, Tuesday, 8 October 1946:

Were You There When They Crucified My Lord	Copper Creek CCCD-0121
When My Blue Moon Turns to Gold	Copper Creek CCCD-0145
Shall I Miss It?	Copper Creek CCCD-0146
Soldier's Joy	Copper Creek CCCD-0145

Program 28, Wednesday, 9 October 1946:

Precious Memories	Copper Creek CCCD-0146
Just a Strand from a Yellow Curl	Copper Creek CCCD-0120
Are You Tired of Me, My Darling	Copper Creek CCCD-0146
Golden Slippers (Curly & Ruel Parker, 2 fiddles)	Copper Creek CCCD-0121
Advertisement	Copper Creek CCCD-0145

Program 29, Thursday, 10 October 1946:

Just a Little Talk with Jesus	
Midnight on the Stormy Deep	
Gathering Buds	Copper Creek CCCD-0120
Turkey in the Straw	
Comedy	Copper Creek CCCD-0145

Program 30, Friday, 11 October 1946:

The Longest Train I Ever Saw	
I Believe It for My Mother Told Me So	Copper Creek CCCD-0121
What Would You Give in Exchange for Your Soul?	Starday SEP-216 (45), Copper Creek CCCD-0120
Arkansas Traveler	Copper Creek CCCD-0121

Program 31, Monday, 14 October 1946:

Life's Railway to Heaven	
Goodbye Maggie	Copper Creek CCCD-0121
Drifting Too Far from the Shore	Copper Creek CCCD-0121
Soldier's Joy	
Comedy	Copper Creek CCCD-0120

Program 32, Tuesday, 15 October 1946:

Ida Red	Copper Creek CCCD-0120	(Partial introduction from Program 23, Soldier's Joy)
Where the Soul Never Dies	Copper Creek CCCD-0121	
Take Me Back to Renfro Valley	Copper Creek CCCD-0120	
Eighth of January (1)	Copper Creek CCCD-0120	

Program 33, Wednesday, 16 October 1946:

Death Is Only a Dream	Copper Creek CCCD-0145
Bury Me Beneath the Willow	Copper Creek CCCD-0121
Won't It Be Wonderful There?	Copper Creek CCCD-0146
Tugboat	Starday SLP-205 (33), Pine Mountain PMR-205 (33), London SLC(M) 353/4 (33), Gusto GT7-0695-2 (CD) (CD)

Program 34, Thursday, 17 October 1946:

Black Mountain Blues	Starday SLP-205, Pine Mountain PMR-205, London SLC(M) 353/4 (all 33), Gusto GT7-0695-2 (CD), GT7-0816-2 (CD), Copper Creek CCCD-0121 (all CD)
Someone's Last Day	Copper Creek CCCD-0120
I'm Going Home This Evening	
Ragtime Annie	Copper Creek CCCD-0146

Program 35, Friday, 18 October 1946:

I'll Meet You in the Morning

Short Life of Trouble

Just One Way to the Gate	
Mississippi Sawyer	

Program 36, Monday, 21 October 1946:

Will You Miss Me When I'm Gone?	
Trail to Mexico	LC LBC-12 (33), Copper Creek CCCD-0120
Dust on the Bible	Starday SLP-205 (33), Pine Mountain PMR-205 (33), London SLC(M) 353/4 (33), Gusto GT7-0695-2 (CD) (These issues may be from Program 7)
Devil's Dream	

Program 37, Tuesday, 22 October 1946:

Precious Memories	Copper Creek CCCD-0146(?)
Mary of the Wild Moor	Starday SLP-205 (33), Pine Mountain PMR-205 (33), London SLC(M) 353/4 (33), Gusto GT7-0695-2 (CD), Copper Creek CCCD-0146
Heaven Holds All to Me	Copper Creek CCCD-0145
Sally Goodin'	Copper Creek CCCD-0146

Program 38, Wednesday, 23 October 1946:

As Long As I Live	Copper Creek CCCD-0145
Lorena	
Let the Lower Lights Be Burning	Copper Creek CCCD-0145
Cacklin' Hen	Copper Creek CCCD-0145

Program 39, Thursday, 24 October 1946:

Where Shall I Be?	
A Picture from Life's Other Side	
Bury Me Beneath the Willow	Copper Creek CCCD-0121
Lee County Blues	

Program 40, Friday, 25 October 1946:

Opening theme and introduction	Copper Creek CCCD-0146
Yellow Rose of Texas	Copper Creek CCCD-0145
Give Me the Roses Now	
Leather Britches	
Comedy	Copper Creek CCCD-0120
Advertisement	Copper Creek CCCD-0146
Request for show dates	Copper Creek CCCD-0146
Closing theme	Copper Creek CCCD-0146

Program 41, Monday, 28 October 1946:

Shake My Mother's Hand for Me	Copper Creek CCCD-0121
The Holiness Mother	Copper Creek CCCD-0120
Answer to the Prisoner's Dream	Copper Creek CCCD-0145
Katy Hill	

Program 42, Tuesday, 29 October 1946:

Farther Along	Copper Creek CCCD-0145
There's No Other Love for Me	
God Sent My Little Girl	
Lost Train Blues	Copper Creek CCCD-0120
Request for cards and letters	Copper Creek CCCD-0146
Comedy	Copper Creek CCCD-0146
Closing theme	Copper Creek CCCD-0120

Program 43, Wednesday, 30 October 1946:

Crying Holy Unto the Lord	
You Give Me Your Love and I'll Give You Mine	
Turn Your Radio On	
Comedy	Copper Creek CCCD-0146
Chicken Reel	Copper Creek CCCD-0146

Program 44, Thursday, 31 October 1946:

Watching You	Copper Creek CCCD-0121 (Partial introduction from Program 43)
We Parted by the Riverside	
Silver Threads Among the Gold	Copper Creek CCCD-0146
Danced All Night with a Bottle in My Hand	Copper Creek CCCD-0145
Comedy	Copper Creek CCCD-0146

Program 45, Friday, 1 November 1946:

Get Along Home, Cindy	Copper Creek CCCD-0121
On the Sunny Side of Life	Starday SLP-205 (33), Pine Mountain PMR-205 (33), London SLC(M) 353/4 (33), Gusto GT7-0695-2 (CD), GT7-0816-2 (CD), Copper Creek CCCD-0145
They're All Going Home But One	
The Girl I Left Behind Me	
Comedy	Copper Creek CCCD-0146

Program 46, Monday, 4 November 1946:

An Empty Mansion	
Speak to Me, Little Darling	

Shall I Miss It	Copper Creek CCCD-0146
Buffalo Gal	

Program 47, Tuesday, 5 November 1946:

A Beautiful Life	Copper Creek CCCD-0146
Little Gal, I Trusted You Too Long	Copper Creek CCCD-0145
I Dreamed I Searched Heaven for You	
Sourwood Mountain	Copper Creek CCCD-0121
Closing theme	Copper Creek CCCD-0121

Program 48, Wednesday, 6 November 1946:

Getting Ready to Leave This World	
Mary of the Wild Moor	Starday SLP-205 (33), Pine Mountain PMR-205 (33), London SLC(M) 353/4 (33), Gusto GT7-0695-2 (CD), Copper Creek CCCD-0146
If I Could Hear My Mother Pray Again	
Turkey in the Straw	Copper Creek CCCD-0145

Program 49, Thursday, 7 November 1946:

Life's Railway to Heaven	Copper Creek CCCD-0146
The East Bound Train	Copper Creek CCCD-0146
This Evening Light	
Whistlin' Rufus	Copper Creek CCCD-0121

Program 50, Friday, 8 November 1946:

Just a Little Talk with Jesus	
Just a Strand from a Yellow Curl	Copper Creek CCCD-0120

Where the Soul Never Dies	
Old Joe Clark	Copper Creek CCCD-0120

Program 51, Monday, 11 November 1946:

Oh, Sister Mary, Don't You Weep	Copper Creek CCCD-0121
Golden Slippers (2)	Starday SLP-205 (33), Pine Mountain PMR-205 (33), London SLC(M) 353/4 (33), Gusto GT7-0695-2 (CD), Copper Creek CCCD-0121
Bring Back My Blue Eyed Boy to Me	Copper Creek CCCD-0145
Hop Light Ladies	
Advertisement (with end from Program 52)	Copper Creek CCCD-0120
Comedy	Copper Creek CCCD-0120

Program 52, Tuesday, 12 November 1946:

The Longest Train I Ever Saw	Starday SLP-205 (33), Pine Mountain PMR-205 (33), London SLC(M) 353/4 (33), Gusto GT7-0695-2 (CD), GT7-0816-2 (CD), Copper Creek CCCD-0120 (all CD)
(The) Sunny Side of Life	Starday SLP-205 (33), Pine Mountain PMR-205 (33), London SLC(M) 353/4 (33), Gusto GT7-0695-2 (CD), GT7-0816-2 (CD) (both CD)
On the Sunny Side of Life	Copper Creek CCCD-0145
Sweet Evalina	
Eighth of January (1)	Copper Creek CCCD-0120
Advertisement (end of ad in Program 51)	Copper Creek CCCD-0120

Program (unnumbered), December 19, 1946 (for broadcast December 25, 1946):

Silent Night (with introduction)
Precious Memories
Her Mansion Is Higher Than Mine
Dust on the Bible
I Need the Prayers of Those I Love

Program (unnumbered), December 19, 1946 (for broadcast December 26, 1946):

On the Rock
Speak to Me, Little Darling
How Beautiful Heaven Must Be
Two Little Rosebuds
Down Home Rag

Program 136, Monday, 10 March 1947:

Opening and Theme	Copper Creek CCCD-0120
When I Reach That City (Partial introduction from program 23)	Copper Creek CCCD-0120
Speak to Me, Little Darling	Copper Creek CCCD-0121
We Parted by the Riverside	
Down Home Rag	
Comedy	Copper Creek CCCD-0121

Program 137, Tuesday, 11 March 1947:

As Long As I Live	Starday SLP-205 (33), Pine Mountain PMR-205 (33), London SLC(M) 353/4 (33), Gusto GT7-0695-2 (CD), GT7-0816-2 (CD), Copper Creek CCCD-0121

A Picture from Life's Other Side	Starday SLP-205 (33), SEP-217 (45), Pine Mountain PMR-205 (33), London SLC(M) 353/4 (33), Gusto GT7-0695-2 (CD)
Nine Pound Hammer	Starday SLP 190 (33), SLP-205 (33), Pine Mountain PMR-205 (33), London SLC(M) 353/4 (33), Gusto GT7-0695-2 (CD), GT7-0816-2 (CD)
The Arkansas Traveler	
Advertisement	Copper Creek CCCD-0121
Comedy	Copper Creek CCCD-0121

Program 138, Wednesday, 12 March 1947:

Opening and theme	Copper Creek CCCD-0121
Precious Memories	
What Does the Deep Sea Say?	
Just a Strand from a Yellow Curl	
Eighth of January	
Comedy	Copper Creek CCCD-0121

Program 139, Thursday, 13 March 1947:

Black Mountain Blues	Copper Creek CCCD-0121
Were You There?	Copper Creek CCCD-0121
Why Should It End This Way? (Partial introduction from Program 138)	Copper Creek CCCD-0120
Fire on the Mountain	Copper Creek CCCD-0145
Advertisement	Copper Creek CCCD-0121
Comedy	Copper Creek CCCD-0121

Program 140, Friday, 14 March 1947:

Introduction	Copper Creek CCCD-0121
The Blood of Jesus	Copper Creek CCCD-0120
There's Been a Change	Starday SLP-205 (33), Pine Mountain PMR-205 (33), London SLC(M) 353/4 (33), Gusto GT7-0695-2 (CD), GT7-0816-2 (CD)
Bring Back My Blue Eyed Boy to Me	
Sally Goodin'	
Comedy	Copper Creek CCCD-0121

RCA SESSIONS, 1947

D7-VB-830-1	Kentucky (Carl [*sic*] Davis)	RCA 20-2296, Cam ADL2-0726 (33), Bb AXM2-5525 (33), Rounder 1006 (33), RCA (Japan) RA-5331 (33)
D7-VB-831-1	I'm Glad (I'm Glad He's Gone and Left You) (Famous Lashua-Bill Boyd)	RCA 20-2380, Bb AXM2-5525 (33)
D7-VB-832-1	The Chapel in the Hills (Karl Davis-Harty Taylor)	RCA 20-3158
D7-VB-833-1	Sold Down the River (Vaughn Horton)	RCA 20-2380, Bb AXM2-5525 (33)
D7-VB-834-1	I'm Going to Write to Heaven (For I Know My Daddy's There) (Chuck Harding-Cousin Joe Maphis)	RCA 20-2296

D7-VB-835-1	Come to the Saviour (E. and B. Bolick-T[homas]. D. Lynn)	RCA 20-3055
D7-VB-836-1	Garden in the Sky (Louisiana Lou)	RCA 20-2570
D7-VB-837-1	There's Been a Change (E. and B. Bolick-C[alvin] Van Pelt)	RCA 20-2570

Earl Bolick: lead voice in duets, guitar; Bill Bolick lead voice (tenor voice in duets), mandolin; Curly Parker: fiddle; Charles Grean: bass. RCA Studio 1, New York City, Wednesday, 7 May 1947, 12:30–3 PM. Stephen H. Sholes and Charles R. Grean, producers,

D7-VB-2693-1	Romans 6:23 (Karl Davis-Harty Taylor)	RCA 20-2900
D7-VB-2694-1	I'll Take My Saviour by the Hand (Whitey-Hogan)	RCA 20-3055, Bb AXM2-5525 (33)
D7-VB-2695-1	I Cannot Take You Back Now (Bill and Earl Bolick)	RCA 20-3158
D7-VB-2696-1	Behind These Prison Walls of Love (Bill Bolick-Hazel Hope Jarrard)	RCA 20-3307, Bb AXM2-5525 (33)

Earl Bolick: lead voice in duets, guitar; Bill Bolick: lead voice (tenor voice in duets), mandolin; Ben Lambert: fiddle; Charles Grean: bass. RCA Studio 1, New York City, Tuesday, 16 December 1947, 9:30 AM–12:30 PM. Stephen H. Sholes and Charles R. Grean, producers.

D7-VB-2697-1	Angel Mother (Bill Bolick-Hugh Anglyn)	RCA 20-2900
D7-VB-2698-1	Let's Not Sleep Again (Leslie York-Louis Buck)	RCA 20-2755
D7-VB-2699-1	Don't Take the Light (From My Dark Cell) (Calvin Van Pelt-Bill Bolick)	RCA 20-2755
D7-VB-2800-1	The Cross On the Hill (Tex Jackson-Deke Mason)	RCA 20-3307, Bb AXM2-5525 (33)

Earl Bolick: lead voice in duets, guitar; Bill Bolick: lead voice (tenor voice in duets), mandolin; Ben Lambert: fiddle; Charles Grean: bass. RCA Studio 1, New York City, Tuesday, 16 December 1947, 1:30–4 PM. Stephen H. Sholes and Charles R. Grean, producers.

The November 8, 1947, issue of *Billboard* reported Curly Parker's departure from the Blue Sky Boys for the Radio Ranchmen show on WARL (Arlington, VA), hosted by Washington country music impresario Connie B. Gay. Ben Lambert and Charles Grean were staff musicians at RCA in New York.

RADIO TRANSCRIPTIONS, 1947-49

Program (WGST unnumbered), December 18, 1947 (Joe Tyson replaces Curly Parker on fiddle):

Precious Memories
Dust on the Bible
Turn Your Radio On
Only One Step More

A recording of a January 10, 1948 guest appearance on the Grand Ole Opry survives, with performances of "Kentucky"and "Sold Down the River."

Audition Disc, WNAO (Raleigh, NC), January 28, 1949:

Old Time Camp Meeting
The Sweetest Gift, a Mother's Smile
The Sinking of the Titanic (Bill solo with banjo)
You've Branded Your Name on My Heart
Down Home Rag

RCA SESSIONS, JANUARY 31, 1949

D9-VB-812-1	The Sweetest Gift, a Mother's Smile (J. B. Coates [Coats])	RCA 21-0034, Bb AXM2-5525 (33)
D9-VB-813-1	You've Branded Your Name on My Heart (Bill and Earl Bolick)	RCA 21-0075, 48-0072 (45)

D9-VB-814-1	Little Mother of the Hills (The Vagabonds-Herald, Dean and Curt)	RCA 21-0108, 48-0111 (45)
D9-VB-815-1	Alabama (Ed Hill-Ira & Charlie Louvin)	RCA 21-0075, 48-0072 (45), Bb AXM2-5525 (33), Rounder 1006 (33), RCA (Japan) RA-5331 (33)

Earl Bolick: lead voice in duets, guitar; Bill Bolick: lead voice (tenor voice in duets), mandolin; Curly Parker: fiddle; Charles Grean: bass. Fox Theater, 660 Peachtree Street, NE, Atlanta, GA, Monday, 31 January 1949, 6:40–8 PM. Stephen H. Sholes and Charles R. Grean-producers.

D9-VB-816-1	One Cold Winter's Eve	RCA 21-0156, 48-0163 (45)
D9-VB-817-1	Paper Boy (Johnnie Wright-Jack Anglin)	RCA 21-0034, Cam ADL2-0726 (33), Bb AXM2-5525 (33), LC LBC-8 (33)
D9-VB-818-1	Shake Hands with Your Mother Today (Pete Roy-Bill Bolick)	RCA 21-0108, 48-0111 (45)
D9-VB-819-1	When Heaven Comes Down (Al Robinson-John Bailes)	RCA 21-0156, 48-0163 (45), Bb AXM2-5525 (33)

Earl Bolick: lead voice in duets, guitar; Bill Bolick: lead voice (tenor voice in duets), mandolin; Curly Parker: fiddle; Charles Grean: bass. Fox Theater, 660 Peachtree Street, NE, Atlanta, GA, Monday, 31 January 1949, 9:15–11:30 PM. Stephen H. Sholes and Charles R. Grean, producers.

WCYB TRANSCRIPTIONS, BRISTOL, VIRGINIA, 1949

Possibly in May or June 1949, [program manager] *Bill Lane called all the Farm and Fun Time entertainers together and told us management felt we should do some early morning programs in addition to Farm and Fun Time. Had management offered a little incentive, such as a small salary, I feel all of us would have been glad to do an early morning program. As it was, none of us felt the early programs would help or benefit us in any way. I think that Bill Lane realized this was asking too much and suggested that we should make some transcriptions that could be used* [on morning shows]. *In addition, they could be used on afternoon programs if the need arose. These recordings weren't made to be used as fifteen-minute programs. There are several opening introductions, a few chats with Uncle Josh, but no sign-offs. These songs seem to be interspersed with other artists and used randomly. So that is the story of why these transcriptions were made.*

When we left WCYB [around December 1949] *I asked Bill Lane if we could have the transcriptions. I'm sure we made more discs than I have but these are all that we could locate. As with the Willys Jeep transcriptions which we made at WGST in 1946, I had no idea as to what we would do with them but I did feel that someday I might have a use for them.*

In the early sixties, ten or twelve years after Earl and I had quit entertaining, my father received a catalog from David Bogen, Inc., that advertised a turntable that would play sixteen-inch discs. For a number of years, Earl and I had used a Bogen public address system and knew their products were very good. As the cost of the turntable wasn't too prohibitive, I had my father to order me one. At the time, I was living in Greensboro and my parents were in Hickory. My wife, Doris, and I usually visited them every four to six weeks. When the turntable arrived, I took it and all my Willys Jeep transcriptions back to Greensboro. I had stored most of my memorabilia and discs at my parents' home as they had a large house. On a later visit to my parents, my mother asked me what I intended to do with the recordings that were stored in the guest bedroom. As soon as I saw them, I recalled that they were the WCYB transcriptions. Truthfully I had completely forgotten about them.

The A-B-C Song	Copper Creek CCCD-0125
Alabama	Copper Creek CCCD-0126
Amazing Grace	Copper Creek CCCD-0126
Arkansas Traveler	
Baby Mine [Going Around This World, Baby Mine] (3)	
Beautiful	Copper Creek CCCD-0126
The B-I-B-L-E	Copper Creek CCCD-0126
Buffalo Gals	
Cacklin' Hen	
The Chapel in the Hills	Copper Creek CCCD-0126
Come to the Saviour	

Cumberland Gap	
East Tennessee Blues	Copper Creek CCCD-0126
Fire on the Mountain	
Getting Ready to Leave This World	
The Girl I Left Behind Me	Copper Creek CCCD-0125
Going Round This World, Baby Mine (3)	Copper Creek CCCD-0126
Golden Slippers	Copper Creek CCCD-0125
Goodbye Maggie	
Hop Light Ladies	Copper Creek CCCD-0126
The House Where We Were Wed	
I Cannot Take You Back Now	
I Dreamed I Searched Heaven for You	Copper Creek CCCD-0125
I Need the Prayers of Those I Love	
I Wish I Had Never Seen Sunshine	Copper Creek CCCD-0126
I'll Be No Stranger There	Copper Creek CCCD-0125
I'm Going to Write to Heaven	Copper Creek CCCD-0125
I'm S-A-V-E-D	
I'm Troubled, I'm Troubled	Copper Creek CCCD-0125
If I Could Hear My Mother Pray Again	
If We Never Meet Again	
Just a Little Talk with Jesus	Copper Creek CCCD-0126
Just Tell Them That You Saw Me. (Bill solo with guitar)	Copper Creek CCCD-0125
Kentucky	Copper Creek CCCD-0125
Kneel at the Cross	
Listen to the Mockingbird	Copper Creek CCCD-0125
Little Joe (Bill solo with guitar)	
Lonesome Road Blues (2)	Copper Creek CCCD-0126
Lost Train Blues	
Mississippi Sawyer	
Mountain Dew	Copper Creek CCCD-0125
My Main Trial Is Yet to Come	
Nine Pound Hammer	Copper Creek CCCD-0126
Oh Those Tombs	Copper Creek CCCD-0125
Old Joe Clark (1)	Copper Creek CCCD-0126
Old-Time Camp Meeting	Copper Creek CCCD-0125
One Cold Winter's Eve	Copper Creek CCCD-0125
Only One Step More	
Roll On Buddy	Copper Creek CCCD-0125
The Royal Telephone (1)	Copper Creek CCCD-0126
Rubber Dolly	Copper Creek CCCD-0125
Sally Goodin'	
She's Somebody's Darling Once More	
Short Life of Trouble (1)	Copper Creek CCCD-0126

Since the Angels Took My Mother Far Away	
Sourwood Mountain	Copper Creek CCCD-0125
The Sweetest Gift	Copper Creek CCCD-0125
Sweetest Mother	Copper Creek CCCD-0126
Take Me Back to Tennessee (4)	Copper Creek CCCD-0126
They're All Going Home But One	
This Evening Light (1)	Copper Creek CCCD-0126
This Train	Copper Creek CCCD-0125
This World Can't Stand Long	
Two Little Rosebuds	Copper Creek CCCD-0126
Unloved and Unclaimed	Copper Creek CCCD-0126
We Buried Her Beneath the Willow	
We Parted by the Riverside	Copper Creek CCCD-0125
What Does the Deep Sea Say?	Copper Creek CCCD-0125
Whispering Hope (1)	Copper Creek CCCD-0126
Will You Miss Me When I'm Gone?	Library of Congress LBC-9 (33)
Worried Man Blues	
You Can Be a Millionaire with Me"	Copper Creek CCCD-0125
You've Branded Your Name on My Heart	

Earl Bolick: lead voice (bass in trios), guitar; Bill Bolick: tenor vocal, mandolin; Curly Parker or (1) Leslie Keith: fiddle, lead vocal in trios; (2) Keith: solo voice, (3) solo voice and banjo, (4) duet with Bill Bolick. WCYB, Bristol, VA, 1949. Leslie Keith replaced Curly Parker in June 1949, playing fiddle and (occasionally) banjo.

LAST RCA SESSION, 1950

Eo-VB-4012-1	The Unfinished Rug (Karl Davis)	RCA 21-0317, 48-0317 (45), Bb AXM2-5525 (33)
Eo-VB-4013-1	Tears on Her Bridal Bouquet (Arthur Q. Smith)	RCA 21-0317, 48-0317 (45)
Eo-VB-4014-1	Lord, Be with Us—Amen (1) (Karl Davis)	RCA 21-0318, 48-0318 (45)
Eo-VB-4015-1	Drop Your Net (Tommy Paige)	RCA 21-0370, 48-0370 (45)
Eo-VB-4016-1	There'll Be No Broken Hearts for Me (William A. Bolick-Earl Bolick)	Bb AXM2-5525 (33)
Eo-VB-4017-1	The New Golden Rule (Karl Davis)	RCA 21-0318, 48-0318 (45)
Eo-VB-4018-1	Where Our Darling Sleeps Tonight (William A. Bolick-Earl Bolick)	Bb AXM2-5525 (33)
Eo-VB-4019-1	Sunny Side of Life (William A. Bolick)	RCA 21-0370, 48-0370 (45), Cam ADL2-0726 (33)

Earl Bolick: lead voice in duets, guitar; Bill Bolick: lead voice (tenor voice in duets), mandolin; Leslie Keith: fiddle, (1) lead vocal on chorus; Ernie Newton: bass. Brown Radio Productions, 240½ 4th Avenue North, Nashville, TN, Sunday, 26 March 1950, 11 AM–3:30 PM. Stephen H. Sholes, producer.

Audition disc, Tar Heel Transcriptions, 116½ West Martin St., Raleigh, NC, late 1950 or January 1951.

Bill: *This disc was made with the intention of selling our programs to various sponsors over different radio stations, probably throughout the South.*

HOME RECORDINGS, AUGUST 1963

Charles Travis recalls: "This Voice of Music tape recorder was used by Bill and Earl to practice for their Starday sessions in Nashville on August 28–29, 1963. Earl came up to Bill's home in Greensboro and, after a few days of practice, they drove together to Nashville. Bill told me they hung the mike over the back of a dining chair and then Bill and Earl were seated to get proper balance. Tapes from this practice session were later used on County 752 records to release an album about 13 years later. Bill gave me this recorder Nov. 04, 2005 which I still possess and treasure."

Beautiful	County 752 (33)
Beautiful, Beautiful Brown Eyes	County 752 (33)
Don't Let Your Sweet Love Die	County 752 (33)
Gathering Up the Shells from the Seashore	County 752 (33)
I Never Will Marry	County 752 (33)
I'll Wear a White Flower for You	County 752 (33)
Just Because	County 752 (33)
The Little Paper Boy	County 752 (33)
My Sweetheart Mountain Rose	County 752 (33)
Why Should It End This Way	County 752 (33)

Earl Bolick: lead voice, guitar; Bill Bolick: tenor vocal, mandolin. 2012 Todd Street, Greensboro, NC (Bill's home), August 1963, taped rehearsals for the Starday sessions.

STARDAY RECORDS, AUGUST 1963

When we quit, we quit entirely. I hadn't seen Earl in six or seven years when we made those albums for Starday. They wrote and asked if we would be interested in recording and I told them that we hadn't sung any in twelve years but we did have some old radio transcriptions that we might work out a deal on.

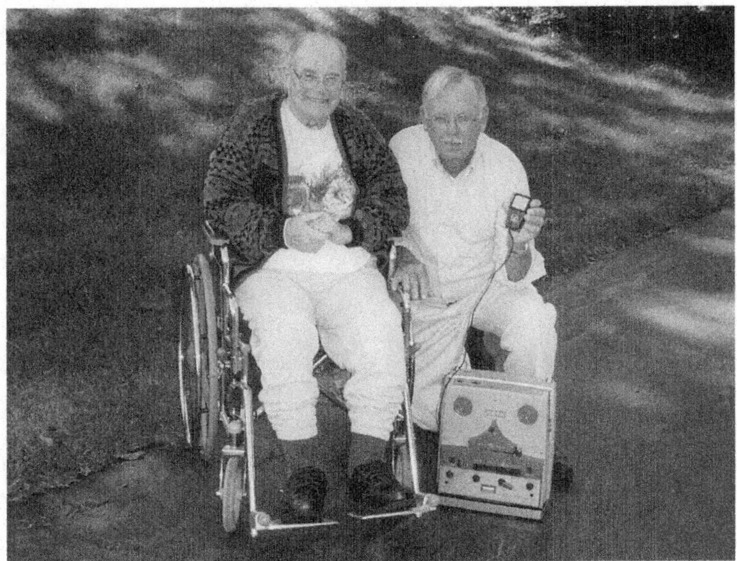

Bill and Charles with a Voice of Music tape recorder, November 3, 2005. Courtesy of Ella Travis.

That's how the Starday album A Treasury of Rare Old Song Gems from the Past [Starday SLP-205] *came about. Later they called and wanted to know if there was some way we could get together again. I got in touch with Earl and we decided to get together at our parents' home in Hickory and we picked out a few old songs we could do with a little rehearsal. We made the hymn album,* Precious Moments [Starday SLP-269], *and* Together Again [Starday SLP-257] *in August of 1963 in Nashville.*

Union wages for backup musicians Starday wanted on Together Again *cost us about $2,500 off the top, so we didn't come out too good on that deal. They wanted to put a Scruggs-type banjo on it but I refused to have anything to do with that, because I said that it would not be bluegrass. We did reach an agreement to add a bass and fiddle on the hymn album, and it is one of the best we've ever done.*

The A B C Song (Bill and Earl Bolick)	Starday SLP-269 (33), Pine Mountain PMR-269 (33), Rimrock STR-3004 (33), Gusto GT7-0549 (CD)
Beautiful (Bill and Earl Bolick)	Starday SLP-269 (33), Pine Mountain PMR-269 (33), Rimrock RLP-1002 (33), Gusto GT7-0549 (CD)
Boat of Life (George Jones-Burt Stephen)	Starday SLP-269 (33), Pine Mountain PMR-269 (33), Gusto GT7-0549 (CD)
Come to the Saviour (Bill and Earl Bolick-T.D. Lynn)	Starday SLP-269 (33), Pine Mountain PMR-269 (33), Gusto GT7-0549 (CD)

God Is Still on the Throne (Bill and Earl Bolick)	Starday SLP-269 (33), Pine Mountain PMR-269 (33), Gusto GT7-0549 (CD)
The Last Mile of the Way (Bill and Earl Bolick)	Starday SLP-269 (33), SLP-303 (33), Pine Mountain PMR-269 (33), London SLC(M) 353/4 (33), Gusto GT7-0549 (CD)
My God Why Have You Forsaken Me? (Dorsey Dixon)	Starday SLP-269 (33), Pine Mountain PMR-269 (33), Gusto GT7-0549 (CD)
Precious Moments (Don Fister)	Starday SLP-269 (33), SLP-308 (33), Pine Mountain PMR-269 (33), Gusto GT7-0549 (CD)
The Promise of the Lord (Leon Payne)	Starday SLP-269 (33), Pine Mountain PMR-269 (33), Rimrock RLP-1002 (33), Gusto GT7-0549 (CD)
Radio Station S-A-V-E-D (Bill and Earl Bolick)	Starday SLP-269 (33), SLP-303 (33), Pine Mountain PMR-269 (33), Rimrock STR-3005 (33), London SLC(M) 353/4 (33), Gusto GT7-0549 (CD)
Whispering Hope (Septimus Winner)	Starday SLP-269 (33), Pine Mountain PMR-269 (33), London SLC(M) 353/4 (33), Gusto GT7-0549 (CD)
Why Should You Be Troubled and Sad? (Dorsey Dixon)	Starday SLP-269 (33), Pine Mountain PMR-269 (33), Gusto GT7-0549 (CD)

Earl Bolick: lead voice, guitar: Bill Bolick: tenor vocal, mandolin; Tommy Vaden: fiddle; Billy Linneman: string bass. Starday Records, Nashville, TN, Wednesday, 28 August 1963. Tommy Hill, producer.

Are You from Dixie? (Yellen-Cobb)	Starday SLP-257 (33), Pine Mountain PMR-257 (33), London SLC(M) 353/4 (33), Gusto GT7-0549 (CD)
Behind These Prison Walls of Love (Bill Bolick-Earl Bolick-Hazel Hope Jarrard)	Gusto GT7-0549 (CD)
Don't Let Your Sweet Love Die	Gusto GT7-0549 (CD)
Don't Trade (Eddie Noack)	Starday SLP-257 (33), Pine Mountain PMR-257 (33), London SLC(M) 353/4 (33), Gusto GT7-0549 (CD)

I Wish I Had Never Seen Sunshine (Jimmie Davis-Johnnie Roberts)	Gusto GT7-0549 (CD)
In the Pines	Starday SLP-257 (33), Pine Mountain PMR-257 (33), Gusto GT7-0549 (CD)
Just Because (Nelson-Touchstone)	Starday SLP-257 (33), Pine Mountain PMR-257 (33), London SLC(M) 353/4 (33), Gusto GT7-0549 (CD)
Kentucky (Karl Davis-Harty Taylor)	Starday SLP-257 (33), Pine Mountain PMR-257 (33), London SLC(M) 353/4 (33), Gusto GT7-0549 (CD)
The Little Paper Boy (Johnny Wright-Jack Anglin)	Starday SLP-257 (33), Pine Mountain PMR-257 (33), London SLC(M) 353/4 (33), Gusto GT7-0549 (CD)
Mommie, Will My Doggie Understand (Jim Eanes)	Starday SLP-257 (33), Pine Mountain PMR-257 (33), London SLC(M) 353/4 (33), Gusto GT7-0549 (CD)
A Satisfied Mind (Hayes-Rhodes)	Starday 677 (45), SLP-257 (33), Pine Mountain PMR-257 (33), London SLC(M) 353/4 (33), Gusto GT7-0549 (CD)
Sweetheart Mountain Rose (Bill and Earl Bolick)	Starday SLP-257 (33), Pine Mountain PMR-257 (33), London SLC(M) 353/4 (33), Gusto GT7-0549 (CD)
Wednesday Night Waltz (Bill and Earl Bolick)	Starday SLP-257 (33), Pine Mountain PMR-257 (33), London SLC(M) 353/4 (33), Gusto GT7-0549 (CD)
Why Not Confess (Ralph Hamrick)	Starday 677 (45), SLP-257 (33), Pine Mountain PMR-257 (33), London SLC(M) 353/4 (33), Gusto GT7-0549 (CD)
Worried Mind (Ted Daffan-Jimmie Davis)	Gusto GT7-0549 (CD)
Your Brand Will Remain on My Heart (Bill and Earl Bolick)	Starday SLP-257 (33), Pine Mountain PMR-257 (33), London SLC(M) 353/4 (33), Gusto GT7-0549 (CD)

Earl Bolick: lead voice, guitar; Bill Bolick: tenor vocal, mandolin; Tommy Vaden: fiddle; Pete Drake: steel guitar; Jerry Shook: guitar; Vic Willis: piano; Billy Linneman: string bass; Harold Weakley: drums. Starday Records, Nashville, TN, Thursday, 29 August 1963. Tommy Hill, producer.

UNIVERSITY OF ILLINOIS, 1964

Title	Issue
After the Ball (traditional, arr. Bill Bolick) (Bill Bolick solo)	Rounder 0236, 11536
Are You from Dixie (intro)	Rounder 0236, 11536
Are You from Dixie (George L. Cobb-Jack Yellen)	Rounder 0236, 11536
Barbara Allen (Bill Bolick solo)	not issued
Beautiful (traditional, arr. Bill Bolick)	Rounder 11536
Behind These Prison Walls of Love (Bill Bolick-Hazel Jarrard)	Rounder 0236, 11536
The Butcher's Boy (traditional, arr. Bill Bolick)	Rounder 11536
Don't Trade (Eddie Noack)	Rounder 0236, 11536
The Fox (traditional, arr. Bill Bolick)	Rounder 0236, 11536
I'm Just Here to Get My Baby Out of Jail (Karl Davis-Harty Taylor)	Rounder 0236, 11536
I'm Saved (traditional, arr. Bill Bolick)	Rounder 0236, 11536
If I Could Hear My Mother Pray Again (Joe Davis)	Rounder 11536
In the Hills of Roane County (traditional, arr. Bill Bolick)	Rounder 11536
It Was Midnight on the Stormy Deep	Library of Congress LBC-2, Rounder 11536
Kentucky (Karl Davis-Hartford Court Taylor)	Rounder 11536
The Last Letter (Rex Griffin)	Rounder 0236, 11536
Little Bessie	not issued
Only One Step More (J. R. Baxter) (Earl Bolick solo)	Rounder 0236, 11536
Quit That Ticklin' Me (Bill Bolick)	Rounder 0236, 11536
The Sweetest Gift (James Coats)	Rounder 0236, 11536
Sweetheart Mountain Rose (Bill and Earl Bolick)	Rounder 11536
Uncle Josh Comedy Skit (Bill and Earl Bolick)	Rounder 0236, 11536
Whispering Hope (traditional, arr. Bill Bolick)	Rounder 11536
Worried Man Blues (A. P. Carter)	Rounder 0236, 11536

Earl Bolick: lead voice, guitar; Bill Bolick: tenor vocal, mandolin. Lincoln Hall, University of Illinois, Champaign, Saturday, 17 October 1964. Rounder 0236 is an LP record; 11536 is a compact disc.

CAPITOL RECORDS, 1965

Capitol contacted us while we were playing at a folk festival at UCLA in 1965, so we recorded an album for them in Hollywood. Ken Nelson promised to put the album in their record club and give us advertising, but I understand that they just printed a few thousand copies and let it go at that.

53691	Wild and Reckless Hobo	Capitol T2483, ST2483, JEMF 104, Arhoolie CD-9063 (CD)
53692	The Unquiet Grave	Capitol T2483, ST2483, JEMF 104, Arhoolie CD-9063 (CD)
53693	Midnight Special	Capitol T2483, ST2483, JEMF 104, Arhoolie CD-9063 (CD)
53694	Who's Gonna Shoe Your Pretty Little Feet?	Capitol T2483, ST2483, JEMF 104, Arhoolie CD-9063 (CD)
53695	Oh, Those Tombs	Capitol T 2483, ST2483, JEMF 104, Arhoolie CD-9063 (CD)
53696	Jack O' Diamonds	Capitol T2483, ST2483, JEMF 104, Arhoolie CD-9063 (CD)
53697	Corina, Corina	Capitol T2483, ST2483, JEMF 104, Arhoolie CD-9063 (CD)
53698	Poor Boy	Capitol T2483, ST2483, JEMF 104, Arhoolie CD-9063 (CD)
53699	Will the Circle Be Unbroken?	Capitol T2483, ST2483, JEMF 104, Arhoolie CD-9063 (CD)
53700	Oh Marry in Time	Capitol T2483, ST2483, JEMF 104, Arhoolie CD-9063 (CD)
53701	Cotton Mill Colic (David McCarn)	Capitol T2483, ST2483, JEMF 104, Arhoolie CD-9063 (CD)
53702	I Don't Want Your Greenback Dollar	Capitol T2483, ST2483, JEMF 104, Arhoolie CD-9063 (CD)

Earl Bolick: lead voice, guitar; Bill Bolick: tenor vocal, mandolin; unknown, string bass. Capitol Records, Hollywood, CA, Monday, 18 May 1965. Ken Nelson, producer.

ROUNDER RECORDS, 1975

Curly Headed Baby	Rounder 0052 (33, CD)
Don't This Road Look Rough and Rocky	Rounder 0052 (33, CD)
Green Grow the Lilacs	Rounder 0052 (33, CD)
If I Could Hear My Mother Pray Again	Rounder 0052 (33, CD)
Just a Strand from a Yellow Curl	Rounder 0052 (33, CD)
The Lawson Family Tragedy	Rounder 0052 (33, CD)

Let Me Be Your Salty Dog	Rounder 0052 (33, CD)
My Main Trial	Rounder 0052 (33, CD)
Searching for a Soldier's Grave	Rounder 0052 (33, CD)
Tramp on the Street	Rounder 0052 (33, CD)
Unloved and Unclaimed	Rounder 0052 (33, CD)
What Does the Deep Sea Say?	Rounder 0052 (33, CD)
When I Take My Vacation in Heaven	Rounder 0052 (33, CD)
You Could Be a Millionaire	Rounder 0052 (33, CD)

Earl Bolick: lead voice, guitar; Bill Bolick: tenor vocal, mandolin. Starday Records, Nashville, TN, Monday and Tuesday, 12 and 13 May 1975.

BILLBOARD REVIEWS OF BLUE SKY BOYS RECORDS, 1944–49

November 4, 1944, p. 66, *Why Not Confess/ Since the Angels Took My Mother Far Away,* Bluebird 33-0516

The harmony singing of Bill and Earl Bolick, as the Blue Sky Boys, is outdoorish with a vengeance. Boys are strictly from the hay-stacks, and for selling the tear-jerking tunes, there's enough cry in their vocal twangs to dampen any disk. Accompanied by mandolin and guitar, they sing it out sadly for "Why Not Confess," complaining of their lost love. For turning on the weeps for honest-to-gosh, what could be sadder than "When the Angels Took My Mother Far Away." It's the kind of singing and song that thrives in the prairie country, and if there is a juke box at the grange hall, they'll run themselves short of nickels in packing the machine for the Blue Sky Boys.

December 7, 1946, p. 96, *Dust On the Bible/Speak To Me, Little Darling,* RCA Victor 20-2022

Strictly backwoods and with a heavy outdoor twang in their song, the Blue Sky Boys, a twosome new to the label, appeal to the rocking chair brigade. Backed by mandolin, guitar and fiddle, the boys sing with a cry for both of these sides. "Speak To Me, Little Darling" is a plaintive folk waltz of a heart-broken husband at the bier of his wife. And in strict spiritual sensitivity urge all within hearing to find salvation for the soul in "Dust On the Bible."

April 12, 1947, p. 123, *I Love Her More, Now Mother's Old/ Have You Seen My Daddy Here,* RCA Victor 20-2151

There's an authentic backwoods twang in the harmonies of Bill and Earl Bolick, as the Blue Sky Boys for both of these mountain ballads, express tender sentiments in their singing with fiddle, mandolin and guitar keeping the tempo bright. For the old folks at home.

June 21, 1947, p. 130, *Kentucky/I'm Going to Write to Heaven,* RCA Victor 20-2296

It's the old-time homespun harmonies of the Blue Sky Boys (Bill and Earl Bolick) for both of these old-time songs with mandolin, guitar, fiddle and bass providing the appropriate musical setting. Boys sing it with feeling in extolling the virtues of "Kentucky," and with full pathos for the tear-jerking "I'm Going to Write [to Heaven]" ballad on the mated side.

September 13, 1947, p. 122, *Sold Down the River/I'm Glad,* RCA Victor 20-2380

Packing plenty of pathos and plaintiveness in their rural harmonies, the Blue Sky Boys (Bill and Earl Bolick), singing to mandolin, guitar, fiddle and bass strums, give it out in good homespun fashion for both of these heartbreak ballads. All the sentiments are expressed for "Sold Down the River," which leads to the port of broken hearts, and in the same moderate tempo, it's deft cowboy dittying for the "I'm Glad" torch. For the Western taps and taverns where they take to torch.

November 20, 1948, p. 104, *I Cannot Take You Back Now/ The Chapel in the Hills,* RCA Victor 20-3158

"I Cannot Take You Back Now": Authentic hill chanting with a male duo doing a heavy nasal, whining vocal on a so-so ballad, backed by a four-piece group. "The Chapel in the Hills": Moralizer doesn't carry much conviction, as the boys' diction is unclear.

February 12, 1949, p. 109, *Behind These Prison Walls of Love/ The Cross on the Hill,* RCA Victor 20-3307

"The Cross on the Hill": Hill country harmony boys yank tears in a ballad about a self-sacrificing war buddy. "Behind These Prison Walls of Love": More of the same effective weepiness here, but the material is more conventional.

April 23, 1949, p. 139, *The Sweetest Gift, a Mother's Smile/Paper Boy,* RCA Victor 21-0034

"The Sweetest Gift, a Mother's Smile": Male duo harmony and guitar accompaniment in the real hill manner project a weeper that appears to have the makin's. "Paper Boy": Saga of a cold, hungry newsboy who dies in the snow. Effective rendition.

September 24, 1949, p. 113, *Little Mother of the Hills/ Shake Hands With Your Mother Today,* RCA Victor 21-0108

"Little Mother of the Hills": Nasal "brother" harmony, sour fiddle, throbbing mandolin, etc., in the deep hillbilly manner. However, it's somewhat clean and studied. "Shake Hands With Your Mother Today": Tearful ditty describes a celestial reunion between a deceased mother and her boy. A clever, effective idea.

Chronology

1753	Johan Adam Bolch arrives in Philadelphia from Rotterdam with his wife and two children
October 20, 1890	Garland Bolick born
October 2, 1892	Annie Ėlizabeth Hallman Bolick born
October 29, 1917	William Anderson Bolick born
November 16, 1919	Earl Alfred Bolick born
1922–26	Perry Kim and Einar Nyland make the first gospel duet records with guitar and mandolin
April 12, 1924	WLS inaugural broadcast, Chicago
April 19, 1924	First broadcast of National Barn Dance on WLS
1924	The Bolick family buys a radio
1925–31	Lester McFarland and Robert A. Gardner sing duets with guitar and mandolin on WNOX, Knoxville
1930	Karl and Harty (as the Renfro Valley Boys) join the National Barn Dance
1931	Lester McFarland and Robert A. Gardner join the National Barn Dance

1934	Bill Bolick meets and jams with Lute Isenhour in Catawba County, NC.
March–June 1935	Bill joins the Crazy Hickory Nuts with Homer Sherrill and Lute, on WWNC, Asheville
October 1935–February 1936	Bill, Earl, and Homer as the Good Coffee Boys on WWNC
March 4, 1936	The Blue Ridge Hill Billies (Homer, Bill, Earl) debut on WGST, Atlanta
June 1936	Bill and Earl resign and return to Hickory
June 16, 1936	The Blue Sky Boys' first records are made in Charlotte
Summer 1936	Bill recovers from nasal surgery and tonsillectomy
September 1936	Blue Sky Boys join J. E. Mainer on WSOC, Charlotte
February–July 1937	Bill, Earl, and Homer return to WGST as the Blue Sky Boys
January 1938–December 23, 1939	Red Hicks joins Bill and Earl at WGST
May 9, 1939	Ruth Walker radio diary begins
December 27, 1939–May 1941	The Blue Sky Boys move to WPTF, Raleigh
May 9, 1940	Ruth Walker radio diary concludes
October 1940	Red Hicks is replaced by Curly Parker
May–August 1941	The Blue Sky Boys (with Curly) join WFBC, Greenville, South Carolina

August 11, 1941	Earl and Bill join the Army
September 22, 1945	Earl is discharged
December 25, 1945	Bill is discharged
March 25, 1946–February 1948	The Blue Sky Boys return to WGST
October 1946	Earl marries Geraldine Bennett of Tucker, Georgia
1947	*Favorite Hymns and Folk Songs* is published
January 10, 1948	The Blue Sky Boys appear on the Grand Ole Opry
March 1948–January 1949	WNAO, Raleigh
March–December 1949	WCYB, Bristol, VA
December 1949–April 1950	WROM, Rome, GA
April–August 1950	KWKH, Shreveport
August 1950–February 1951	WNAO, Raleigh
February 1951	Blue Sky Boys retire
1954	Bill hired at Railway Mail Service in Washington, DC; Doris Eileen Wallace leaves Bellaire, Ohio, to join him
February 1957	Bill and Doris marry
September 1957	Bill and Doris move to Greensboro, NC

August 28–29, 1963	The Blue Sky Boys record for Starday in Nashville
November 17, 1964	University of Illinois concert
May 14–16, 1965	UCLA festival, Capitol LP recorded
April 19, 1974	First appearance at Duke University
Summer 1974	Carlton Haney bluegrass festivals from Memorial Day through Labor Day
1975	Bill and Doris move from Greensboro to Hickory
April 1975	Second Blue Sky Boys appearance at Duke University, and their last public performance
May 12–13, 1975	Final recordings made for Rounder in Nashville
April 19, 1998	Earl dies in Tucker, Georgia
March 13, 2008	Bill dies in Hickory

Sources and References

Pat J. Ahrens. *A History of the Musical Careers of Dewitt "Snuffy" Jenkins, Banjoist and Homer "Pappy" Sherrill, Fiddler.* Columbia, SC: Pat J. Ahrens, 1970.

———. "The Role of the Crazy Water Crystals Company in Promoting Hillbilly Music." *JEMF Quarterly,* vol. VI, part 3, no. 19 (Autumn 1970): 107–9.

———. "Crazy Water Crystals and Its Union with Pioneer String Band Performers." *Bluegrass Unlimited,* vol. 36, no. 2 (August 2001): 56–60.

Annie and Garland Bolick. Interview with David Whisnant, January 31, 1974. Southern Folklife Collection, University of North Carolina, Chapel Hill.

William Anderson "Bill" Bolick. "Bill Bolick's Own Story of the Blue Sky Boys." *Sing Out!* vol. 17, no. 2 (April–May 1967): 18–21.

———. "I Always Liked the Type of Music That I Play." Notes to *Presenting the Blue Sky Boys,* John Edwards Memorial Foundation JEMF 104 (LP reissue of Capitol ST 2483), 1976. Included in the CD reissue Arhoolie CD 9063 (2012).

———. Interview with the Blue Sky Boys, Bill and Earl Bolick. Interviewer: Douglas B. Green, also present: Richard K. Spottswood. Camp Springs, NC, May 26, 1974 (transcription of audio cassette, Country Music Foundation Oral History Project). Nashville: Country Music Foundation, 1974.

———. Interview with the Blue Sky Boys: Self-interview by Bill Bolick, Hickory, North Carolina, July 1974 (transcription of audio cassette, Country Music Foundation Oral History Project). Nashville: Country Music Foundation, 1974.

———. Interview with the Blue Sky Boys: Self-interview by Bill Bolick, Hickory, North Carolina, March 1975 (transcription of audio cassette, Country Music Foundation Oral History Project). Nashville: Country Music Foundation, 1975.

———. Letters to John Dodds in England, 1984–2005.

———. Letter to author, July 7, 2004.

———. Videotape interview with Walt Saunders, August 27, 2005. International Bluegrass Music Museum, Owensboro, Kentucky.

Kyle Crichton. "Thar's Gold in Them Hillbillies." *Collier's National Weekly,* vol. 101, no. 18 (April 30, 1938): 24–25.

Wayne W. Daniel. "Bill and Earl Bolick Remember the Blue Sky Boys." *Bluegrass Unlimited,* vol. 16, no. 3 (September 1981): 14–21.

———. *Pickin' on Peachtree: A History of Country Music in Atlanta, Georgia.* Urbana and Chicago: University of Illinois Press, 1990, 152–58.

———. Notes and correspondence with Bill Bolick, 1980–81. Special Collections Department, Georgia State University, Atlanta.

Ed Davis. "Blue Sky Boys." *Muleskinner News* (March 1975): 5–13.

Favorite Hymns and Folk Songs As Sung By the Blue Sky Boys (Bill & Earl Bolick), Folio No. 1. n.p., n.d.

Brian Golbey. "The Blue Sky Boys: Bill and Earl Bolick, Among the Last of the Old Time Traditionals (Roots: An Ongoing Survey)." *Country Music People* (September 1996): 48–49.

Archie Green. Notes from audiocassette interview with Bill Bolick and Ken Irwin, 1986. Southern Folklife Collection, University of North Carolina, Chapel Hill.

Douglas B. Green. "The Blue Sky Boys on Radio, 1939–1940: A Newly Discovered Log of Their Daily Programs, Kept by Ruth Walker." *Journal of Country Music*, vol. IV, no. 4 (Winter 1973): 108–58.

Pamela Grundy. "'We Always Tried to Be Good People': Respectability, Crazy Water Crystals, and Hillbilly Music on the Air, 1933–1935." *Journal of American History*, vol. 81, no 4 (March 1995): 1591–1620.

Bill Malone. *The Blue Sky Boys: The Sunny Side of Life* (book with compact disc set). Bear Family BCD 15951, Germany, 2003.

Greil Marcus. Untitled essay in notes to *Harry Smith's Anthology of American Music, Volume Four.* Austin, Texas: Revenant RVN 211 2000, 79–82.

Rodney McElrea. "Bill and Earl Bolick—the Blue Sky Boys—'a Duo of Distinction.'" *Country News and Views*, vol. 3, edition 1 (July 1964): 6–15.

Gary Reid and Bill Bolick. Notes to Copper Creek and Blue Tone records (see discography).

Kinney Rorrer. *Back to the Blue Ridge.* WVTF broadcasts, Roanoke, Virginia, Christmas week 2006, and February 4, 2007.

Kinney Rorrer and Seth Williamson. Interview with Bill Bolick. Recorded by Jeremy Stephens, Hickory, NC, November 26, 2006.

Joe Ross. "The Brotherly Soul of Bluegrass." *Bluegrass Unlimited*, vol. 32, no. 10 (April 1998): 54–58.

Tony Russell. "Bill Bolick, Mandolin Player and Half of Hillbilly Brother Act, the Blue Sky Boys" (obituary). *The Guardian*, June 10, 2008.

Walt Saunders. "Earl A. Bolick, 1919–1998" (obituary). *Bluegrass Unlimited*, vol. 32, no. 12 (June 1998): 17.

Ossie Lee Setzer and Vernon Lafone (compilers). *A History of the First Church of God[,] Hickory, North Carolina.* n.p., n.d.

Cameron Shipp. "Expert Comes Here to Direct Making Phonograph Records," *Charlotte News*, January 26, 1938, reprinted in *The Dixon Brothers: A Blessing to People* by Patrick Huber (book accompanying CD set). Bear Family BCD 16817, 2012.

Seba Smith. *The Life and Writings of Major Jack Downing, of Downingville, Away Down East in the State of Maine. Written by Himself.* Boston: Lilly, Wait, Colman and Holden, 1834.

Shelby Stephenson and Ben Niblock. "The Blue Sky Boys: An Interview with Bill Bolick." *Pembroke Magazine* 39 (2007): 186–98.

Charles Travis. "The Boys from North Carolina." Unpublished manuscript, 2005.

Walt Trott. "Earl Bolick of the Blue Sky Boys Passes Away." *Country Music People* (June 1998): 5.

Charles K. Wolfe. *Classic Country: Legends of Country Music.* New York: Routledge, 2001, 97–102.

———. "On the Sunny Side of Life: Gospel Roots of the Blue Sky Boys." *Precious Memories* (July–August 1989): 4–11.

———. *The Blue Sky Boys in Concert, 1964* (record notes). Rounder CD 11536.

Marshall Wyatt. "Kentucky Songbirds: The Monroe Brothers and Byron Parker in Greenville, South Carolina, 1935-1936." *Bluegrass Unlimited,* vol. 51, no. 12 (June 2017): 26-30.

Index

CPSIA information can be obtained
at www.ICGtesting.com
Printed in the USA
BVOW08s0311280118
506263BV00002B/2/P